Praise for Organizing For Dummies

"*Organizing For Dummies* covers it all. This book will save you time, money, and many headaches."

> — Lillian Vernon, Founder and Chief Executive Officer –
> Lillian Vernon Corporation

"Eileen is a no-nonsense organizer and Elizabeth is a witty writer. Their book is fun to read but even better when the job is done. You are clutter free and proud of the results!"

> — Jean Brown, Travel Advisor

"This is an organization book that has been a long time coming. After all of the well-meaning – albeit failed attempts – to organize, you *can* do this, enjoying the journey all the while. You'll applaud yourself thereafter for the new world that opens up once the clutter is gone. Your life will no longer be just filled, it will be fulfilled."

> — Eve Flor,
> former Executive Secretary/Organizational Consultant

"An organized office offers visual reassurances that you are in control. Eileen Roth has covered organizing your office from every possible angle. You can't help but feel more efficient after applying her techniques."

> — Gloria Petersen, President –
> Global Protocol, Inc.

"I don't know how I got by before. Not long ago, I was the winner of the "messiest desk" award at my office. I had a hard time finding my files, I couldn't see my desktop, and the floor was so cluttered with stacks of papers that it was difficult to walk around. Now, using these organizing tips and techniques, I have one of the most organized filing systems in my office. I can see my desktop again, and I can always find the information I need very quickly. Do yourself a favor – read this book, and make the time to put these principles into practice. It *will* make a difference."

> — Steve Paolella, Network Engineering Manager –
> ACCO Brands, Inc.

"As a perpetual organizer, I can attest to the fact that *Organizing For Dummies* takes the decision making and stress out of organization. It is the next best thing to having a personal organizer at your side. Eileen's experience makes this a must-have book for the most experienced, as well as the "Dummie" organizer."

> — Carole R. Sandner,
> former *Everything in its Place* student

"The time saved from an organized work space is amazing. You should buy a copy of this book for every member of your team! This book is a wealth of valuable information, written in clear, commonsense language. Organizing my work space made the difference. I wish I could have had this book years ago!"

> — Scott Baumruck, executive vice president, COO –
> Paper Industry Management Association

"This book is written for anyone who's ever felt overwhelmed. It can teach you the process that leads to enhanced creativity and confidence in everything you do. It's a gem."

> — JoEllen Weiss

by Eileen Roth with Elizabeth Miles

Wiley Publishing, Inc.

Organizing For Dummies®

Published by
Wiley Publishing, Inc.
111 River Street
Hoboken, NJ 07030
www.wiley.com

Copyright © 2001 by Wiley Publishing, Inc., Indianapolis, Indiana

Published by Wiley Publishing, Inc., Indianapolis, Indiana

Published simultaneously in Canada

For general information on our other products and services or to obtain technical support, please contact our Customer Care Department within the U.S. at 800-762-2974, outside the U.S. at 317-572-3993, or fax 317-572-4002.

Wiley also publishes its books in a variety of electronic formats. Some content that appears in print may not be available in electronic books.

Library of Congress Cataloging-in-Publication Data:

Library of Congress Control Number: 00-107683

ISBN: 0-7645-5300-3

Printed in the United States of America

15 14 13 12 11 10 9 8

1O/SV/QR/QV/IN

About the Authors

Eileen Roth: When asked how long she's been organizing, Eileen Roth relies on the estimate made by her dad: since age five. At an evening dinner party in her native Chicago, the sweet young systematizer would go downstairs to say goodnight to the guests. Spotting the candy dish they'd been passing, she'd make a beeline for the bonbons — not to grab a treat, but to return the dish to its original place! Despite this early prowess, Eileen insists she wasn't born with an extra organizing gene. Instead, her parents had been teaching her to put things away from the day she could walk, and she draws on those simple lessons today in helping people see that organization isn't inherited — it's a learned skill.

Through her company Everything in its Place®, Roth consults with clients including Fortune 500 companies, trade associations, entrepreneurs, and busy individuals and families. Her success shaping up even the organizationally impaired has landed her spots on *Oprah*, the *Today* show with Bryant Gumbel, *Handy Ma'am* with Bev DeJulio, and NBC, ABC, and WGN news. Eileen's organizing fixes been featured by the *Chicago Tribune* and *Chicago Sun Times* and on a number of radio stations, and she uses her advanced time management skills to squeeze in workshops across the country.

Roth was sixteen when she first brought her organizing skills to the workplace. Her after-school job at SS Kresges (now Kmart) turned into a management coup when she became the only part-time person asked to run several store departments. After graduating from the University of Illinois, Roth was ready for a bigger challenge: organizing business executives. She started as a secretary and went on to spend fifteen years in office and association administration, honing the systematic skills that keep her in demand at companies seeking a competitive edge.

Motherhood brought balance to Roth's organizing talents by taking her out of the office and back home. Eight months pregnant with her second child, Eileen attended her first Tupperware® party and fell in love with the organizational advantages of the plastic food storage system. When the local sales manager told her that she could earn a free set by hosting six parties of her own, she did it — all before the baby was born. Five more years selling Tupperware® enabled Eileen to stay home with her two young daughters while she perfected her domestic organizing techniques in the kitchens of her party hostesses.

When her daughters were older, Roth returned to her career. In 1992, as organizing became recognized as a profession and after being laid off twice in one year in a job market slump, Eileen called on her entrepreneurial spirit and her extensive experience in both home and workplace organizing to found her own company. Everything in its Place® caught on like wildfire, and Roth was soon a consultant, speaker, and trainer for companies such as Northwest Airlines and Argonne National Laboratories.

With her first book, Roth brings a lifetime of the lessons learned while organizing in the trenches to readers everywhere. Written for any level and to cover the full spectrum of a busy life, *Organizing For Dummies*®, says Eileen, could even reduce the national stress level and improve GNP. No matter what, this tell-all reference will help people put everything in its place and put their disorganized days behind them for good.

Eileen Roth has recently moved from her hometown of Chicago to Phoenix, AZ to be closer to her college-age daughters. She is a member of the National Association of Professional Organizers (NAPO), National Speakers Association (NSA), and American Society for Training and Development (ASTD).

Elizabeth Miles: Looking for a better way to strengthen your mind, feed your soul, get healthy, wealthy, or wise? Turn to author, media personality, and entrepreneur Elizabeth Miles. Known to her fans for her user-friendly approach to peak performance on many fronts, Elizabeth offers answers that pop off the page and onto your to-do-now list. She's miles of smiles as she tells you how to tune into success, new-millennium style.

With a professional career that's run the gamut from banking on Wall Street to booking rock concerts and developing gourmet recipes, Miles relies on a broad range of experience in making the good life easier for busy people. She puts her graduate degree in ethnomusicology to work with her book and CD series *Tune Your Brain*®: *Using Music to Manage Your Mind, Body, and Mood* (Berkley Books, Deutsche Grammophon 1997-2000), which draws upon the latest neurological and medical research about music's effects on the body and mind to create an applied system for listeners. As creator and host of the daily "Braintuning Break" radio feature, she's taken her advice to the airwaves and earned listener loyalty over three seasons on the California Classical Network.

Music is food for the ears, says Miles — but you can't live on sound waves alone, and you'll often find her in the kitchen cooking up something tasty and targeted to your personal energy needs. *The Feng Shui Cookbook: Creating Health and Harmony in Your Kitchen* (Birch Lane Press 1998) is the first book to reunite the Chinese art of feng shui with its age-old partner of nutritional medicine. Elizabeth's contemporary take on tradition helps readers of all tastes and lifestyles eat for optimal energy, health, and prosperity — the "good *chi*" that spurs achievement. If you prefer a scientific slant when serving up dinner, Miles has partnered with Hollywood nutritionist Carrie Latt

Wiatt to pen *Portion Savvy: The 30-Day Smart Plan for Eating Well* (Pocket Books 1999), which pairs science with psychological and lifestyle factors to produce mind-body prescriptions for fitness.

Miles' popular approaches to achieving potential have been extensively covered in national and international media from *Self* to *Success*, PBS to the BBC, while the *Tune Your Brain* CD series has enjoyed long Top Ten runs on Billboard's classical chart. Miles lectures and consults for organizations such as Kaiser Permanente, the Los Angeles Unified School District, the Young Entrepreneurs' Organization, the Wellness Community, and many more concerned with health, education, and performance. As a previous self-professed organizational dummy, Elizabeth enjoyed applying her trademark knack for making things easy to Eileen's expertise and proven techniques to help bring *Organizing For Dummies* to life. A native of Madison, Wisconsin, Miles holds a Master's degree from the University of California, Los Angeles, and a BA from Dartmouth College. She lives in Los Angeles, halfway between UCLA and the beach, amidst musical instruments, cookware, books and CDs that are all finally finding their place.

Dedication from Eileen

To my mother and father, Millie and Marv Roth, who taught me how to get organized and so are largely responsible for this book. If she's watching from heaven, my mother is surely proud.

Acknowledgements

Big thanks to Tami Booth, the original Acquisitions Editor for Hungry Minds who invited Eileen to write this book, and Betsy Amster, our literary agent, who tracked Eileen down, broke it to her that she didn't have the humorous writing style for the series, and teamed Eileen and Elizabeth together. To Sherri Fugit, Project Editor at Hungry Minds and our trusty guide to the *For Dummies* world, who gamely endured all our efforts to make things "just right" and contributed welcome shape, substance, and finesse to the final results. To Karen Young, the new Hungry Minds Acquisitions Editor who worked with us on illustrations, marketing, and cheerleading. To Esmeralda St. Clair and her colleagues for copy editing to please a perfectionist's soul. To our expert reviewers — Shelly Cohen, who gave a CPA's view of the Information Flow chapter; Ken Braly and Charles Miles, whose technological expertise brought the Cyberorganization chapter up to the minute; Ann Gambrell, NAPO founding member, who reviewed the Home section; and Jackie Tiani, current NAPO board member, who reviewed the Office and Time Management sections. Thanks also to those who helped picture our thoughts on the page — David Hochberg and Kathy Mosechella at Lillian Vernon Corporation, Frank Rakawski, Maggie Scillia and Donna Miserendino at Get Organized!, Cathy McMannis and Jeremy Reiss at Stacks and Stacks, Dave Brown and Nancy Deptolla at Hoffman York, and especially our illustrators at Precision Graphics.

From Eileen

It's been a long year for me, what with a divorce, getting my youngest daughter off to college, and moving from Chicago to Phoenix all while writing my first book. For all the support, personal and professional, during this transitional time, I thank my children — Mindy and Julie Parelman; my family — Marsha Buck, Allan Roth, Marv Roth, and even my ex-husband Joe Parelman; my friends, especially Vicki Schneider; my colleagues in the NSA-Illinois Chapter, especially the Forum Group; Windy City Toastmasters; and all my clients, consulting and speaking, whose belief in my organizing skills has made my career possible. Most importantly, thank you Elizabeth, for working with me to create this book, for polishing a diamond in the rough. I couldn't have done it without you! I tip my hat to you. From the bottom of my heart, I thank you. (*Was that enough trite phrases to a writer? Whoops, I should have created an acronym!*)

From Elizabeth

As always, I have my friends and family to thank for keeping me centered and sane with generous input, insight, and unending patience when I disappeared from the scene for weeks on end to tend to my prose. Special thanks to my parents — the house at 200 North Prospect served as my mental model for each room of the Home section — to all the roommates who've shared the challenge of living in small spaces with me and so made me organizationally sensitized, and to the colleagues, creative partners, and clients who motivate me to find better ways to reach the finish line at work. Last but not at all least thank you Eileen, for entrusting me with your life's work and passion, for not laughing too hard when you saw my house and making me laugh lots of other times, for being a true partner even when your burden was heavy. Thank you for teaching me the deep power of putting everything in its place, a life-changing lesson that has made co-creating this book a pleasure with eminently practical results!

Thank you all.

Eileen and Elizabeth

Publisher's Acknowledgments

We're proud of this book; please send us your comments through our online registration form located at www.dummies.com/register.

Some of the people who helped bring this book to market include the following:

Acquisitions, Editorial, and Media Development

Project Editor: Sherri Fugit

Acquisitions Editor: Karen Young

Copy Editor: Esmeralda St. Clair

Technical Editors: Ann Gambrell, Jackie Tiani

Editorial Manager: Jennifer Ehrlich

Editorial Assistant: Jennifer Young

Composition

Project Coordinator: Maridee Ennis

Layout and Graphics: Matt Coleman, Leandra Johnson, Jill Piscitelli, Julie Trippetti, Jeremey Unger

Proofreaders: Laura Albert, John Bitter, Corey Bowen, Melissa D. Buddendeck, Angel Perez

Indexer: Norcross

Publishing and Editorial for Consumer Dummies

Diane Graves Steele, Vice President and Publisher, Consumer Dummies

Joyce Pepple, Acquisitions Director, Consumer Dummies

Kristin A. Cocks, Product Development Director, Consumer Dummies

Michael Spring, Vice President and Publisher, Travel

Brice Gosnell, Associate Publisher, Travel

Suzanne Jannetta, Editorial Director, Travel

Publishing for Technology Dummies

Richard Swadley, Vice President and Executive Group Publisher

Andy Cummings, Vice President and Publisher

Composition Services

Gerry Fahey, Vice President of Production Services

Debbie Stailey, Director of Composition Services

Contents at a Glance

Cartoons at a Glance

By Rich Tennant

page 7

page 43

page 141

page 181

page 251

page 333

Fax: 978-546-7747
E-mail: richtennant@the5thwave.com
World Wide Web: www.the5thwave.com

Table of Contents

Introduction

Organizing for the Millennium

What's the favorite four-letter word of less-than-fully organized people? "Help!" Answering that call has given me a satisfying career and my 15 minutes on the *Today show* and *Oprah*. In case you missed the shows or absorbing life-changing information takes you more than 15 minutes, I'm here to answer the call for you with *Organizing For Dummies*.

If you think of yourself as an organizational dummy, don't feel bad; everybody is born that way. Organization isn't inherited. With the human genome decoded, the evidence is clear: DNA strings dedicated to putting things into place and managing your time like a pro are nonexistent. Instead, organization is a learned skill set, just like driving a car. In fact that's a pretty good analogy. If you think back, learning to drive probably seemed pretty daunting at first, but driving may now be so automatic that you can practically drive in your sleep (though national safety experts don't recommend this). Organization is acquired, and as in any learning process, you need help. This book offers you that help.

I learned how to be organized through a combination of luck and sheer force of will. The lucky part is that I was born with organized parents. My mother and father *taught* me to clean up my toys, put the dirty dishes into the dishwasher, and make my bed every day. They showed me that everything had a place, and that some things should be put away before others came out. Lucky me; I learned all this before I even learned to read. (*Organizing for Dummies* didn't exist at that time, so being able to read wouldn't have helped anyway.)

After college, I landed my first job as a typist. That was fine, especially back then, before the days of career women, but I wanted more, so I decided to come up with better ways to do things to build my own rungs up the corporate ladder. I learned office organizing skills to add value to my work, and soon I'd moved from typist to secretary. The next stop was as an office administrator and eventually I ended up in association administration, juggling the workings of huge organizations, honing the systems that made events and processes run smoothly, and accomplishing my company's strategic goals. I discovered organization by doing in my office career because otherwise all the executives I worked with never would have made it through the day, let alone reached the company's bottom-line objectives.

Then things really got complicated: I became a mom. Determined to spend as much time as possible with my two daughters but committed to working and staying involved, I left the office and became a Tupperware rep. Yep, parties and all. Tupperware soon had me organizing kitchens all over the city of Chicago, coming in with my containers and leaving the place completely transformed. Being organized is a great way to win friends and influence people when you sell Tupperware. Meanwhile, I was busy with my family, attending all the girls' school and sporting events, acting as a teacher's aide and Girl Scout leader, washing a million loads of laundry, and racking up miles in the carpool lane. I discovered efficient ways to work and live because I had to. I couldn't be in two places at one time but my organizing systems were in place everywhere, 24/7, and I was supermom. (Sorry about the bragging, but they say it's okay for the Introduction.)

As my daughters grew old enough to need me less, I reassessed, set some goals (you can find out how in Part V), and became a professional organizer and trainer. Boy, was there a need out there! Today, through my company, Everything in its Place™, I help clients from Fortune 500 companies as well as trade associations, entrepreneurs, and busy individuals and families get organized. What I learned in the process is that anyone can learn organizing skills and put them into practice. So if you feel like an organizational dummy now, just open up your eyes and read, open up your mind and do, and you can create an organized you. All the pieces of your personality can remain in place, even as each element of your life and work finds its place too.

Being Busy versus Being Productive

So many technological, social, and economic changes impact your life every year that you probably need organization just to keep up, let alone advance. Many people have two jobs, one at the office and one taking care of things at home. If you have a family, you may have a third. Elderly relatives or community commitments? You can count off four, five, and keep right on going. No matter what life stage you're in, getting organized can make every day better and help you achieve your long-term goals.

Read this book if you'd like to have

- ✔ More time
- ✔ Less stress
- ✔ Greater productivity
- ✔ Fit finances

✔ Better relationships

✔ An improved professional reputation

✔ Space to live, work, breathe, and be

Don't have time to get organized? All the more reason to read this book. I can make the time for you and deliver the goods, and you may wonder how you ever had time to be any other way.

How to Use This Book

Did you notice I wrote how to *use*, not *read,* this book in the heading above? That's because reading is only half the battle. To get organized, you have to act.

I'm offering you a shortcut to my lifetime of learning. In these pages, you can have all my professional secrets. Still, all the organizing secrets in the world won't do a thing for you if all you do is read them. You must put the principles into practice. This is not a novel or a book to read through and toss into one of your many piles. *Organizing For Dummies* is a reference book for real life, so you have to bring the pages to life by doing.

Thinking of a task as a pie and taking just one slice at a time is a time-management trick. Do the same thing with this book, read just one part, chapter, or a section within a chapter — depending upon your attention span and reading speed — then act on what you just read. Don't wait until you finish the whole book. That day may never come (I'm a realist), and furthermore, you're sure to forget all kinds of good tips and tricks by then. So read, and then do, and then read some more, sort of like an organizing sandwich.

First things first: Start with Part I. Chapters 1 to 3 contain the guideposts, the principles of organization that are key to understanding the rest, and they're a pretty quick read.

Next, go where you want to go. Perhaps you're currently single and aren't too concerned about what's going on at home, but your office is a certifiable war zone; start with the office chapters in Part IV. You can always go back to the home when you get inspired or after you have children and need to organize their clothes and playthings. (It happens!) On the other hand, if your home is the war zone in your life, that part is your starting point. Pressed for time? Skip to the time-management section in Part V.

When it's time to tackle Part IV (office) or V (time management), you may ultimately save yourself some time by reading the whole part through first, and then going back and working on individual sections. You can get an edge by getting the big picture because the organizational ideas and skills you will gain can all work together to reinforce each other.

Psychologists say it takes about 18 to 21 days to make or break a habit, so give yourself some time to absorb this information. Read a section over again. Three times if you like. No one will think less of you for it. At school, you wouldn't read something once and then take the test. (Or if you did, you know what usually happens.)

How This Book Is Organized

I set up *Organizing For Dummies* to support the quick-hit reference process I just described, so you can skip around and easily find the organizing advice you need for any aspect of your life. Here's a quick rundown of what's where.

Part I: Basic Organizational Tools and Tenets

Chapters 1 through 3 give you the who, what, where, why, when, and how of getting organized by showing you the principles and systems that are used throughout the book. If you really want to get going, this is the beginning.

Part II: Getting Organized at Home

Here's a room-by-room rundown of all the places you live in — the kitchen, living room, dining room, den, playroom, bedroom, and bathroom. The part opens with the front hall, because that's the entrance to your home (very important in the ancient Asian tradition of *feng shui* that harmonizes the physical placement of objects in our daily surroundings for the sake of flow). Go where you want to get organized first, and learn how to apply the five principles of P-L-A-C-E™ to systematize each space: purging, placing like things together, accessibility, containing, and evaluating.

Part III: Organizing Storage Spaces and Other Secret Places

Part III takes a good look at many spaces of your home that you don't live in and therefore may overlook. Hopefully you don't live in the laundry room, which is included here. (If you do, read the chapter on how to do your laundry in two days so you can get the heck out of there!) The basement, attic, and garage are covered too, to help you organize your storage and secret places so that you can reclaim this real estate.

Part IV: Professionally Organized: Your Office

Turn here if your desk is a mess or your files have gone wild. Think you don't need files when you have good piles? Do not pass go! Proceed directly to Part IV. The tricks and tips using W-A-S-T-E™, R-A-P-I-D™, and R-E-M-O-V-E™ will get you through your papers quickly and show you what you need to pitch, what to retain, and how to store and find things from your stapler to your strategic plan. My clients say that the Take Action File™ alone is worth the cost of this book.

Part V: Time Management Strategies for Home, Office, and Travel

Whether you wonder where the time goes, need to accomplish more at work, or simply want to make the most of your day and your life, this part can get you started and take you to the time-management finish line. From the new to the tried and true, here are all the time-management techniques that you need in one place, presented in systems that you can start using today. If all you get out of this section is "plan today for tomorrow," I will have accomplished a great goal. (Planning today is easy when you follow the four steps of P-L-A-N™.) If you grasp all the other good stuff that's there, I can die happy and you can squeeze in a lot more living before you go.

Part VI: The Part of Tens

These five chapters have ten ideas each for organizing a particular process or space. If you're looking for storage ideas for apartments and condos, want to be better prepared for emergencies, or need some pointers about pets, this is the place to turn for quick ideas. Anyone gearing up to move may want to jump into Chapter 24 and have a great garage sale, then go to Chapter 23 to make your move smooth.

Icons Used in This Book

I direct your attention to all sorts of helpful hints for getting organized in *Organizing For Dummies* with a system of icons that help you scan right to the juicy stuff on any given page. Here's an overview of what you'll see.

Extra ideas to aid the points made.

This warns you of possible problems.

Points to remember that will save you time and trouble later.

Shortcuts to shave time off tasks and leave more for living.

Cut-to-the-chase ways to clean up that mess.

High-level hints for advanced organizing.

You Don't Have to Be Organized to Get Organized

I want to conclude all this talk of what's where with a reassuring word and a promise. First, there's no wrong way to use this book. Read it however you please (though if you go from right to left your comprehension may be seriously impaired). The point is simple: Read and do, and you can't go wrong.

My promise is that if you read and do just a little bit at a time, you *will* get results. Really. Twenty old papers tossed is an inch of free file space and the beginning of a new habit, and you can do it in five minutes or less. So get organizing today, and by tomorrow, you may start seeing things in a whole new way.

Part I

Basic Organizational Tools and Tenets

The 5th Wave By Rich Tennant

"The funny thing is he's spent 9 hours organizing his computer desktop."

In this part . . .

*O*rganized people aren't born . . . they're made. So if you wouldn't know a time-management technique if you tripped over one and can't figure out how cleaning out your closet can make your life better, where do you start?

This part introduces you to the why and how of getting organized, giving you both the convincing pep talk and the basic principles you need to put everything in its place. You can discover the many benefits of being organized, how to develop an organized mindset, and six tricks that make quick work of any organizing challenge. Read it and you'll be raring to go!

Chapter 1

Dealing with Clutter

· ·

· ·

1 know you think clutter-busting is going to hurt. For many people, getting organized sounds less appealing than a trip to the dentist and more complicated. You may have put off cleaning up your life by figuring that if you're not organized yet, you must have the wrong personality type. Getting organized goes against the grain and only causes pain.

Then there are the more specific antiorganization arguments. "I don't have time," say many, mixing up the excuse with the exact reason to do it. Others worry that organization will limit their creativity or rob them of their spark. Some people steer clear because they fear that organizing systems might turn them into uptight rule-makers or rigid control freaks.

If a broad range of people didn't share these concerns, I wouldn't have a booming business as a professional organizer. My job, in my business and in this book, is to prove the power of putting everything in its place and how that improves all aspects of your life, from work to home, play, personal relationships, and professional reputation. Why get organized? How about recovering the 15 minutes a day you spend looking for your car keys, or the hour lost last week searching for a critical computer file saved in a dark corner of your directory? Getting dinner on the table with ease and cleaning up like a breeze? Inviting guests into your home without shame? What about finally winning the promotion you may have been passed up for because your desktop piles or late arrival at meetings have undermined your credibility? Wouldn't you like to leave the office earlier so you can get to know your friends and family again and earn more per hour than you did when you were 16?

The techniques in this book provide simple and proven ways to organize your life *the way you like to live it*. Get organized to achieve peak potential and enjoy lifelong peace.

Organizing myths and truths

Myth:	Truth:
I wasn't born with an organized personality.	Organization is learned, not inherited.
Getting organized will make me less creative.	Organization frees the mind to think outside the box, and leaves you more time to do it in.
I don't have time to get organized.	Organization saves time, yielding huge payoffs for the small amount of time invested in setting up systems that will last for life.
Getting organized will turn me into a control freak.	Organization reduces your need to exert control. Everything is already in its place — so you can relax instead.

Living in an Overstuffed World

Imagine that a tornado hit your house and whisked it away. What would you really need to start over again? What would you truly miss?

Say that an earthquake levels your office to rubble. How many missing items would you have to reassemble to get back to work? An accident lands you in the hospital. How much would the world really suffer because you didn't attend to all the obligations on your calendar? How much of the confusion could you have prevented with good systems that someone else could manage while you recovered?

It often takes dramatic thinking to help people sort out the productive elements from the clutter in their lives. Why? Because the world is overstuffed. Houses and offices are filled to the brim, and yet advertisers still beg consumers to buy more. Sandwiches get bigger all the time, and people do too. Cities are bursting at the seams, schools are overcrowded, and they've jammed so many seats onto airplanes that passengers are practically sitting on each other's laps. Society has adopted an overstuffed mentality, and then you wonder why you can't think clearly or feel peaceful and calm.

Getting organized is about *unstuffing* your life, clearing out the deadweight in places from your closet to your calendar to your computer, and then installing systems that keep the good stuff in its place. Organizing is a liberating and enlightening experience that can enhance your effectiveness and lessen your stress every day, and it's all yours simply for saying "No" to clutter.

Clutter happens when you don't put things in place, whether on your desk-top, inside the filing cabinet, in your calendar, or atop the kitchen counter. Bringing things into a room and not putting them back where they belong creates clutter. Leaving toys in the hallway, newspapers in the living room, or e-mail in your incoming queue clutters up your space. Unimportant obligations are clutter in the day. Jamming too many things in your home, office, or schedule — filling every space, littering your life — doesn't give you more power or pleasure. Random articles and activities give you clutter. By getting organized with the techniques in this book, you can leave space free to work, play, and be.

Piled-up clutter

Then there's that special form of clutter you may recognize with a guilty smile: the pile. While making a pile could seem like putting things away, nothing could be farther from the truth. Think about what happens when you make a pile: Now you have to dig through everything on top to find what you need, instead of simply going to the file or drawer or shelf where the item should be. Whether it's papers, toys, clothes, or computer disks, making piles makes work and wastes time.

Organization turns pilers into filers and helps you to put things away naturally and easily, because everything has a place.

Mental clutter

The most disorienting form of clutter is mental. Mixing up your mind with commitments you can't keep track of, things you can't find or don't know how to do, or chaotic surroundings can cause stress and block basic cognitive processes. If you find it hard to make a decision; if you frequently have to go back to the office, the store, or home to pick up something you left behind; if you're worried that you can't accomplish what's expected or needed, from cooking dinner to finalizing a deal, then you're probably suffering from the confusion caused by mental clutter. When you get organized, you'll gain planning, time-management, and placement techniques to clear your mind and de-stress your life. Getting organized is like growing new brain cells — an all-natural upgrade to your gray matter.

The Cost of Clutter

The reason for reading and using this book to organize your life is simple: Clutter of all kinds costs you dearly.

The costs of clutter range from hard cash to time, space, health, and your relationships with people. You may be unaware of the price you pay for over-stuffing your life, but when you analyze the cost of clutter, the rewards of getting organized become clear.

Time

What's the one commodity we can never replace in this life? Time. Once it's gone, it's *gone*. Not a moment can be retrieved, relived, or replayed. Time is the most precious gift, yet we casually throw it away every day. Did you spend time looking for something this morning? Miss an appointment, train, or plane? Drag your way through a report after wasting your peak work time on opening the mail? Maybe you waited in rush hour traffic because you left too late. Perhaps you lost an hour of relaxation time because it takes too long to get dinner on and off the table, your laundry room is set up wrong, or you went to the grocery or office supply store without a list.

Every second counts. Getting organized helps you get things done fast so you can spend the extra time enjoying life.

Money

Hello, bottom line! The wallet is often where people feel things first, and disorganization could be draining yours. Consider your own situation, and take a minute to calculate the dollar cost of the clutter in your life based on the following:

- **Rent or mortgage:** All the square feet filled with junk in your home, office, or storage locker

- **Wage or salary:** The time you waste doing things inefficiently, twice, or without a plan *plus* the raises you haven't received because you're not working at peak potential

- **Overpaid for purchases**: Excess costs from buying at the last minute, from the wrong source, or in the wrong quantity

✔ **Duplicate purchases:** Cost of things you've bought duplicates of because you couldn't find yours, forgot you had one, or lost the instruction book or warranty to use it or get it fixed

✔ **Penalties:** Fees, interest, and penalties for late payments and bounced checks

✔ **Depreciation:** Loss of resale value of cars and other equipment you're not maintaining properly

✔ **Medical bills:** From doctor's visits to aspirin and stomach medications, all the money you spend because stress is sabotaging your health

Now imagine: What can you do with all that money when you get it back by getting organized?

 Don't waste your money renting storage lockers or warehouse space. If you're using something so rarely that it's in offsite storage, you don't need it, so throw it away, sell it, or give it to charity. One of my clients paid to have the contents of two storage lockers moved to his new house in a faraway state, only to realize when the stored contents arrived that he didn't want most of the items anymore. Poor Robert; he could have used that money for fixing up his house instead.

Health

Getting things done when you're disorganized is hard enough, but how about when you're sick too? Over time, disorganization can actually contribute to disease. Stress can cause disorders from headache and fatigue to ulcers, high blood pressure, even heart disease. Missing checkups or neglecting treatments can allow conditions to get worse. Simply can't make the time to exercise? You could be shaving years off your life.

Just as being disorganized can make you sick, getting organized is a sound investment in your well-being. Reducing physical and mental clutter and creating easy self-care systems can give you the gift of health, now and far into the future.

Space

Close your eyes and imagine you're in a park, on a mountain, at the beach. What makes you feel so great to be there? It's that rarity of modern life — wide open space.

People today are so accustomed to being crowded that forgetting the value of physical space and letting yours get overstuffed with things you don't want or need is easy to do. Yet space creates appreciation for everything it contains. As they tell you in music class, without the rests, the notes lose all their interest. When you get organized, you can find out how to stop filling up space and let it stay empty, so you have room to breathe, dance, and dream.

Reputation and relationships

Missing birthdays. Blowing deadlines. Greeting guests with a harried face and house. Letting clients, colleagues, and your boss see you surrounded by piles of papers and supplies. What do you think clutter does to your reputation and relationships?

Clutter comes between people. At work, looking or acting disorganized presents a picture of incompetence that may make your boss hesitant to assign you projects or put you up for promotion. Teammates might be reluctant to work with you if they doubt your act is together. A messy desk, missed meetings, or misfiled memos can all inhibit your potential for money and growth.

In your personal life, the toll is just as high. A cluttered home puts your family on edge and discourages guests from having fun or even coming by. High-stress holidays and parties, late or poorly chosen gifts, leaving the kids waiting at soccer practice, forgetting to follow up on a sick relative or pick up your partner's dry cleaning when you promised can all lessen the love and laughter in your life. Is that a price you're willing to pay?

Getting organized can enhance all your interpersonal relationships by letting your talents shine. Order and clear expectations create a comfortable environment, freeing everyone up to enjoy and express themselves. Organization can boost self-esteem and the regard in which others hold you. This confidence will reflect in everything you do.

The Causes of Clutter

Clutter is costly but not inevitable — clutter is caused by patterns and practices that can be changed. If you have clutter-causing habits, I'm here to tell you that you are not alone. The age of abundance has affected everyone, and I have clients of all ages, backgrounds, and occupations who are equally unequipped to process all the information, products, and activities being pushed upon us today. You are living in a unique historical period in which people generally have more things and thoughts than ever before but are finally facing the limits to growth. You may want to simplify, streamline, get to the essence of what's important, and at the end of the day have more time and money and less stress and stuff. But how?

Let's tackle the problem at the root, by looking at the causes of clutter.

You've got mail and other forms of information overload

Whether you're hooked up to the Internet, surfing a few hundred satellite TV channels, or simply trying to get through your mail and the daily paper, you're probably faced with all the facts you can handle and more, 24 hours a day. Just a short century ago, books, newspapers, and mail were about it in terms of information arriving at your door. Today the telephone has become a fifth limb that travels everywhere you go. Radio and television bombard the population with messages around the clock. E-mail, faxes, and the Internet broadcast information instantaneously, keeping millions up-to-the-minute on a world's worth of minutiae.

Knowledge is power, but information you don't need is clutter. Whether data is printed on paper, electronically encoded, or just bouncing around in your mind, information without a proper place is a waste of time and space. Getting organized will help you filter information flow and turn the tide of this new age to your advantage at work and play.

The drive to buy

Though the information age is still a little new, the consumer age is so well entrenched that buying has become second nature — whether you need it or not. The Sunday paper beckons you out to stores. The exciting ads in the evening entertainment can leave you dissatisfied with your lifestyle and eager to make up the difference for a few (or many) dollars. A culture built on free enterprise encourages people to compare themselves to their neighbors, not on the basis of inner riches or personal fulfillment but by the number of things in their houses and yards.

My main message when it comes to managing the drive to buy is: Be very afraid. Salespeople are pros. Advertisers go to school, attend training sessions, and earn advanced degrees finding ways to sell you things without regard for your needs. Their sole purpose is to sap your bank account and fill your available space. Then, surprise! You don't end up with the more fulfilling lifestyle they promised. Your big reward is an empty savings account and an overstuffed house. Driving the drive to buy are the standard, full-price temptations. And then there are the sneaky ones.

Sale: Your favorite four-letter word

You walk into any store and what's the first sign you see? SALE!

So you make a beeline to the display behind the sign to see all the ways you can save money by buying more today. Suddenly, shopping is not a matter of looking for what you came for but of choosing from what the store has put on sale. You're no longer matching a solution to a need. The seller takes over, telling you what to buy — even if you already have a sweater in that color, or own nothing to match, so now you need to buy a pair of pants — at full price — too. As you organize yourself and your home, you'll find it easier to put up a stop sign between you and the sale sign. You'll think of your nice neat closet . . . your nice full wallet . . . and you'll just say no.

Freebies

Even more appealing than a sale to our bargain-hunting soul is that other four-letter word: free. Free lunch, free toothbrush, free trip for two to Bermuda — this single syllable is a siren call to all acquirers. But free offers usually have a price. Either the item comes attached to something else that you have to buy and might not want, or you have to buy more later, or you have to spend time filling out rebate forms and matching them to receipts and getting them in the mail.

Let's say a certain brand is giving away a free toothbrush when you buy a tube of toothpaste. Great, you think, I need a toothbrush, so you buy it. But you use a different brand of toothpaste specially formulated for sensitive teeth, and the new tube sits around forever. Was that toothbrush free? Nope. It cost the price of the toothpaste you didn't use and the space to store it.

Maybe you spend 15 minutes filling out a $1 rebate. Isn't your time worth more than $4 an hour? Add in the cost of the stamp and envelope, and you're really in the hole.

Then there are the notorious offers where you get a free book or CD if you agree to buy ten more during the year. Would you buy ten books otherwise? Do they have the books you want? At the end of the year, will you have read them all? Any? Do you have space on your shelf for ten more books?

Even true giveaways — pens, mugs, calendars, caps, knickknacks — that promote a company or product aren't free. You're advertising at the cost of the space in your life.

I've already talked about the costs of clutter. As you read this book and become more clutter-conscious, you'll free yourself from free things that come at a price.

Warning: This car stops at garage sales

Many cars have such a bumper sticker. The warning can at least help prevent accidents from the sudden stops, if not the clutter disaster that can result from garage-sale shopping.

I admit that I once had a garage sale problem myself. When my girls were young, they liked to take their little wallets full of pennies, nickels, and dimes and go trolling for clothes, costume jewelry to play dress-up, puzzles, games, books, toys; once we even landed a pair of roller skates. But as I started to see my house fill up, I realized what was happening: Everyone else was putting out their clutter, and I was taking it home and making it mine. How did I recover from this organizing error? I turned around and had my own garage sale. What came in the front door went out the garage door. (Now, of course, I don't let clutter in any door at all.) For ideas on having your own garage sale, see Chapter 24 in the Part of Tens.

Organizing principles show you that if you do buy something used, you should check to be sure you need it and that it works. Are all the parts there? Does it look nice? If it needs repair, can you take care of it easily, cheaply, within the next week?

Getting organized will also help you drive on by those garage sales and get on with your life.

The cute effect

One quick definition of the word *cute* is useless. Cute things are rarely high-value purchases, but they have a way of getting you to open your wallet. Probably the reason the thing is sending a smile across your face is because it's so silly — a wild and crazy dress you'd never wear outside the fitting room, a really dumb joke on a coffee mug, a talking tie. The problem is that cute (or stylish, or wild, or silly) wears off fast. Puppies are cute too, but you better not buy one unless you eventually want a grown-up dog.

As you discover how not to clutter up your life, you'll find yourself less attracted to things of only momentary meaning. You'll gravitate to acquiring items that will last and matter. You'll buy less "cute."

Gifts that keep on taking

A gift, almost by definition, is something you didn't choose — so you may or may not want it. But a gift is also a token of affection or esteem, so you have to keep it, right?

The important thing to remember about gifts is that they're meant to make you happy. Clutter doesn't do that. Clutter messes up your life. So observe the true spirit of giving by returning gifts you don't want to the store, exchanging them for something you can use, or putting the refund money in the kids' college fund. Maybe you know someone who really wants or needs the item. Give it to them. (Don't just pass on clutter, though. That is *not* the spirit of giving.)

There are occasional cases, usually involving good friends or relatives, in which the giver expects to see the gift in use. Does that mean you have to display the ugly vase from Aunt Susie or wear the so-not-you sweater from a friend all the time? Of course not. The true clutter-busting solution is to tell Aunt Susie the vase broke and your friend that the cat clawed the sweater to shreds or you spilled coffee all over it and the ugly stain won't come out — then quietly return or donate the gifts. If you prefer not to fib, put the vase away in a remote cupboard and the sweater on a high closet shelf. Get the vase out when Aunt Susie comes to visit. Wear the sweater once in awhile when you see your friend. Don't let things you don't like take up prime space in your life.

Saving for later

Did your parents teach you to save for a rainy day? Great. Go have a garage sale, get rid of all the junk, and put the cash in the bank for the day you lose your job, leave your relationship, or make another major life change. Clothes you can't or don't wear anymore, old appliances and dinner plates, outdated files and papers, and extra boxes of staples simply aren't going to make the difference on that rainy day. Though *someday* may always seem just around the corner, the chapters that follow will help you make more of today by clearing away the clutter you're saving for later. Focusing on the present can yield many future benefits.

Souvenirs and mementos

Souvenirs are another form of saving for later, trying to capture a moment in a thing. When travel becomes a quest to acquire objects to remember you were there instead of devoting yourself to being there, you're cheating yourself now and cluttering up your later. Why not skip the souvenir shops and loll on the beach, lay back in a café, or take in a museum or show instead? The word *vacation* comes from *to vacate,* which is hardly what you're doing when you fill up your suitcase with *tchotchkes* to take back home.

You want to remember special moments. This book offers hints on how to snap photos and shoot videotapes packed with personal meaning; catalog your archives for easy, anytime enjoyment; select the special accents from your travels and adventures that spice up your life, and leave the junk behind.

Aunt Babe's gifts

I was the only relative living nearby when my Great-Aunt Babe decided she was getting old and wanted to start passing on some of her things, which she had plenty of. She and Uncle Abe had lived in their house since the 1930s or so, and though it was very neat; boy, was it packed full, so I greeted her announcement with some trepidation. Still, she was like a grandmother to my girls and very dear to me, so I dealt with her gifts and learned some good strategies in the process.

Gift #1: Don't want or need it. Aunt Babe's first gift was simple: some cloth doilies for the holidays. Though I didn't want them, it was easy to take them and pass on to my sister, who did.

Gift #2: Needs work but useful. The next visit to Aunt Babe's house was a little more nerve-racking. She had some chairs, she said. Oh no, I thought. I have zero appreciation for antiques (what can I say?), and it would be tough to get rid of an entire set of chairs, let alone explain their absence when Aunt Babe came over. But lo and behold, Babe pulled out these light wood chairs with gorgeously carved backs that I absolutely loved. The only problem was that they were upholstered in an awful shade of green. I took them directly to the furniture shop — and the key word here is *directly* — and

had them recovered in a shade I liked. Transformed by a simple fix from ugly to beautiful and very useful for parties and holidays, those chairs are still with me, though Aunt Babe's been gone for more than ten years.

Gift #3: I hate it, the kids love it. The next time, Aunt Babe pulled a grandmother's trick and applied her gift-giving wiles directly to my daughters. "Girls, would you like those shell collections on the wall?" she innocently asked. We're talking two truly bad-looking spray-painted shell collections that had me groaning and the girls, age 3 and 5 at the time, jumping up and down with glee. Nothing to be done here. To them, the shells were a piece of Aunt Babe. Those shell collections hung in my basement for 15 years until I moved. Some gifts you just can't fight.

Gift #4: I hate it, the kids hate it. The fourth time, Aunt Babe bypassed me again, offering the girls an old chenille bedspread. Chenille apparently has none of the appeal of shells to little girls, and it went over like a lead balloon with them. The spread looked old and decrepit to me too. I didn't want it, they didn't want it, but what were we going to do, hurt an old woman's feelings? We took the old spread.

Why get organized? To collect the payoff of putting everything in its place: More time and less stress. Cash in your pocket and peace of mind. Peak productivity, better health, and more rewarding relationships.

Flip through the pages of this book to see how you can put organization to work for *you,* from planning a meal to pulling off a strategic project; from beautifying your home to cleaning up your computer. Get organized so you can make more of your life while working less, and let these proven systems take care of the rest.

Chapter 2

Training Your Mind to Be Organized

In This Chapter

▶ Organization as a state of mind

▶ Setting your organizing goals

▶ Making time to get organized

▶ Breaking down organizing jobs into bite-size pieces

▶ Personalizing your organizing plan

▶ Maintaining an easy mindset to end yo-yo organizing forever

*I*n the last chapter, I hope I convinced you that organization isn't inherited — organizing is learned. That means that whatever disorganized secrets lurk in your past or what a mess you see when you assess your present condition, you can become organized and stay that way for a lifetime.

"But organizing sounds hard!" you may think, and that could be the case if I were talking about calculus and you'd only gone as far as basic algebra. But I'm not. Though there are many useful principles and tips behind getting organized in every aspect of your life — a whole book's worth in fact — thinking like an organized person isn't rocket science. Being organized is simply a habit, just like brushing your teeth, which, believe it or not, you once didn't know how to do.

Organization begins in the mind. Once you've got those synaptic connections in place, you can start to see what to do even before I tell you. Take a few minutes to read this chapter to get a jump start on the organizational mindset, as well as how to organize the process of getting organized. After all, how can you get started if there's a mess in your mind?

Letting Go to Find Flow

Begin by clearing the decks. Sit back for a minute and close your eyes. Dream up a picture of perfect peace. Do that now, and then come back and read on to the next paragraph.

What did your picture of peace look like? Was it full of papers and old clothes and tightly packed days on the calendar? Probably not. The first thing most people do when they picture peace is let go of all that stuff that seems so important in daily life, and return to a clean, clear state that you may consider original. The way people were meant to be.

Flow is a word used by psychologists, artists, coaches, and other performance-minded people to describe the state of mind and body when everything's perfectly in tune. You're completely focused on your task. Nothing stands in your way. To get there, you have to let go.

What blocks flow? Time wasters, distractions, and frustrations. Items out of place. Disorder, and the disaster that can result when you don't plan ahead. Freeing your life from things and tasks that aren't necessary and streamlining those that are is the best way to attain flow, find fulfillment, and achieve your peak potential. I'm not talking about being a minimalist (though you're welcome to take that course if it's your way). Bare skin and bones don't make a person. The builder builds a house, but until you put things inside, the house is not a home. Sometimes, new clients are afraid that when I come in I'm going to throw out their favorite possessions or interfere with their daily rituals. Getting organized is not about stripping away the extra touches that make us who we are. I'm not a minimalist, nor am I trying to turn you into a robot. I simply want you to get organized so that you can enjoy life.

Your Organizing Plan

The first step in wrapping your mind around the organizational challenge is to make a plan. How to begin? What next? Start with a basic planning tool that will pop up throughout the book. To make a plan, simply think like a journalist. No, not "man bites dog." This technique is what I call the Five Ws Plus How — six questions reporters ask when writing a story, and that can put any plan into place: Who? What? When? Where? Why? How? These are easy questions, but actively answering them can help you make a concrete plan.

Organizing your mission

Why do you want to get organized? To create an organized mindset, you need a mission. Saving time, saving money, reducing stress, enhancing performance, building self-esteem, and improving relationships may figure into your organizing mission. For me it always boils down to my trademark phrase, which you just read a few paragraphs back: Get organized to enjoy life.™

Aren't those little trademark signs nifty? By the way, you definitely need to be organized if you ever want to deal with the Office of Trademarks and Patents. But that's a story for another day.

Take a minute now to decide on your organizing mission statement. Here are a few examples:

- ✔ My mission is to get organized so that I can enjoy more time with my family and friends.

- ✔ I want to improve my organizing skills to achieve my true potential at work.

- ✔ Our group's objective is to use organizational techniques to speed processes, facilitate communications, and reduce individual stress levels.

Have you got your mission statement? Good. Write it down here.

_____

_____

_____

Your organizing goals

What are your organizing goals? Once you've got a mission, you can set specific objectives. Do you want to organize your home? Your office? Your time? One after the other in priority order? The point is not to try to take on everything at once, but to focus on what you want to do now. You can select a single closet or an officewide process. You might want to shape up your computer files or finally find the right containers for your kids' toys. Maybe the main immediate goal is to clean up your living room so you can welcome friends and family into your home. You may have one goal or ten, big ones or small ones. Perhaps your goals have a domino effect — if you get one done, then you want to do another. Can you guess what I'd like you to do with your organizing goals? That's right — write them down.

_____

_____

_____

_____

_____

Your organizing time

When's a good time to get organized? Eventually, the answer may be "all the time," but when you're just getting started, being more specific helps. Spring cleaning, fall cleanup, the new year, or start of the school year are all natural times to get organized. A big deadline at work may spur you to organize at the office. Knowing the family is coming for Thanksgiving can get you in gear at home. Moving? You better get organized from bottom to top. (I'm moving from Chicago to Phoenix as I finish this book, so I know what I'm talking about. You should see me opening up one of my carefully catalogued and numbered packing boxes to pull out a reference book when my co-author Elizabeth asks a question I need to research. Trust me. This book would not be in your hands if I didn't practice all the principles you're discovering here.)

To find out more about setting goals by the season, you can peruse Chapter 18. But for now, you can get going simply by reading on.

One of the most frequent complaints I hear is, "I don't have time to get organized!" Have you ever made such an assertion yourself? As I said in Chapter 1, the less time you have, the more you stand to benefit from organization, so break down the time barrier with five easy techniques for managing your organizing time.

Chunking your chores

Looking at the whole picture of what you need to organize can be so overwhelming that you don't get started at all. Or maybe you do, but then you quit in an hour because there's still so much left to do. Biting off more than you can chew isn't comfortable in your mouth or your mind — so chunk it instead.

When you don't have the time or concentration to complete the whole Herculean job, simply break up tasks into bite-size pieces that you can reasonably accomplish. Choose one file drawer at a time, and soon you can have the whole filing system down. Start with a single kitchen cabinet and do the second one tomorrow or next week. Rome wasn't built in a day. Chunk what you want to do and get under way.

Setting a time limit

The kitchen timer lets you know when something is done cooking. Use it to signal when you're done organizing too. When you set a time limit, things get done. You know there's a deadline, and you may even find yourself racing the clock to accomplish as much as you can before it rings. If you think you have about an hour to work, take a timer, whether your watch or a clock or the one you use while you cook, and set it for your stop time. There's a trick to this: Subtract 10 minutes from the time you want to work — for instance, an hour becomes 50 minutes — so you have time to put away what you've "decluttered."

Delegating tasks

The best way to get the job done when you're short on time is to let some-body else do it — delegate. In an office with staff at your disposal, this is rela-tively easy. You may simply give a copy of this book to your assistant, along with a priority list (desk first, and then files, and then calendar, and so on) and a timeline for what needs to be done by when. Or you could do the read-ing yourself, and then have a meeting with your office manager or staff to assign projects and establish deadlines.

At home, delegating can be a little bit harder. If you live alone, delegating is called *outsourcing*. If you have a spouse and/or children, delegating is referred to as *delicate family management*. Starting out as a team often helps, working side by side to purge and organize the toy collection and home media center or clean out the garage. Eventually, as your children (and your partner) grow up, you can hand off tasks altogether, which helps them grow up further. You can find many hints for involving the family in your organizing efforts in the chapters to come, as well as for hiring out jobs when it makes sense to do so.

Whether you're at work or at home, see Chapter 19 in Part V on time manage-ment for everything you need to know to delegate productively and politely.

Being accountable

Have you ever had someone assign you an important project upon which other people's decisions, schedules, or success rode? If so, you know what being accountable is like. The repercussions of a sloppy job or missed dead-line could range from wrath or a ruptured relationship to losing a job. The result is that you work hard and fast. You can put the power of accountability to work in your organizing projects simply by telling someone — a sibling, spouse, colleague, neighbor, or friend — what you've promised yourself to do. Once you've told someone else your plan, you won't want to disappoint that person or look like a failure. Being accountable spurs achievement.

Want to make your accountability really stick? There are two ways to up the ante. One is to tell someone who truly cares about the outcome. Promise your boss you're going to clean off your desk, and I bet you won't delay. Say to your best friend or significant other, "I won't be late to meet you again because I'm finding ways to organize my time," and you may be doubly vested in planning your day. The second way is to set a definite date and/or time for your accountability buddy to call you back and ask you if you did what you said you would. Do you know how great it feels to say, "Yes?"

Pretending to move (or really moving)

Last but not least, a powerful motivator for getting organized is to move. When you consider the cost of moving all that extra junk, and the excess stress that your lack of planning and time-management systems will cause in the process, you'll get on the stick. No immediate plans to move? Well, you could make some in the interest of the cause — or just pretend. Set a real date for the move. Schedule it on your calendar, planning backward from the move date to today about what needs to be organized by when. Put the sub-goals on your calendar too, and get moving!

Organizing your space

Organization takes place in space, and a question I commonly hear is, "Where do I start?" My answer is that you have two possibilities, depending upon the situation and your personal style. They are the following:

✔ Beginning with the hot spot: Choose your organizing space by selecting the place that frustrates or bothers you the most — the hot spot. After that, everything else will be downhill. If you go crazy every time you drive into the garage, skip straight to that chapter and spend your first organizing weekend creating a nice, welcoming home.

✔ Starting slow and easy: If the hot-spot approach has you splayed out on the couch in dread and defeat, simply turn 180 degrees and start in the space that's easiest for you. If your desk is fairly clear but your file drawers are a mess, begin with Chapter 15 to see how simple bringing organized perfection to your desktop can be, and then use the energy of your accomplishment to move on to the next project.

Wherever you start, you want to work where the organization is taking place. Don't pull all your clothes out of the closet and take them into the living room to sort and toss; it requires an extra step and leaves you nowhere near a mirror or a rod for rehanging. You may need to clear off some space first because empty surfaces are vital to most organizing tasks. Make like a snow-plow and push it all aside.

Organizing for the people who work, live, or play here

Organization is a people-based process, designed to make people happy and productive on a daily basis — so do ask "Who?" in all the organizing you do.

To personalize your organizing systems, ask yourself, "Who works, lives, or plays here?" What do they want and need? If you're reorganizing your file system, your new setup can affect whoever retrieves or files records there, so you might want to work with your assistant, staff, colleagues, or other family members to design the system together. At the very least, let them know what you've done. If you've just reorganized the pantry, a few labels are worth a thousand words in terms of guiding cohabitants to finding the snack center and putting the potato chips back. Are you single or in business for yourself? Use the tips in this book to organize in ways that work best for you but remember that you may also want to set up systems that meet client needs or make a visitor comfortable.

Getting organized is one of the most personal projects you can undertake in your life. Everyone thinks, acts, and feels differently, and no single system works for every person on the planet. If there was, someone would have packaged it into a pill long ago and I wouldn't have had the pleasure of writing this book.

How You Do It

This is a trick title because, of course, the rest of this book is about how to organize all the specifics of your life. But I'm training your mind here, so take this opportunity to discover how getting organized can be as simple as 1-2-3.

1. **Pick your target:** The good news is that getting organized can improve every aspect of your life. That's the bad news too, because you can't possibly do everything at once. The first step toward using my system to organize your life is skimming the Table of Contents and choosing the target chapter you want to start with. You've already established your mission and set your goals, so this presents no problem.

2. **Read this book:** Sit back, relax, and read the chapter for your first target project. You can take notes or scribble in the margins, or get ultra-organized and read the section in Chapter 19 on how to underline and highlight for maximum reading retention. No matter what, you can find what you need to know and keep the text on hand as a reference all along the way.

3. **Schedule your organizing project:** Write your first organizing project in your calendar and set a deadline for completion. Break down each goal according to the sections or subsections of the chapter and set aside the time to work toward your objective. Match the length of the session to the scope of the task, whether the timeframe is 15 minutes or an hour a day, 3 hours a week, or a few work days or a weekend. Set aside the time on the schedule and go.

Maintaining Organization

Many people are hesitant to put the effort into getting organized because they doubt they can maintain an organized state of affairs. Like going on a diet, why bother if the excess pounds or clutter are just going to come back?

The beauty of getting organized is that it *does* retrain your mind, and there are no biochemical cues trying to confuse the message. In fact, organization is one of those self-reinforcing pleasures in which a mind and body, grateful for the reduced stress and strain, are eager to explore more. Enter maintenance.

If you follow the systems I describe, you may only need to have a major organizing session once a year or less to clean up any given area. A few basic tactics common to all these systems make maintenance easy. Here they are, for the benefit of your newly organizing mind:

- **Right now.** Clean up clutter as soon as you create it.

- **Every day.** Spend 15 minutes at the end of each day putting things away so tomorrow is a brand new start.

- **The one-year rule.** Every time you come across an object or piece of paper, ask yourself if you've used it in the past year. If the answer is no, chances are the item can go.

- **Plan and schedule.** If a major organizing job arises, don't sit around waiting to have the time to take on a grand action. Break it down into chunks today and write each upcoming task into your calendar.

- **Set routines.** Establish patterns, from the annual purging of everyone's closets before buying new school clothes and repaving the blacktop driveway to weekly grocery shopping, laundry, or housecleaning on the same day each week, and so on. Clean out the china cabinet and the garage each spring and fall. Write the car's oil changes into your calendar. Straighten up the house the day before its weekly cleaning. Purge a few files every day. The more routines that you can set, the faster and smoother things can go and the stronger your organizational systems can be.

- **Share.** Remember that maintenance isn't your job alone. Set up systems to share with or delegate to staff, family, and roommates.

The seeds are planted in your mind. All you need to do is fertilize them with all the information herein, and then watch your organized self blossom forth.

Chapter 3

Assembling the Tools, Supplies, and Systems

● ●

In This Chapter

▶ Organizing systems for your space, work, information, and time

▶ Disposing in environmentally and socially conscious ways

▶ Using containers to put everything in place

▶ Choosing the right supplies and avoiding the wrong ones

● ●

Getting organized is a systematic process, so it makes sense that there are some systems and supplies that go into making it work. On this subject, I have good news and good news. First, the right resources, from pullout drawers for your desktop to a calendar/planner matched to your scheduling needs, can make organizing far easier than you may have thought. Second, when you assemble the right resources to get organized, you don't need many. Some key containers and time-management tools, a small selection of information-management supplies, and six simple organizing procedures you can easily carry in your head to handle any organizing question are the sum total of what you need to change your life for the better.

This chapter will introduce you to organizing resources that you'll meet more specifically in the chapters to come. *Important note:* Sit still and put your checkbook away. Don't buy a single thing or redo a space until you read the chapter for the area you're working on. That's where you can fill in the details you need to know to choose right the first time and accomplish your organizing goals. In the meantime, here's a big-picture view of how you can turn your organized mindset into action.

Paper Clips, File Folders, Binders: What's It All About?

Stocking your desk and office right is half the fight for productive and efficient work. In Chapter 15, you can find out how to divide and organize your desktop and drawers into task-driven *centers,* and how to choose and use office supplies. For instance, why you may want to toss out most of your sticky notes and find a better way to white things out. An organized approach to office supplies saves time and money and makes every job easier, so no matter what your position or post, take the time to simplify and supplement your supplies as Chapter 15 describes.

Whether you're organizing at home or the office, you probably have plenty of paper and electronic information to deal with. The right tools can keep info in its place, which is right at your fingertips.

At work and home, all active papers are best kept in file folders inside hanging files. Loose files fall over, and loose papers do not make the organizing grade. The same goes for *loose* computer files, running around your hard drive with no rhyme or reason. Inactive papers and electronic files need a space of their own, located outside your prime productive area and with the same system for easy additions and retrievals.

The basic tools for any paper filing system include:

- Drawers or containers
- Hanging files
- Hanging file tabs
- File folders
- File folder labels

Add in binders and perhaps a few file pockets and wallets, as well as a color-coding system for your tabs and labels, and there's no piece of paper you can't tame. Discover everything you need to know about the ABC's of filing for office or home in Chapter 16, and carry the same concepts through to your computer in Chapter 17.

Organizers and Planners: Lists to Live By

Organized people don't trust their memory — they trust their lists. You can find out how to live by lists and their close cousins, calendars, in Chapter 18, to help you get everything done and leave your mind free for more important things.

Two lists can manage your time, plain and simple. You start with a Master List, which, just as it sounds, covers everything in your life, sort of an ongoing download from your mind. The Master List flows to your To Do List, the tool for scheduling your day, meeting your deadlines, and achieving your goals.

Once you have your lists in place, filling in your planner and putting it to work is as easy as pie. Chapter 18 explores all your organizer options — electronic or paper or both; daily, weekly, or monthly; large or small; filled with this feature or that. You'll even find out what color to write which engagements in. If you haven't tapped the full power of a planner before, getting organized on this front can fill a big gap in your potential.

When you go shopping for your organizer, which you shouldn't dream of doing until you read Chapter 18, here are a few formats and names you may see.

- ✔ **Paper and paper-to-electronic systems:** At a Glance, DayTimers, Day Runners, Filofax, Franklin Covey. Old-fashioned paper has several advantages even in the twenty-first century: easy access, portability, and the ability to flip quickly and scan your schedule at a glance.

- ✔ **Electronic systems:** Palm Pilot and other portables (Casio, Hewlett Packard Jornada, and Royal daVinci) and various computer programs such as Microsoft Outlook. With the power to carry and categorize vast amounts of information, many electronic organizers also offer access to the Internet and e-mail via your Internet connection for computer programs, and through a wireless connection for portable devices.

You can spend anything from less than $10 to several hundred clams on an organizer, depending upon whether you choose paper or electronic and how many features and add-ons you want. The information in Chapter 18 will help you reach the right cost-benefit ratio when it's time to shop for your planner.

Office supply stores, as well as mass-merchandise stores, carry various brands of organizers. The Franklin-Covey organizer is sold only in its own stores, and stationery stores are the place to spot Filofax planners.

Though most organizing vendors are online, I recommend examining an actual organizer up close before you buy, to view what's on a page and determine which brand you want to try. If at first you don't succeed, try again with another type. Finding the one that works for you is worth the search, and fortunately, many organizer refills fit in other binders. Be sure to buy a size that you can carry around with you, because you may quickly discover that this single volume can contain your entire life.

Putting Things in Their Place: Containers

Every time you set out to organize a space, you need containers to clean out the deadwood and create homes for the survivors. Whether you're working in the garage or getting your office into shape, the following tools and techniques can help put everything into place.

No-strain containers: Types, shapes, and sizes

Containers can organize things by like type, such as trays for cosmetics or pens and pencils or dividers for desk or underwear drawers. They can keep food fresh, as a sealed canister does your pasta or pet food. Containers can facilitate cleanup — for instance, preschoolers' toys in big open baskets children can easily access. From the kitchen to the office, the boardroom to the bath, containers are your organizing friends.

Remember, don't dash out and go shopping yet. Just review some container basics here, and then I'll make loads of specific suggestions in the following chapters for matching containers to the job. I don't want you to end up with a closet full of unused crates because you really needed drawers instead.

Whenever you aim to contain, measure the item(s) and storage space first, and then search the house or hit the store for what you need. Containing options include:

- Cabinets
- Shelves
- Drawers and drawer dividers
- Bookcases and bookends
- Magazine racks
- File drawers and boxes
- Baskets, boxes, and a variety of closed containers
- Tiered and stacking racks

Each class of container comes in a range of materials, shapes, and sizes. Matching these characteristics to your containing criteria is your goal — so isn't it great that manufacturers have come out with just about every container you could ever need?

Selecting the material

In selecting material, consider the container's weight, durability, safety, and looks, and whether you can lift or carry it easily. In general, plastic is lightest, lasts long, and doesn't break. However, plastic is often not as scenic as glass or a pretty basket. You probably don't want plastic in your living room, but boy, is it great in the kitchen, inside cupboards, and for storage areas.

Choosing clear or colored containers

Clear containers have a clear advantage: You can see right through them to identify the contents inside. Unless you're trying to hide what's in your container, choose clear and save yourself a step. Transparent containers are also great for showing young children how to get organized. Seeing what's hiding inside — crayons, blocks, toy trucks — sends an easy visual cue for what gets put away there.

When visual neatness is your goal, go opaque with your containers to keep their contents hidden. In this case, you may want to use color as a code — for instance, a blue container to hold kids' gloves and green for adults.

Doing geometry: Shape and size

Round containers waste space. Want to picture why? *Square* off a round container in your mind's eye, and you can see the corners that you're losing. Or put several round containers together and look at all the empty space in between. Whenever you can, choose squares or rectangles for your containers to avoid this geometric rip-off. Yes, you'll need some round bowls, and a big round basket works well for balls, but otherwise stick to the squares.

Once you have the basic geometry down, match the shape and size of containers to what you're storing there. Allow enough space to group things by like type, but not so much that things get lost or jumbled within the container or you're left with a lot of room to spare.

Also ask yourself whether you need a lid on this container. Does it need a tight seal or stackable surface? Some containers, such as Tupperware's Modular Mates, stack easily on top of each other, which can make good use of vertical space.

If you're containing food, you might consider a pouring spout. Try this concept on your containers for cereal, sugar, rice, pancake mix, and biscuit mix.

Identifying with labels

A label can save loads of time by identifying a container's contents with a quick look. Best for things you're storing out of sight (nobody wants to sit on the living room couch and read a label that says "Extra Ashtrays"), container labels add information to your organization. Here are a few tips:

✔ Be sure to use a washable label if you may be cleaning the container in question (for instance, the one you store your flour in). Skip the white computer labels and use a clear, plastic one or a tape made on a label-maker instead.

✔ Clear labels are hard to see on clear containers. If you use a clear, washable label on a clear container per the preceding point, place the label low so that the contents behind it can serve as a background.

✔ Use colored labels to code containers by type. Maybe all your baking supplies are in containers with blue labels ("b" is for blue and for baking), while pasta and grains are labeled with green ("g" for green and grains).

Just as firefighters talk about containing fires, use containers to contain clutter and spend less time putting out organizational fires. Containers provide a place for every important item in your life.

The Three Ds: Using containers as clutter busters

A major contributor to clutter is a basic law of physics: Matter is inert. The way to unclutter is to make matter mobile, and the Three Ds can help. What are the Three Ds? Three containers — boxes, baskets, or big sturdy bags — that you use anytime you tackle a space to distribute, donate, or dump the stuff you find there. Here's how the Three Ds can ease the flow of things and keep you clutter-free.

Distribute box

Have you ever noticed how things tend to end up where they don't belong? To bring them on home, take a container and dub it "Distribute." When you find a cereal bowl in the bedroom, don't rush downstairs to take it to the kitchen, and then go back up to collect the dirty clothes and run them down to the laundry room, followed by a stop in the front hall to grab the suntan lotion you had out for yesterday's tennis game and return it to the upstairs linen closet, and so on and so on until you're utterly exhausted. Five minutes of simple cleanup can wipe you out for the day unless you centralize operations with a distribute box.

Any time you need to leave the room to put something away, don't. Put it in the distribute box instead, and then carry it along to the next stop, just like riders on the bus waiting to exit until they reach home.

Donate box

Maybe the item is not out of place but it no longer has a place in your life. ·
When that's the case, consider donating. Anything useable but no longer
useful to you goes in the donate box, which sits there waiting to go to your
sister, neighbor, or your favorite charity for a tax write-off. For instance, if
you have three sizes of clothes in your closet, you obviously aren't wearing
two of them, so donate those. You probably don't want to go back to the
larger size, and when you reach the smaller one, you'll deserve a treat of
some new clothes in today's styles. The same goes for appliances, equipment
(donate or sell computer stuff the second it gets disconnected from your
system; those things aren't getting any younger), dishes, furniture — you
name it. Letting things move on to people who can use them makes the world
a better place, and your donate box can help.

Dump box, bag, or can

Then there are things that nobody wants or needs. You can designate a box,
trash can, or big garbage bag for things you choose to dump as you unclutter.
The trick is to keep it close at hand as you work and put anything you want
to discard directly into the garbage. Don't forget to recycle when you can.
Garage sales, consignment stores, and charities are great ways to recycle.

You can organize your giveaways by establishing a donation center in the
basement or another storage area where you collect things until you have
enough to warrant a pickup or a trip to a drop-off center.

A Halfway House: A container for the undecided

I am well aware that some of you have a hard time parting with things. If you
didn't, you wouldn't need to hire me. Sometimes, though, all you really need
is time.

Let time heal the pain of parting by putting the items you can't quite say
goodbye to but know you need to into a box. Mark it with "Halfway House"
and the date. If a year rolls by and you haven't gone into the box for something you wanted, then give it away, unopened. This is important. If you open
the box, you're likely to pull something back out into your home. So don't. If
you really want something from your Halfway House during the cooling off
period, go get it. Then close up the box and proceed to give the remaining
contents away if you don't pull them out within a year's span.

The Six Organizing Secrets

Every professional organizer has her or his secrets, and when I was invited to
write this book, the publisher asked me to give away mine. So here they are:
six surefire ways to think through organizing any space or job, from the dining

room to the desktop, from tomorrow's meeting to where you want your marriage to be five years from now.

Five of the organizing secrets are acronyms, words in which each letter stands for a step of the process to make each one easy to remember. Technically, this is called a *mnemonic device,* also known as a way to help your memory. Whether you remember the technical term or not, this is a very organized way to think, and simply remembering the six organizing secrets and putting the secrets to work can help train your organizing mind.

Designing any space with a layout

When you start out to tackle a space, the ideal first question takes in the big picture: "Where do things *go*?" Is that the best arrangement for the desk and filing cabinets? Can you open up more space by moving the bed? What's the most efficient use of the room's wall space? To answer the big picture question, I simply ask you to think like an architect.

Even if you've never sat down at a drafting table, you can lay out any space by drawing, cutting, and playing. Specific goals and considerations for rooms in the home and office are covered in their individual chapters. For now, take a moment to review the basics of how easy it is to make like an architect and create your own blueprint for high-performance rooms. Just follow these simple steps:

1. **Draw the basic blueprint:** First, get out a tape measure and measure the dimensions of the space you want to organize, including the width of each wall, window, door, and closet, as well as the height underneath windows. Jot down each measurement as you go.

   Now swap your tape measure for a ruler and draw your room to scale on a blank piece of paper, using 1 inch to represent 1 foot. Tape two sheets of paper together if you need to. After sketching the basic outline, mark the windows, including a note about the wall clearance underneath, the closets, and the doors.

2. **Create cutouts:** Now think about what furniture and equipment you want in the room, which may include what's there now, new items as recommended in the chapters, or something that's been on your wish list. Measure these items if you already have them or estimate their dimension if not. Next, take some colored paper and cut out a rectangle, square, or circle to represent each piece, again using 1 inch to represent 1 foot as your scale. A typical desk is about 6 feet long and 3 feet wide, so that becomes a 6-x-3-inch rectangular cutout.

   Continue until you cover all the furniture and equipment you'd like to include in your layout. Be sure to write what each cutout represents on the front so you don't lose track.

3. **Play with your layout:** Finally, put glue that allows you to reposition your layout on the backs of the cutouts so you can move them around on your blueprint but not lose their place, and play with your layout. Remember to use the space under windows for smaller pieces — a desk or two-drawer file cabinet in an office, or a dresser or short bookcase in the home. Also keep in mind that doors need room to open and close, so don't put the fax machine in the door's path.

Keep playing until you come up with one or more layouts you like. You may discover a whole new look for your room, or that there's not enough space for the bedroom and bureau to share a wall, all without lifting a finger or straining your back. Not bad for your first organizing secret.

Saving or tossing

From clothes bursting out of closets to the constant assault of information, most people in our affluent part of the world are buried in a daily inflow and existing excess of stuff. How do you decide what to keep and what's a waste of space and time — not to mention energy and money? Simply ask the five W-A-S-T-E questions, and you're well on your way to an informed keep-or-toss decision.

I know from my experience as a professional organizer that the process of deciding what matters in your life and what to let go of goes as deep as it gets. I developed W-A-S-T-E to help separate the wheat from the chaff. As you work through the questions, think like a judge, considering past precedent, future ramifications, and sometimes-subjective differences between right and wrong:

✔ **Worthwhile:** Do you truly like the dress or shirt in question? Is that article actually important to your job? Does the fax cover sheet contain any information you need to know? If the item isn't worthwhile, toss it out now. If it is, move on to the next four questions.

✔ **Again:** Will you really use this thing again, or is it just going to sit in a kitchen cupboard or take up space in your files? This question could also be rephrased as, "Use it or lose it." If you don't foresee needing something in the next year or you haven't used it in the last one, clear it out. Maybe your waffle iron was used weekly for awhile but hasn't been touched in months, because you broke up with the boyfriend you cooked them for or got tired of cleaning out the grooves. It was once worthwhile, but now, goodbye!

✔ **Somewhere else:** Ask yourself: Can I easily find this somewhere else? If you have to make waffles for a special brunch, can you borrow a maker from a neighbor? Can you find a memo in your assistant's files or in another department, or get the details by making a quick phone call? Can you hit the Internet, the library, or the local discount store if the need for this item or info should arise in the future? If so, you don't need to save it. Sometimes, the somewhere else is quite close at hand, such as in your own closet, cupboard, or office. Do you really need half a dozen *fix-it* outfits for painting or messy plumbing jobs when you only wear one at a time? How about the old dot matrix printer; are you actually going to send documents there with that new high-speed laser on hand? A good way to avoid this sort of redundancy is to say, "Out with the old and in with the new."

✔ **Toss:** Many things have ways of slipping and sliding by the first three questions, so here's the acid test: Will anything happen if you toss it? If not, go ahead, unless it must be legally retained. (Chapter 16 will give you guidelines for retaining information.)

This question often ends up taking people on a sentimental journey. Maybe something passed the first three questions because it had sentimental value, but the world wouldn't stop turning if it were tossed. This question is the toughest to judge because it can't be measured by anyone but you. The sentimental value of things generally accrues from the people who gave them to you, whether a family elder such as my Aunt Babe, a good friend or lover, or — here's a hot button — a child.

✔ **Entire:** Do you need the entire thing? The whole magazine, document, or draft? Every coordinate of the outfit, even if you only ever wear the pants? The complete catalog, when you only intend to order from one page? If not, keep what you need and toss the excess.

Breaking things down into components can help with any save-toss decision but especially when sentimental attachment is involved. Maybe you've held onto a high school newsletter that features a picture of you. Can you cut out that picture and the name of the newsletter with the date and paste it into a scrapbook, where you may actually look at it from time to time? Perhaps you inherited a painting from your grandmother that you don't like or that clashes hopelessly with your décor, but you don't want to forget. Take a photograph of it, add it to your album, and give the painting away to someone who likes it better, within or outside your family. This trick works with all sorts of things, from collections you no longer want to display to every gift you ever received that's not quite you but represents an important memory or moment. A picture says a thousand words!

Everything is the sum of its parts, but some parts count more than others. Use the *entire* question to trim the things you do keep down to size.

Everything in its P-L-A-C-E: Organizing space

In the course of my practice, I've developed a reliable process to clear an area of clutter, organize items for easy access and neat appearance, and fine-tune the results to your needs. P-L-A-C-E is the way to organize space and put everything in its place. What could be easier to remember?

You can clean up any area in the world with the following five steps:

✔ **Purge:** First, break out the Three Ds and the five W-A-S-T-E questions and clear your space of clutter by dumping, donating, or distributing everything you no longer need. Whether you toss the dried-up glue sticks in your desk drawer, discard outgrown toys in the playroom, or clean the hall closet of unmatched gloves and ratty old sweatshirts, purging can empower all your organizing efforts.

✔ **Like with like:** The second step in putting things into place is to organize like things together. Not only does grouping help you know where to look, whether you're searching for a file or a first aid lotion but placing similar items together also often creates what I call *centers,* one-stop spots with everything you need to complete a task. You can create a mail center in your desk drawer in Chapter 15, a media center in Chapter 9, a cooking center in Chapter 5, and more, all to tap the clarifying effects of categorization — grouping like with like.

✔ **Access:** Once you have things grouped, placement is the next priority — and here, think easy access. Where do you usually use these items? Put them there. Pots and pans should be near the stove and file cabinets close to your desk. How close is close? Literally at your fingertips.

Placing items for fingertip management can enhance concentration, whether you're making coffee (hey, brewing can be hard first thing in the morning) or working on a report with multiple research sources. To fine-tune your access decisions, consider your fingertips first.

On the flip side, something that you don't use often can be moved farther away because you access it less. If you rarely use the warming tray, keep it on a hard-to-reach shelf.

✔ **Contain:** Containers do double duty from an organizing perspective: They keep like things together, and move things out of sight to clear the landscape and your mind. You can contain things on shelves, in drawers, with bookends or magazine holders, in hanging files, or in baskets, boxes, or closed containers in a variety of materials, shapes, and sizes. Contain within containers by adding dividers to drawers. The more you contain, the better you may feel, and you can find an abundance of practical ideas, complete with pictures and illustrations, in the coming chapters.

✔ **Evaluate:** After you complete the first four steps of P-L-A-C-E, Evaluate: Does it work? Organization is an ongoing process, and organizing can often be improved upon as your needs change or you sharpen your skills. I provide evaluation questions throughout these chapters to help you size up the success of each project as you finish it and in the future. Is a system coming up short? Adapt, change, and fix the function until you're happy that your system is doing the best possible job.

When you evaluate and adjust over time, your organization systems become self-maintaining. Some good occasions to assess your systems include job changes, starting college, getting your first apartment, getting married, getting divorced, and any time you move. But you don't have to wait for these major events to evaluate. A yearly checkup can help you keep everything working at peak level and up-to-date with your current needs.

Clearing your desktop with R-E-M-O-V-E

One very common reason people call me is that they can't see the surface of their desk and have no idea how to fix the situation short of a snowplow. That's why I developed R-E-M-O-V-E, six steps to clear off even the most snowed-under desktop and set a desk up for success. I go through this in detail in Chapter 15, but here's a quick preview to get you thinking:

✔ **Reduce distractions:** Is your desk covered with pictures, knickknacks, or this morning's mail? These may be distracting you and reducing productivity. The reduce principle helps you to identify distractions and get them off your desk.

✔ **Everyday use:** Only things that you use every day may stay on top of your desk. Don't worry; you'll find homes for everything else you need.

✔ **Move to the preferred side:** You use one hand for most daily operations, and your desk can be arranged accordingly. Placing pens, pencils, and pads where you reach for them most gives you fingertip management and makes everything from writing notes to taking phone calls faster and easier. See Chapter 15 for the big exception to the preferred side rule. Can you guess?

✔ **Organize together:** Just as with P-L-A-C-E, organizing like things together on the desktop forms centers so you can find and use items easily.

✔ **View your time:** Everybody hates to be late, so give yourself a leg up by making time visual on your desk. An organizer and a clock are important desktop elements for keeping time in view.

✔ **Empty the center:** Finally, chanting my mantra that "The desk is a place to do work," clear off a space in the center of the station so that you can work on the project at hand. Behold, a long-lost surface — your desk.

Responding to your mail with R-A-P-I-D

Even before e-mail came on the scene, mail overload had slowed many people down to snail's pace, so this system is designed to help you pick up speed with a R-A-P-I-D sort that doesn't even require opening an envelope. Five sort categories help you bring order to incoming mail and get it opened and filed in a flash. Here they are:

> ✔ **Read:** Anything that you need to read — later, please — goes in this stack. You may often find *to read* items at the bottom of the mail pile because they're big ol' magazines and newsletters.
>
> ✔ **Attend:** Notices and invitations for seminars, workshops, meetings, performances, parties, and so forth go in the *to attend* stack.
>
> ✔ **Pay:** If somebody wants your money, *to pay* is the pile to put the item in. Window envelopes are an easy cue. If it looks like one more credit card offer you don't want, just rip right through the envelope to protect your identity and toss, all without taking the time to open it. Time is money, and all these folks are already after yours.
>
> ✔ **Important:** Presume important until proven innocent, and put all unknown incoming mail into this stack.
>
> ✔ **Dump:** If you know at a glance that you won't read or need it, *do not* break the seal on the envelope. *Do dump* that piece of mail in the nearest available trash can.

Chapter 16 will walk you through R-A-P-I-D in detail and tell you what to do with mail after you open the envelope.

Maximizing your time with P-L-A-N

The most important thing you can plan is your time, that precious and irreplaceable commodity. Yes, there's more to it than simply marking dates in your calendar but planning time doesn't have to be hard. All you need are four steps formulated to take you to your goals, large or small, soon or later on. Put time on your side and achieve your peak potential with the power of P-L-A-N.

> ✔ **Prepare:** The step you all too often skip in dividing up your time on Earth is defining missions and setting goals. The result can be that instead of pursuing what you want and need, you simply do whatever presents itself to you. *Prepare* repairs this problem by taking you through the "Five W's Plus How," forming the foundation for plans from next week's party to long-range career development or finding the love of your life.

✔ **Lists you can live by:** Out of your goals flow things to do, and the Master and To Do Lists keep track of all these tasks over the short and long term so you can do more and stress less. Once you find out how to use these lists along with your daily planner, you need never let a small detail or top priority slip again.

✔ **Act with rhythms and routines:** Time has rhythms, like the ticking of the clock, the beating of your heart, and the biochemical changes your body and brain go through every day. When you learn to act with your personal rhythms and establish time-saving routines, you may find more minutes in the day and reap better results from all your efforts. From sleeping to peaking to pacing, acting with rhythms and routines helps you go with the flow.

✔ **Notice and reward your accomplishments:** Here comes the fun part: Whenever you accomplish a goal, you earn yourself a reward, and the P-L-A-N system makes sure you get one by building a prize right into the time management process. When you notice and reward your accomplishments, you create an even stronger incentive to reach your goal the next time around. Pretty soon you have a positive feedback loop that can spiral you right to the moon.

P-L-A-N is such a pivotal part of getting organized so you can enjoy life that I devoted an entire chapter to it. You can read Chapter 18 and start putting its principles to work at any point in the organizing process, and the sooner the better.

By now, you know why you want to get organized. You have a plan for tackling organization in your mind. You've met the systems and supplies, so you can expect no confusing surprises as you work with this guidebook in the priority order of your choice. You know what you need to know. So what are you waiting for? Go!

Part II
Getting Organized at Home

The 5th Wave   By Rich Tennant

It was the last time Darlene stored her shoes in Luke's holster.

In this part . . .

*I*f home is where the heart is, how can you possibly find the old ticker amid all that stuff? Each of these chapters covers a room and its contents, helping you enlighten your living space to create a haven of peace and a home you can show off with pride. With a clean kitchen, beautiful bathrooms, uncluttered living and dining rooms, systems to simplify your entertainment center, even a closet setup that enables you to get dressed in the dark, your heart will leap with joy every time you walk through the front door. Home, sweet organized home.

Chapter 4

Where It All Begins: The Front Hall

*F*irst impressions count, and when it comes to your home, the front entryway creates the immediate and lasting frame of reference for everyone who walks through the door. Clean up the front hall and you can go forth with a clear mind and come home happy. Your guests will be delighted to arrive and take glad memories when they leave. The front hall is your house's face, and getting the entryway organized can give your home a facelift in form as well as function. Welcome home.

The front entry doubles as a showpiece and a dressing room, which presents a special organizational test: How can you keep everything you need close at hand to get everyone out the door, yet also create a clean and uncluttered space? The answer: Put everything in its P-L-A-C-E so that whatever the weather, you can get in and out in a snap and still leave the entryway spotless and tidy. Here's how the P-L-A-C-E system (see Chapter 3 for more) summarizes the steps to simplifying your front hall:

✔ **Purge:** Toss or donate coats, hats, boots, and scarves that don't fit or you no longer use, unmatched or torn gloves or mittens, and any old clothes that no one claims anymore.

✔ **Like with like:** Arrange coats by owner, and sort hats, gloves, and scarves into separate groups for children and adults.

✔ **Access:** Keep this season's accessories on the lower closet shelf and out-of-season items on the upper shelf. Move off-season coats to another closet or basement storage. Sports equipment can be relocated to the garage or storage area. Reserve the hall table strictly for mail and notes. Put everything you need for leaving in the morning by the door the night before. Anything unrelated to leaving or entering the house can find another home.

✔ **Contain:** Put hats, gloves, and scarves into clear boxes or open baskets, separating adults' from children's for quick retrieval. Hang keys on a rack near the door you use most frequently. Use baskets or a sorter on the hall table to hold incoming mail for a family.

✔ **Evaluate:** Can you easily get dressed and find everything you need to leave the house? Can you find a place for your outerwear, the mail, your keys, and what you're carrying after a long, hard day? Does the front hall stay clean with quick and easy pickups? Do you, your family, and your guests feel warmly welcomed upon walking through the front door?

Getting In and Out of the Door: The Flight Deck

The first function of the front hall is as an exit and entry, the point of takeoff and landing for every member of the house. Just as airports employ tight air traffic control to keep this process running smoothly, you need a system for easy exits and entries. If you find yourself running around like the proverbial chicken with its head cut off when it's time to leave the house, you can put your head back on straight with a fast-start plan for using the front hall as a flight deck.

To create a front hall flight deck, place everything you need by the exit door the night before. This may include the following:

✔ Briefcase

✔ Purse

✔ Backpack

✔ Keys

✔ Laptop computer

✔ Cellular phone

✔ Gym bag

✔ Tapes/CDs for the car

If you have an armload-plus to carry, consider taking a load to the car trunk in the evening but beware of leaving sensitive items (electronics, the pet goldfish for show and tell) outside overnight.

If you leave the house by the back or garage door, put your flight deck there for easiest access.

What goes out generally comes back in, raising the question of where all those things can go. The front hall can't be an undifferentiated dumping ground for whatever you have in your hands when you walk through the door, so think about fingertip management before you decide where to drop.

If you plan to tackle work in your briefcase or laptop computer, take the case to your work site — office, kitchen, or bedroom. Kids' backpacks can go wherever homework is done, generally the bedroom or a special spot in the kitchen (conveniently positioned to receive lunches the next morning).

Leave by the door — neatly, please — items that will go out with you tomorrow and you don't need in the meantime. *Exception:* Purses and wallets. Even if you live alone, your front hall can be a very public place, and keeping your cash out of temptation's way is best.

Men's wallets can go on a valet tray in the bedroom.

Women can designate a spot in the bedroom, perhaps next to the dresser or on a certain shelf, to drop your purse every time you walk in the front door. Keeping your handbags in the same spot enables easy switching from one purse to another and eliminates the guesswork of where you left your purse last.

See Chapter 21 for a full discussion of organizing for trips from your daily commute to farther journeys.

Mirror, mirror

The front hall is a great place to hang a mirror to take a last-minute look before leaving the house. In fact, *feng shui* practitioners hang mirrors here to aid the flow of positive energy into the house and reflect the space to make the room seem larger. Because of its prominent position, any mirror you hang in the front hall should be beautiful and in accord with your décor. If you're using a humbler model (including many full-length mirrors), consider hanging the mirror inside the closet door instead.

Coats, Boots, and Outerwear: The Closet

The front hall closet tends to become a catchall, which can wreak havoc on your sanity and schedule when you're missing a glove. P-L-A-C-E principles can restore order to this space. Soon you may even open the door to hang a guest's coat without shame.

If you have a standard-issue front hall closet — one rod and one shelf — the first thing to do is add another shelf. Front closets usually have plenty of extra space above, and if need be you can usually lower the rod a little to make space for the second shelf.

Next, think one-stop centers in setting up the closet, dividing items by like type and owner, and arranging them for easy access.

Family coat center

Human nature encourages people to hang their coats in the hall closet any which way, which doesn't work very well. Wouldn't you rather see all your outerwear options in a row than sort through the kids' down parkas, your partner's running jackets, and who knows whose faded, stretched-out sweatshirts? Group coats by the identity of their owner so that whoever opens the closet door can easily match their choice to the occasion, the outfit, and the conditions outside. Start with the adults' coats on the side that's opened first and work your way down to the youngest child.

You may be tempted to economize on space by installing an extra closet rod closer to the floor for shorter children's jackets. Bright idea, but the additional rod doesn't work so well in this closet. Children grow up quickly and get longer coats. In the meantime, grown-ups and guests need a place to stow their full-length wraps without short rods in the way. Have your front closet's insides overflowed onto pegs on the hall wall? Pull them out. Pegs are not nice to look at and create an instant clutter zone. If you want pegs for children to hang their own coats on, install them by the back door to keep the front entrance clear.

The neat and tidy boot and shoe center

A fact of life when it rains or snows, boots are also a big logistical problem. Boots are wet, messy, and tend to pile up in chaotic mounds bound to trip you up on your way in and out of the house. The solution is to create a boot-drying space right next to the front door as an immediate landing spot, and institute a storage system in the closet to keep boots out of sight when they're not in use.

To dry boots, set a rectangular indoor/outdoor carpet in front of the door and stretching out to the side. You can give your boots or shoes a second swipe on the carpet as you walk in. Then take them off and set them on the out-of-the-way end for easy access in and out of the door. An alternative is a ridged plastic tray with a ledge to catch water. Move dry boots to the floor inside the hall closet.

As for all those unsightly sport shoes, move them to a tiered shoe rack by the back door or in a first-floor laundry room. If you don't have a back door or close-by laundry room or would rather not look at a bunch of sweaty sneakers, purchase a closed cabinet with shelves.

Organize shoes by person, ideally on different tiers of your shoe rack, so all household members can easily find their own.

Getting your mitts on this: Accessory center

Many households accumulate acres of accessories and few have devised an optimal system for storing and accessing mittens, gloves, earmuffs, scarves, sun hats, ski caps, or the dog's leash. In fact, my client Fran was putting unnecessary extra miles on her car due to accessory chaos. Every morning her kids raced around the house from bedroom to kitchen to den looking for hats and gloves at the last minute, often missing the school bus in the process. By putting the children's gloves in a green basket, their hats in a red basket, and their scarves in a black basket when they came home from school, Fran was able to stop the morning hide-and-seek game and get the kids on the bus instead of driving them to school herself.

Here's how to solve your own accessory overload:

1. Purge unmatched gloves and mittens, worn or torn items, and anything no one's worn in a year.

2. Sort your gear into winter and summer groups. Put rain-related stuff with the current season because rain can fall in either half of the year.

3. Organize each seasonal group by putting like items together: gloves, hats, scarves, and so forth. Separate kids' stuff from the adults'. If your family's really big and you have space, make a separate stack for each child.

4. Contain each group in its own colored basket — for instance, adult gloves in blue, kids' gloves in green, and so on. If you'd rather see contents than basket color, opt for clear containers instead. Label the baskets or containers.

5. Access what you need now by placing the out-of-season containers on the closet's upper shelf, and then arranging this season's accessories on the easy-to-reach lower shelf.

If your closet has enough clearance, you can use the back of the door to hang hats and scarves for easy access. A hanging hat rack can do the trick, and Figure 4-1 shows you one way to do it. Unfortunately, this is not an option for folding or sliding doors.

Figure 4-1:
Buried in baseball caps? Try a rack inside the front hall closet door to separate or stack your hats.

You can seriously simplify the process of dressing kids for winter by using clips to keep their mittens with their coats. Buy the same color clips and at least one extra set (two if you have four or more children) so that if a clip gets lost, you have a matching replacement on hand. Clip the mittens to the coat each child wears most.

Umbrellas can stand in a corner of the closet, or you can use the handle or loop to hang them on a closet wall hook, over a hanger, or (for the hook-style handles) over the closet rod. If you're in a rainy spot or season, a stand by the door can receive wet umbrellas; relocate the whole thing to the garage or basement during sunny months.

Keep an umbrella in each car at all times. Talk about needing access — you never know when that sunny day may segue into a downpour. Likewise, put a pair of sunglasses in the glove compartment or car door pocket so you always have glare protection when you drive. See Chapter 21 for more information on organizing your car.

The return and repair center

Making returns and taking things to be repaired are rarely at the top of anyone's fun list. The result can be a forlorn pile by the front door awaiting a willing errand-runner — hardly anyone's idea of a happy sight. Handle the rejects in your life by establishing a return and repair center in a basket or container kept in the front hall closet. If the volume of items exceeds your closet space, try a spot near the back door instead. Under a sink is another idea, but being so out of sight may put your errand out of mind.

Keep the original receipt in the bag with return items so you don't have to search the house when it's time to hit the store.

Secret Storage: The back of the front closet

Some front hall closets go extra deep for additional storage behind the row of coats. If you're one of the lucky ones, use this space to store items that are seasonal or seldom used:

- Luggage
- Sports gear: tennis rackets, golf clubs, swim and ski equipment
- Picnic baskets and coolers
- Punch bowls and other entertaining/holiday items
- Folding chairs
- Archived tax papers and files

Hall Table

If you have room, you may elect to put a table in the front hall. A front entry surface is likely to attract items from all who pass by, which makes the table very handy, or an organizational hell, depending on the way you use it. See Table 4-1 for a quick reference about how to optimize your hall table.

Table 4-1:	Optimizing Your Front Hall Table
Good Uses for the Hall Table:	*Bad Uses for the Hall Table:*
Incoming mail area	Mail filing area
Outgoing mail drop	Return and repair center
Key depository	Anything-goes repository
Communication center for notes	

For a power hall table that facilitates flow through the front entryway, find one with a drawer or two to hold and hide keys, sunglasses, and paper and pen for notes. Give the drawers a ruthless cleaning every week and watch this spot like a hawk.

Keeping it neat and moving: The mail center

Even if much of your mail now comes over the Internet, most people arrive home eager to see what the postal service has brought today. Immediate access and proximity to the mailbox make the hall table a good place to sort and distribute incoming mail. The key to good mail handling, in the hall or anywhere, is to keep it neat and moving.

- ✔ If you live alone, place the mail on the table when you come in and make sure that it moves off by the end of the day. (See Chapter 16 for a sorting system that can speed incoming mail to the proper destination.)

- ✔ If there are two or three of you, have whoever brings in the mail sort it by recipient. You can stick to simple piles or get fancy with attractive baskets or trays. Again, the rule is that all mail be taken from the table by day's end.

- ✔ For a household of four or more, consider buying a small mail sorter. Daily removal of mail from the front hall is even more important for a crowd this size.

Your key center

How many hours of your life have you lost looking for your keys on your way out the door? Having one fail safe storage spot and never yielding to the temptation to put keys somewhere else is an easy cure for the common condition of keylessness. The closest use for keys is near the door or the car, so depending on your setup, your key spot should be the front hall or by the garage door. A drawer in the hall table or key rack on the wall provides the place; you provide the willpower to put your keys in the drawer or on the rack.

Use your head when deciding what keys to carry each day. If you leave the house with 20 pounds' worth and you don't work as a jail warden, then lighten your load. Carry just the keys you need, which means you can leave the keys for the storage shed and your spouse's or children's cars at home. Keep the office filing cabinet keys . . . you guessed it, at the office.

If your key-toting habits have torn holes in your pockets, don't toss the garment. Look for *half-pockets* that you can easily sew in to make your holey pockets whole again . . . then clean out your key ring. Organizing the front entryway is the first step toward achieving a house of high order. Do it and you can consider yourself a member of the cleaned-up club. Congratulations! You crossed the threshold!

Chapter 5

What's Cooking: Organizing the Kitchen

Cooking station, dining area, phone center, study hall, and party hangout, the kitchen is often the most used and multipurpose room in the house. You're also likely to find yourself in the kitchen when you're tired, hungry, and short on patience. In such a state, causing an avalanche every time you pull a pan from the cabinet can easily send you running for takeout. The price of a disorganized kitchen can be high — but the payoff of cooling down the hot spot with organizational savvy is sweet. Clean up your kitchen systems to add flow to the heart of your home, and you may find yourself and your family better fed in mind, body, and soul.

Organizing the kitchen can seem like a big job, so don't try to tackle the task all at once. Choose a single section, such as straightening up the pantry or arranging pots and pans, to get started. Whether you work your way straight through this chapter or skip around from one section to another, your successes can inspire you to continue until everything is in its P-L-A-C-E — the word that summarizes the five steps to cleaning up your kitchen as follows:

> ✔ **Purge:** Toss out broken or worn items, from appliances you haven't fixed to dull kitchen knives that you don't plan to sharpen. The same goes for outgrown kids' dishes and cleaning supplies you tried but didn't like. In the pantry, fridge, and freezer, anything old or unidentifiable goes in the garbage. Say goodbye to expired coupons and untried or unsuccessful recipes. Do you have appliances, dishes, or pans that you don't use but someone else could? Donate!

✔ **Like with like:** Group items of similar type together, including dishes, utensils, pots and pans, appliances, and cleaning supplies. Arrange pantry, refrigerator, and freezer shelves like supermarket sections.

✔ **Access:** Place appliances, dishes, pots and pans, and utensils closest to their most frequent use, creating one-stop centers to make coffee, cook at the stove, serve meals, package leftovers, and wash dishes. Heavier items can go on lower shelves, while lighter things can be kept in cupboards above the countertop. Move seldom-used items to out-of-the-way cabinets or their deepest corners. Sink stuff that you don't use every day can be stored in the cabinet below. Relocate papers, warranties, receipts, and manuals to the office/household information center (unless you have a kitchen desk) and return toys and books to their original homes.

✔ **Contain:** Move noneveryday items (appliances, cutting boards, knives) off countertops and into cabinets and drawers. Add dividers to drawers to contain their contents by type. Transfer grain products from boxes and bags to sealed plastic or glass containers. Organize recipes and restaurant reviews into binders and coupons into a 4-x-6 inch file box.

✔ **Evaluate:** Do you have enough counter space to prep foods, accommodate dirty dishes, and serve meals with ease? Can you make coffee, clean and chop vegetables and get the trimmings into the garbage or disposal, and wash dishes from start to finish — each without taking more than a step? Are you comfortable cooking, eating, and hanging out in the kitchen?

Clearing Off Your Countertops

You may have noticed that working in the kitchen can be akin to aerobic exercise, with all that bending, stretching, reaching, twisting, and the occasional hop to reach a high shelf that most of us do to prepare a simple meal. Working out while you cook may seem like a good idea in theory. However, aerobics rarely feels like a good thing first thing in the morning as you hustle to get everyone fed and out the door, or at the end of a long day when you're stumbling around bleary-eyed wondering if you can serve dinner from bed.

Surfaces you can see are a good place to start organizing your kitchen, because visible areas have both aesthetic and practical importance. Clear counters provide space to work and promote peace of mind while you cook, as well as looking much nicer than the appliance junkyard that clutters many a kitchen.

Identifying countertop criteria

Access is the key criterion to apply when clearing off countertops. Three cardinal questions can qualify an item, be it an appliance or a knife block, for residence on your counter. Ask yourself

- Do you use it every day? If the answer is yes, that's a countertop contender. Qualifying examples may include the coffeemaker, toaster, microwave, can opener, and knife set. The popcorn popper is probably not on this list, so put the machine away until popping day.

- Do they make a convenient under-the-counter version? Kitchen basics from paper towel holders to clock/radios to can openers and even toasters are now made to mount under counters and free up valuable space.

- Can the item fit into an easy-access cabinet close to where you use it? If the answer is yes, and this is not an everyday item, you've just found its new home. *Exception:* Take into account the heaviness of the item and the height of the cupboard. You may not mind reaching overhead for a coffee grinder, but wrestling a Mixmaster out of a high or low cabinet is asking for trouble. Leave that behemoth on the counter unless you're only an occasional baker or have a cabinet that *lifts* the equipment to counter height. Figure 5-1 gives you an inside view of this inventive new technology.

Figure 5-1:
A lifting cabinet to carry heavy equipment up to countertop height.

Photo courtesy of Merillat Industries.

Do you have a specialty appliance you haven't used in years but are saving for a future someday? It could be a crock-pot, a waffle iron, a donut maker — but whatever the genius idea, someone will have improved upon the appliance by the time you want it again, so go ahead and give the space-waster away.

Arranging the countertop

After passing countertop clearance, an item needs a location. As with any prime real estate, carefully consider the space on your counter, including where an item is most commonly and conveniently accessed. The key to a cool kitchen is fingertip management, in which you arrange everything from soap to soup bowls according to a *work center* concept of accomplishing basic tasks without taking a step. Apply the fingertip management concept to everything you do to cook, serve, clean up, pack lunches, and unpack groceries. Tap the power of fingertip management in the kitchen, and even making your first cup of morning coffee can get easier. Here are some principles for easy-access counters:

✔ Electrical appliances need to go near an outlet the cord can reach.

✔ Put the toaster near the plate cupboard for easy early-morning serving.

✔ To create a coffee center, situate the coffeemaker somewhere near the sink so you can fill and empty the pot in the same spot. Store the coffee, filters, mugs, sugar bowl, and creamer in a cupboard overhead. For you purists who grind your own, put the grinder and beans here too.

My own coffeemaker is nowhere near the sink because I'm allergic to caffeine and only make coffee for guests. The highest pantry shelf holds my regular coffeemaker, which is easy enough to take down when there's company. My 30-cup percolator in basement storage rarely comes upstairs, but boy is it handy with a houseful of guests.

✔ A can opener located near the sink makes draining off liquid and wiping up spills nice 'n' easy.

✔ The microwave should be in easy reach — lifting down hot dishes is a home safety hazard — and near a heatproof surface (tile counter, stovetop, or wooden board). Take into account the direction the door opens and make sure that you have adequate clearance. Microwave carts make a great solution for kitchens with limited counter space.

✔ The food processor, blender, and juicer are swing items. Store them in a cupboard if they're rarely turned on; otherwise, find a spot on the counter somewhere near the refrigerator, if possible, so ingredients are within close reach.

Clearing off your countertops can have an immediate enlightening effect that inspires the rest of your kitchen makeover. With all this wide-open space, you can shift your focus to the food you're preparing and the pleasure of the people around you. Do you feel it? Then don't stop there.

Simplifying Your Sink

The phrase "and the kitchen sink" was coined to describe anything and everything thrown together any which way. If your kitchen sink is in such a state of chaos, simplify. Stand at your sink and ask yourself: What do I do where? Answering that question can help you create your sink centers.

Creating the dishwashing center

If you have a two-sided sink, you probably wash the dishes in one side, and in the other scrape, if the sink has a garbage disposal, or rinse. Start by putting your soap, sponge, scrubber, and brush on the washing side.

Cleaning tools and supplies can get cluttered around the sink pretty quickly, so clutter-busting is definitely in order here. Soap (detergent) and sponges are the usual culprits because they're used on a regular basis. Soap may make things clean but the process can get messy. Try these ideas for spotless suds:

- If your sink boasts a built-in pump for dish soap, use it. This gets the bottle out of the way and provides easier, neater dispensing.

- As an alternative, try an attractive pump bottle for the dish soap, one purchased for the purpose or a recycled hand soap bottle (in colors that match your kitchen. To prevent clogging, rinse the spout after use.

- Go tubular with a single soap-sponge unit, a sponge attached to a tube that you fill with soap, which means your sponge is always soaped up and ready to go. The downside is that the device can make a soapy mess while lying around, and the tube requires refilling more often than a soap bottle does.

- Try a nifty little sponge basket with two suction cups on the back that gloms onto the wall inside the sink and keeps two or more sponges — maybe a soft one for wiping counters and a nylon rib sponge for scrubbing pans — virtually out of sight. See Figure 5-2 for a sponge basket in action.

- Presoaped pot scrubbers can go into a raised soap dish with a drain to keep them out of rust-making, soap-leaching water.

- You can install a tilt-down panel/drawer at the front of the sink. Just the spot for your sponges.

Photo courtesy of Get Organized.

Figure 5-2:
An in-sink sponge holder keeps sponges handy and dry.

Do you really need a vegetable brush out on top of the sink? If you're actually scrubbing vegetables every day, more power to you — but those of you who eat mostly frozen veggies or packaged salads can move this brush to a nearby drawer.

Under the sink: Cleaning and supply center

The term *sinkhole* may come to mind when you consider that dark place down under. Rediscover this treasure trove of usable space by setting it up as a cleaning and supply center. Placement is everything under the sink, and if yours is a tangled thicket, think access in front-to-back layers. The front layer includes anything you use every day or so — dishwasher soap, kitchen cleanser, rubber gloves (for those who are good to their hands or their manicures), and a small garbage can for things that don't go down the disposal. This is also the row for a return/repair center if you keep one here. The next layer is for less-frequently used items such as other cleansers and cleaning supplies, soap refills, and laundry detergent (if you don't have a laundry room). In the back, put your spare paper towels and sponges. Within each layer, keep like things together, using the left and right sides as natural subdivisions — for instance, the return/repair center goes on the left, cleansers on the right. Don't forget to use vertical space by stacking when you can.

Buy duplicates of cleaning supplies you also use in other parts of the house —
scouring powder, spray cleanser, disinfectant, glass cleaner — and keep the
extra sets close to where you use them so that you can accomplish your task
without a trip to the kitchen. You may welcome the time and effort saved and
be more likely to do the good deed.

To prevent unforeseen floods, keep your cleaning bucket under the kitchen
sink pipes in case of leaks.

Classifying Your Cabinets and Drawers

Cabinets and drawers can attract clutter and make clatter. Nevertheless,
properly classified, the secret space behind closed doors can be a cook's
best friend.

Pots, pans, dishes, casseroles, and mixing bowls are usually best stored in
stacks. Though retrieving an item at the bottom of a pile can be a major
weight-lifting chore, so much space is saved that I recommend accepting
stacks as a fact of life. Use racks with as many tiers as your shelf can accommodate to create stacks on top of stacks, making item removal and return
much easier. Try the ones that expand to the height of your shelf for maximum
stacking. Note that the skinny little legs of wire racks can only stand steady
on a solid shelf, not on racked or grid shelving.

Two-tiered lazy Susans waste horizontal space with their circular shape, but
the extra vertical tier and easy spinning access may be worthwhile if reaching
is a problem for you.

Dishes: Serving centers

Decide where to put dishes depending upon where and how often you access
them. The closer you keep frequently used dishes to the dishwasher and/or
dish drainer, the quicker you get them put away. On the other end of the
equation, you're well served to keep dishes close to where you usually use
them — the stove for dinner plates, refrigerator for sandwich plates, and so
on. Look for the best tradeoff between serving and stowing locations.

There are matters of altitude to consider too. Save your lower cupboards for
hefty pots and pans and place dishes on shelves above the counter. Heavy
dinner plates work well on the lowest shelf of an upper cabinet, with salad
and sandwich plates and bowls just above.

TIP

Make more out of a tall shelf with a three-tiered coated wire rack like you see in Figure 5-3. Putting dinner plates on one tier, salad plates on another, and bowls on the third beats making one big stack and having to move the whole mountain every time you want something from the bottom.

Figure 5-3:
Tiered racks expand the space of any shelf and make for stable stacks.

Photo courtesy of Stacks and Stacks.

Glasses, cups, and mugs: Beverage center

Most people get past one sorting criteria here: If you can drink out of it, the vessel goes in the beverage cupboard. After that, it's the luck of the draw. If you ever courted disaster while reaching over a tall glass to grab a short one, you probably guessed that there is a better way.

If you have children, consider putting glasses and tall cups at a kid-friendly height so you don't have to be bothered every time a child wants a drink. Mugs can go higher up, because (unless you're raising coffee hounds) kids only use them for the occasional hot chocolate.

Make the organization of your glass cupboard crystal clear by starting with the shortest glasses on one side and working your way to the tallest on the other, in columns of the same height or glass type. No more fumbling toward the back for the glass you want. Again, if your cupboard is tall, a coated wire rack can double your usable space. Make sure the clearance between shelves accommodates your tallest glasses.

Expanding your cupboard's capacity by hanging coffee cups and mugs from hooks in the bottom of the shelf above is best for those with good hand-eye coordination. Otherwise you risk knocking a cup off its hook as you grab your favorite mug from the back.

If there are no small kids to cater to, arranging your dishes and glasses all in a single cabinet enables you to set the table by opening only one door. Glasses are easily grabbed off the higher shelf, plates and bowls from the lower one — and dinner is served.

Pots and pans: Cooking center

Though modern metals technology has taken us a long way from the days of ten-ton cast iron skillets, pots and pans are still big and heavy. That's why you want to think *low* when you consider cabinet space for cooking vessels. Lifting up is always easier than bringing down, and don't forget to bend your knees.

You don't need access to pots and pans that only get occasional use — a big stockpot, the turkey roaster, specialty cake pans — so it's a good thing that most kitchens have so many inconveniently located spots to keep them in. Put these items in the back of deep cupboards, wedged under the support bar, in the dark and awkward corner — anywhere you wouldn't want to reach on a daily basis but don't mind once in awhile.

Remembering what you've got stored in hard-to-reach cabinets can be hard. Give your brain a break by posting a list of contents on the inside of the cabinet door.

Once you divvy up the least-desirable space, put the rest of your pots and pans in the slots closest to their point of use. Skillets and saucepans can go in the bottom drawer of the stove, and baking sheets and cooling racks into a tall, narrow cabinet alongside. (If you don't have such a cabinet, get a set of dividers designed to stand baking sheets and racks on end as you see in Figure 5-4.) Casseroles, baking dishes, mixing bowls, cutting boards, and cake and pie tins are conveniently stored under the food prep counter.

To store lids space-efficiently, put one lid knob side down inside of your stack of pans, and then layer on another lid knob side up, like a sandwich. If your lids outnumber your stack-topping slots, get a rack to stand them on end as in Figure 5-4.

Square edges align and round ones don't, so the simple truth is that anything round wastes cabinet space. Choose square pans when you can.

Skip hanging pots on the wall where they accumulate dust and grease, and you can spare yourself the trouble of washing them before cooking. You may also appreciate the cleaner look.

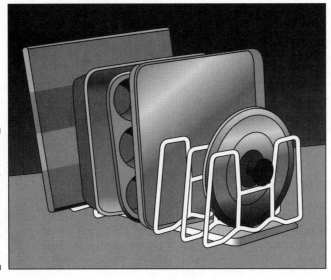

Figure 5-4:
A rack keeps lids or baking pans organized from smallest to largest.

Get a step stool with two steps (three if you're on the short side) to keep folded against a pantry or kitchen closet wall and put your highest cabinets within easy reach.

The Drawer Doctor Is In

Kitchen drawers can easily fall into disarray, with jumbled utensils and unsorted silverware getting in the way when you need a whisk to stir something on the stove or seek a salad fork. For drawers that do more, use the idea of work centers to create quick access to the tools for each type of task.

The essential, five kitchen drawers are:

- **Tableware center:** Placed near the kitchen table, the tableware center drawer can include forks, spoons, table knives, and serving pieces.

- **Baking and prep utensil center:** Located near the counter and cutting board, the baking and prep utensil center should include measuring cups and spoons, mixing spoons, rubber scrapers, whisks, rolling pin, beaters, hand can opener, vegetable peeler, apple corer, garlic press, zester, egg separator, grater, food processor discs, strainer, and kitchen shears.

- **Cooking utensil center:** Near the stove is the spot for the cooking utensil center, including spatulas, tongs, meat fork, ladle, slotted spoon, thermometers, potato masher, baster, and gravy separator.

Utensils can stay cleaner inside a drawer — but if you simply don't have room, use a utensil stand on the counter by the stove instead.

- **Linen center:** Designate a drawer near the stove for potholders, mitts, kitchen towels, and cloths. No linen drawer? Hang your dishtowel on the oven bar and potholders from hooks on a wall above or near the stove. Keep extras in a pantry or cabinet shelf.

- **Office supply center:** Freezer marker, masking and transparent tape, pens and pencils, scissors, ruler, stapler.

If you have a few more kitchen drawers

If you're blessed with a decadence of drawers and have more to spare, here are some other ideas:

- **Knife center:** Chopping, slicing, paring, and steak knives can go here.

  If you have small children, skip the countertop knife block and keep everything sharp put away in a drawer instead. Safety locks can keep small ones out of dangerous places such as a drawer full of knives or a cupboard with household cleaners and chemicals.

- **Wrap center:** Aluminum foil, plastic wrap, wax paper, storage bags, and twist ties.

- **Coupon, box top, and proof-of-purchase center:** Keep these items only if you redeem them regularly; otherwise, they count as clutter and should go. (Read on for hints on coping with coupons.)

- **Basic tool center:** Screwdriver, hammer, nails, and pliers. You can add tools to your office supply center if you don't have a separate drawer to dedicate. Move tools to a high cabinet if you have young children who may hurt themselves.

Divide, conquer, and contain

Once you have the right things in the right drawers, divide and conquer. Free-form drawers waste time and try your patience as you sort through in search of what you need — so measure your drawers, take stock of the size of the various items in them, and hit the store in search of dividers. Look for sections tailored to the length and width of the various things you store: standard tableware, measuring cups and spoons, gadgets, long knives, cooking utensils. Take advantage of the opportunity to give the insides of your drawers a good wipe-down before installing your new dividers. The doctor is in!

Don't buy dividers with slots molded to specific shapes, such as spoons. They limit your flexibility and drawer capacity. Get ultra-organized with the new self-adhesive section dividers that allow you to design the space to your needs.

Sectioning Off Your Pantry

The pantry has primal meaning for most of us. We worry that if old Mother Hubbard goes to the cupboard she'll find it bare — but more likely she may come across a crowded, topsy-turvy place nonconducive to putting dinner on the table or grabbing a snack.

Think of every visit to the pantry like a trip to the supermarket: You're shopping for what you need right now. Stores help you find things by arranging shelves by like type and making all items easy to access. You can do it too. To put your pantry in the pink, use these eight great pantry sections:

- **Baking:** Sugars, flour, oatmeal, cornmeal, mixes (cake, brownie, pancake, muffin), baking powder and soda, salt, extracts, oil, shortening, chips, chocolate, pie fillings

- **Cereal:** Hot and cold breakfast cereals

- **Pasta and grains:** Dried pasta, noodles, rice, rice mixes, other grains, potato mixes, bread crumbs, stuffing

- **Canned fruits and vegetables:** Fruits, vegetables, applesauce, tomatoes, tomato sauce and paste, beans

- **Canned soup, entrees, meat, and fish:** Soup, broth, pasta, chili, tuna, salmon, chicken

- **Condiments:** Mustard, ketchup, mayonnaise, salad dressings, vinegar, sauces (marinara, hot sauce, barbeque, steak, chili, cocktail, soy, Worcestershire, salsa, and so on), peanut butter, jam and jelly

- **Snacks:** Chips, crackers, pretzels, rice cakes, cookies, ice-cream cones

- **Drinks:** Coffee, tea, iced tea, hot chocolate, powdered creamers, sweeteners, drink mixes, soda, canned drinks, juice boxes, bottled water

I've seen too many pantry shelves succumb to the pressure of supersized foods and cases of soda. Avoid shelf sag or even breakage by putting your heaviest items on the floor or near support bars, and splitting up cans and jars. For instance, put fruits and vegetables on one shelf, canned soups and pastas on another, and condiments on a third.

After sectioning off the pantry, arrange items on shelves for easy access with two principles: above-below and front-to-back.

✔ **Above-below:** First group each of the eight pantry sections on vertically adjacent shelves. For instance, you may place flour and sugar on the shelf directly above boxed mixes, chocolate chips, and other baking needs. The two-shelf approach helps compact the space for each section and distribute weight more evenly.

✔ **Front-to-back:** Next, put the tallest items at the back of the shelf and the shortest in front. That means tall cake mixes line up against the back wall while pudding, gelatin, shortening, and nuts go in front. You can also use step shelves to add different levels to your front-back arrangements, as you see in Figure 5-5.

Figure 5-5: Step shelves keep jars, cans, or your spice collection from playing hide-and-seek.

Reconfiguring the Refrigerator and Freezer

Whether a science project in the vegetable drawer or a mystery package on the back of the shelf, the fridge can get scary fast. Fight the fear with some basic configuration.

Five steps to a reconfigured fridge

Like the pantry (but colder), the ideal refrigerator is arranged in supermarket-type sections with the taller items in back. You can adjust the height of most refrigerator shelves to accommodate your items without wasting space. But, you protest, I'd have to take everything out and start over! Yep. That's *exactly* what you need to do. (It's a great time to clean it out too.)

The following steps can take you to a cleaner, more organized refrigerator:

1. **Take it all out:** Pull up a trash bag and take everything out of the refrigerator, tossing fuzzy and old things as you go. Haven't used that mustard in a year? Goodbye! Give the whole thing a good swipe with a soapy sponge. Add an open box of baking soda to soak up refrigerator odors.

2. **Start with the obvious:** Fruits and vegetables go in the bins — fruits on one side, vegetables on the other — cheese and deli items in the drawer if you have one, butter and cream cheese in the butter compartment, and eggs in the little indentations in the door.

   If you don't go through eggs quickly, keep them in their carton instead of on the door. The carton blocks air and food odors to keep eggs fresh longer.

3. **Stock the door:** Fill the door shelves with smaller items grouped by like type — salad dressings, mustards, sauces, jams and jellies, and so on. Soda or milk up to quart size can go in taller door shelves; superspacious doors can handle liters or even gallons. The door is also a convenient spot for a carton of half-and-half or creamer for splashing into coffee.

4. **Work from the top:** The top shelf is the tallest, so this is the place for drinks. Adjust the shelf to suit your tallest pitcher or bottle. If you have split shelves, you can shorten up the other half and put your most frequently used items there (usually dairy).

   Organize your bottles and cans with wire racks. Try the two-tiered type that sit on the shelf for soda cans, and a basket that hangs underneath for liter bottles lying on their sides.

5. **Group foods by type and arrange them for easy access:** Look at what you have left to store and sort. Your sections may include:

   - Cooked foods and leftovers

   - Dairy products and eggs

   - Meat, poultry, and seafood

   - Condiments. For each group, gauge the maximum height and adjust the shelf height accordingly.

Split shelf alert: A big sheet cake or lasagna waiting to hit the oven may not fit on a half-shelf. Get friendly with big foods by aligning at least one set of shelves to reach all the way across the fridge.

The feng shui way to an enlightened kitchen

The Chinese art of *feng shui,* using placement and other techniques to improve your life force energy, is clear on its view of the kitchen: The center of the home and the place where *qi,* or essential energy, begins. Feng shui advises that you paint your kitchen walls white to cool down the heat of the stove and clear out all traces of clutter to give energy room to flow. It's nice to know that the ancient sages were organized too.

Freezer freedom

Now that you're cooled off, dig into the deep freeze. The same principles apply in the freezer as in the fridge: You want supermarket-like sections that make items easy to find by type. Achieve this by clearing out the contents, sorting items into sections, and selecting the freezer spots that afford best access to each group.

1. **Toss the fossils:** Anything you don't recognize or remember or can't see through the frost gets tossed.

2. **Section items off:** Seven good freezer sections include: Meat, poultry, seafood, prepared entrees (store-bought or leftovers), sauces and side dishes, vegetables, juice concentrates, breads, and desserts.

3. **Configure for access:** Freezer setups vary depending upon whether you have an above-fridge, below-fridge, side-by-side, or stand-alone unit. Whatever yours is, if you don't have enough shelves to make sense of your space, buy freestanding coated wire units with a few tiers. (Measure your freezer before shopping.) Next, arrange your food by section, with the items that you use most frequently closest at hand. Juice, breads, frozen vegetables, and desserts are often small enough to slip into door shelves.

"Wrap and date" is the mantra that will keep your freezer straight and your food safe. Freeze anything you won't use soon, in appropriate serving sizes. If that bargain pack of ground beef ends up wasted after thawing, you won't save money. A pound-and-a-half or so (a quarter of a 5-pound package) is the right amount to freeze for a family of four, while singles may opt to make and freeze individual patties.

Keep a reusable ice pack or two in the freezer for keeping lunches cool or icing down an injury.

Fast-Track Food Storage

You can get more out of your groceries when you store them right. Once you set up your system, unpacking groceries and putting away leftovers becomes a snap — and the contents of your kitchen stay organized and fresh.

Don't take the word *storage* too seriously. Most meats and seafood shouldn't stay in the refrigerator more than a few days or the freezer for more than three to six months. The optimal shelf life on most unopened pantry items is six months to a year. So go do a big purge right now, and then get on a spring and fall cleaning schedule to keep your food supply fresh.

Cool container solutions

Clear is the color of choice for food containers, whether plastic bags, glass canisters, or rectangular tubs. The instant visual ID a clear container offers can save you hours, maybe even years over the course of a lifetime. Colored labels and lids can provide aesthetic relief for your eye and a coding system for your mind.

Containers that go from the freezer to the microwave serve a dual purpose and save transfer time. Remember to go square for the best use of space. Stock a variety of sizes and stack the empties inside each other. If you're storing more containers than you're using, that's a tip to toss, as are any containers without a lid or vice versa. Lid holders help contain everything in its place.

Opened packages of grain products — including flour, oatmeal, cornmeal, rice, pasta, noodles, bread crumbs, stuffing mix, and dried beans — can be protected from insect invasion by storing them in containers with tightly sealing lids. Simply match the size of the container to the contents of your package, make the transfer, and then — don't forget this part or you may be sorry later — cut out any preparation instructions from the original package, wipe them clean, and put them right into the container for reference at cooking time. Tape prep instructions on the outside if you prefer, but removing the tape and paper when it's time to wash the container can be inconvenient.

You may want to keep a few disposable containers, such as whipped cream or butter tubs, for toting food to other people's houses or sending care packages to college kids; purge the rest. Likewise, a couple of glass jars are great for storing frying oil to be reused or bacon grease until full to toss, but any more is clutter.

Some containers come preprinted with codes to match the bottoms to the lids. Use a permanent marker to code the rest with letters of the alphabet. While you're at it, write your name or initials on any pieces you take to other people's houses.

Wrapping center

A wrap and packaging center can make quick work of leftovers, lunches, and food that you want to freeze in a one-stop spot. Find a drawer or cupboard shelf that can hold all your wraps — plastic wrap, aluminum foil, wax paper, sandwich bags, resealable bags, and lunch bags — and food containers in a variety of sizes. Containers can stack inside each other according to size.

You may want to slide your wraps into one or two wire racks to keep them easily stackable. These can be a shelf-top model, or designed to mount inside a cabinet door; check out this alternative in Figure 5-6. (Be advised that large-size boxes won't fit into most racks.)

If you're short on drawer or shelf space, store your wrap center under the sink.

Resealable bags are a perfectionist's idea of nirvana. Stock all the sizes — snack, sandwich, pint, quart, and gallon — and watch yourself come up with novel ways to use them, from freezing sauces to storing children's game pieces, toting cosmetics or pencils, and making ice packs for your weekend warriors.

Once you get your wrap center set up with all of your wrapping stuff, you're ready to prepare lunches, keep leftovers, and use your freezer to maximum efficiency. Here are some pro tips:

- ✔ Wrap foods in freezer paper, aluminum foil, or a double layer of plastic wrap, zip them into resealable plastic freezer bags, or slip them into plastic containers.

- ✔ Use a permanent marker or freezer pen to label and date everything as it goes in. Just a date will do on purchased items in their original wrapping. You can skip items you go through fast and use quickly.

- ✔ Color-code your labels or container lids according to the section they belong to or your own criteria. For instance, I top beef gravy containers with orange lids and turkey gravy with beige. A quick-reference chart can help you decode your colors later; use the same ones all the time to remember better.

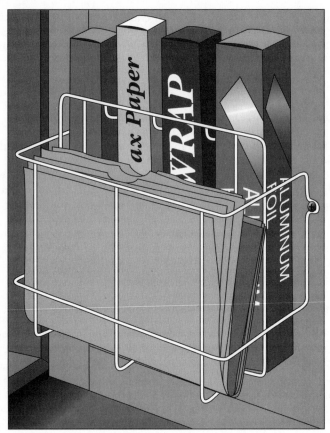

Mealtime or Hassletime: The Organized Meal Planner

Attention take-out addicts: A simple plan turns "I don't have time to cook" into "I can!" and saves time, money, and stress along the way. You may also be amazed by how much more your house feels like a home and your family like blood relatives when you fill your kitchen with enticing aromas and all sit down to break bread together. For those of you already in the nightly cooking trenches, prepare to discover some powerful secret weapons.

The first step to master meal planning is to know what you eat. Take a minute to jot down what you ate for dinner each night for the past week. (If this is straining your brain, just keep a log for the next week or two.) Now look for the pattern — maybe pasta on Monday, chicken Tuesday; meetings and school events on Wednesday mean leftovers or frozen entrees as everyone fends for themselves. Thursday is tacos or wraps, Friday dinner is out,

Saturday is a slightly gourmet effort with fish or meat, Sunday night is take-out for the day of rest. Looks like you need to plan and shop for four nights. Not so hard, right (especially when you consider that most weeks run pretty much the same)?

Writing your master menu and grocery shopping list

Write up your typical week of meals, throwing in the lunches and breakfasts eaten at home. Add in any missing favorite and/or frequent meals. This is your master menu list.

Now use your menu list to create a master shopping list. Remember to account for fruits and veggies, side dishes, snacks, desserts, drinks, and school lunches. Organize your list by supermarket section, and then type it up and make a bunch of copies or enter it on your computer.

Keep your master lists on the bulletin board or in the office supply drawer in the kitchen. Use the menu list to choose tomorrow's dinner before going to bed each night (okay, it still works as you walk in the door that evening because you did your shopping in advance — haven't you?). Pull out a fresh copy of the shopping list each week and use a highlighter to indicate what you need. Add items to your current shopping list when they're halfway down. Stock a backup of anything you go through fast. Do you live in snow, earthquake, hurricane, tornado, or flood country? Keep some nonperishable items on hand for an emergency. Those who live alone can stock some soups and canned foods for days that you're sick and can't go to the store.

Add to and edit your master menu and shopping lists as you make new discoveries and favorites fall out of favor.

Create your master menu and shopping list in a word processing table or spreadsheet on the computer so you can easily make additions or changes as your choices change.

Is making a master shopping list more than you can manage? There are two other solutions for you:

- ✔ Keep a wipe-off board on the refrigerator door to write down things you need as you think of them during the week. Let kids add their requests but tell them you make no promises. On shopping day, jot the items on the board down on a piece of paper. Look through your pantry and fridge and add whatever's running low as well as needs for the week's meals.

- ✔ Less customized but better than going listless is a magnetic shopping list with pieces to slide over the items you want to buy. Now that was easy, wasn't it?

Shop like a jock without dropping

An organized kitchen begins in the supermarket. If, like most people, you usually hit the store with frayed nerves and a scattered mind and come home with a predictably mixed bags of goods, try these shopping strategies to procure like a pro.

Shop at the right store.

- Keep a separate list for bulk purchases — paper goods, cleaning supplies, soda, liquor, and nonperishable foods — and shop once a month at a warehouse or club store.

- The supermarket is the place to get your fresh foods and specialty items. Plan to do your main shopping once a week and run in a second time only if you need to pick up perishables.

- Convenience stores are hard on your budget, but oh-so-easy in emergency situations.

Just be sure to buy only what the emergency requires — and the first time you find yourself there for toothpaste, add it to your backup list.

Shop at the right time. Try to resist the urge to shop when you and the rest of the world want to most: just before dinner. You may be competing at the meat counter and standing in line forever — and you're likely to buy more when you're hungry. Morning and late evening make great grocery times in today's 24/7 environment, as does the day after your favorite store stocks its shelves (ask a friendly manager).

Shop in the right sections. The hot service counter, salad bar, gourmet sauce shelf, and prepared foods section are great when you're in a hurry, not so good when you're on a budget.

Cooking in bulk truly saves time — and often money, because you can buy ingredients in value packs, and a well-stocked freezer or fridge can forestall many a stop at a restaurant or take-out place. Roasts, soups, stews, and casseroles are all great candidates for cooking ahead. So break out the big pots and leverage economy of scale. Remember to package the fruits of your labor in serving sizes right for one meal.

Unloading the goodies

After grocery shopping, unloading efficiently can save time and stress. Keep a collapsible crate in the trunk of the car to help carry bags into the house. If your garage is already organized, you will have remembered to back the car into the garage for easy unloading (see Chapter 13). If you live in a high-rise building, a folding shopping cart can help you get your groceries upstairs with ease. Just remember to put the heavy items on the bottom, or they'll squish your vegetables and bread!

As you unload the groceries, be thinking about how and when each item can be used. Organizing as you unpack items can give you a headstart on busy mornings and harried meal times. For instance, wash and ice the minicarrots for the kids to snack on. Seal pretzels into resealable plastic bags to tuck into lunches. Toss out all those old and spoiled things you come across as you put away the new.

Are you a victim of grocery bag buildup? Here's how to keep bags neat until you recycle or reuse: Open one brown grocery bag, close the rest, and slip them lengthwise into the open bag. Plastic grocery bags can be packed inside one open bag too, or purchase a cylindrical container that hangs from the wall to hold them. Unless you only go to the grocery once a year, you shouldn't need more than a bagful of empty bags on hand for reuse, so recycle the rest.

Cookbooks and Recipes

The recipes that tell us what to do for delicious success can be a source of vital sustenance and heritage — when they're not cluttering the kitchen with information overload. Systematize your cookbooks and recipes into accessible references instead of acres of meaningless paper, and watch your culinary prowess soar.

Cleaning up your cookbook collection

How many cookbooks is enough? Everybody needs at least one all-purpose cookbook, so that whether you wonder what to do with the fresh Muscovy duck you just bought or are summoned to provide oatmeal cookies for the school bake sale, you have somewhere to turn. Beyond that, it's a question of how much you (really, actually) cook. Go through your cookbook collection and purge anything you haven't consulted or cooked from in a year, even if the book was a gift or a quaint collection from your local junior league. Remember that the library is well stocked with cookbooks for that special occasion when you need an appetizer from Afghanistan. Resist the urge to buy new cookbooks you don't need. Store cookbooks in the kitchen, where they're used. You can contain them on a pantry shelf, install a shelf on the wall, or, if your collection is legitimately large, arrange them in a small free-standing bookshelf, grouped by type. If you're stuck with a wire rack shelf, lay a board or sheet of clear, hard plastic over it so you can slide books in and out easily. Don't forget bookends to keep everything standing up straight.

While you cook, slip your cookbook into a clear stand that holds it upright and keeps the book open for easy viewing while screening out the splashes and spatters.

Reducing your recipe burden

Now, as for all those recipe clippings, that ragged and yellowing pile — yes, you know you have one, so put your guilt aside. Notice how they just sort of fall out all over the place when you have to find a recipe? This calls for some action. Your step-by-step solution is as follows:

1. Get two three-ring binders and a stack of plastic sheet protectors.

2. Sort your recipes into two piles: *to try* and *tried and true.* Toss out anything you tried and haven't loved, lost interest in, recipes dated over a year back or those so old the paper the concoction is printed on turned yellow.

3. Write today's date on the recipes in the *to try* pile.

4. Slip recipes into sheet protectors, fitting in as many as you can see. File the recipes, one pile per binder, according to sections marked with tabbed dividers — appetizers, meats, poultry, seafood, pasta, desserts, and so forth. Label the binder spines so you can distinguish the tried from the new. (See Chapter 16 for more information on setting up binders.)

Voilà! — now you know just where to go to find your favorite no-cook pasta sauce or the hazelnut-crusted halibut recipe that looks so fabulous for your next dinner party.

Card files are a hard-work way to store recipes. You have to do amazing feats of origami to get the recipes clipped in a way that they fit on the card, or rewrite the whole thing from scratch. Try the binder approach and spare yourself the extra effort. To maintain your binders, throw away any recipe you try but don't like, and move those you do into the *tried and true* binder. Date all new *to try* recipes as you file them, and toss them after they've sat around for a year. Chances are that the dishes don't really fit your lifestyle, and there are plenty of new ones coming.

If you collect restaurant reviews, use the same two-binder system to file them and guide your decision when it's time to go out. Make sections like restaurant guidebooks — business lunch, romantic dinner, family, ethnic cuisines, and the like.

If you're a serious cook and computer-savvy, you may want to consider filing your recipes on your computer, in special recipe software that also runs nutritional analyses and generates shopping lists, or in your word processing program. Recipe programs are set up to organize your recipes by section; if you use a word processor, create a different folder for each type of dish. Getting recipes entered takes extra time, but you save storage space and can print a fresh copy whenever you need one.

Healthy eating made easy

Many of us are trying to eat more healthily, but need some new habits to make healthy eating as easy as it should be. Here are a few ways you can organize your kitchen to help you keep your best resolutions:

✔ Clear unhealthy foods out of your cupboard. Unopened items can be donated to charity.

✔ Keep plenty of fruits and vegetables on hand — fresh, frozen, and canned.

✔ Buy lowfat soups, canned beans, pasta, and marinara sauce for quick throw-together meals.

✔ Use cooking sprays and chicken or vegetable broth for fat-free sautéing.

✔ Stock your pantry with fat-free flavor sources: spices, hot sauce, mustards, chilies, horseradish, vinegars, soy sauce, and so on.

✔ Package desserts and snacks into individual serving sizes as soon as you make or buy them.

Coupons: Turn Clutter into Cash in Hand

Coupons appeal to our most basic instinct: to get a good deal. Of course, manufacturers wouldn't offer them if coupons weren't a good deal for them too, and purveyors love nothing more than consumers buying stuff they don't need or wouldn't buy otherwise — preferably in the extra-large size stipulated on the coupon — simply to *save* 50 cents. The first rule for turning coupons into cash in hand is *don't clip* anything you don't need. Because bagel bites are on sale is no reason to introduce bagel bites to your diet; a single person doesn't need a 2-pound pack of lunch meat; and yes, you can have too many cans of tomatoes.

However, when coupons are properly clipped, filed, and redeemed, they can be great money-savers, especially for larger families. The trick is to be efficient enough that you don't spend more time than the money you save is worth. Here's the plan:

1. Get a 4-x-6-inch file box (3-x-5 inches is too small for wider coupons).

2. Add tabbed dividers and label them by five categories: food, household items, paper goods, personal, and other (batteries, camera, office and school supplies). Depending upon your shopping habits, subdivide further for easy retrieval.

3. Tackle your coupons as soon as they arrive — the Sunday paper is a good source — and clip items you commonly use, know you need, or genuinely want to try. Don't bother with things that you already stocked up on unless the expiration date is fairly distant.

4. File your coupons by section, putting the newest ones in back and weeding out those that have expired.

For fast-food and take-out coupons, contain them in a big (6-x-5-inch) magnetic pocket posted on the less-visible side of the refrigerator. Keep menus in front and coupons in back, organized by type of food: burgers, pizza, chicken, Chinese, and so on. Purge expired coupons every month or two.

When you shop, look for a place that redeems coupons at double their face value — usually large supermarkets, where you can do much of your drugstore shopping these days too. Mark the coupons that you know you want to use on your shopping list, and then take the whole box along for the ride so you never leave one behind or miss an opportunity to double up with an in-store special. Set your box in the child seat of the shopping cart for easy browsing as you stroll the aisles.

Many Web sites offer coupons for items from groceries and sundries to electronics, books, and flowers. The great thing about cybercoupons is that the Web stores them for you; just print and clip them when it's time to shop, and go!

Sweeping the Kitchen Clean

Keeping the kitchen clean is a daily challenge, but with a few tricks up your sleeve you can create a self-cleaning kitchen. Well . . . almost. Here are some ideas for keeping daily kitchen cleanup organized and easy.

✓ **Wash up while you wait** for the water to boil, the chicken to roast, the sauce to reduce. Washing pots and pans as you use them leaves a smaller pile to clean up at the end.

✓ **Sweep after every meal,** or at least at the end of each day, so crumbs and fallen food don't get ground into the floor and create a tough cleanup job for later.

✓ **Put a plastic mat under the baby's high chair** to catch drips and spills, and then just rinse it off in the sink after feeding time.

✓ **Keep your tools close by.** If you don't have a utility closet in the kitchen for the broom, dustpan, and mop, various organizers are available to hang them from a pantry wall. A first-floor laundry room is another place to put these implements.

Use a plastic dustpan for easy washing when you sweep up something messy.

✔ **Indulge your trashy side.** Most kitchens generate a great deal of garbage, so go ahead and get a nice big, plastic wastebasket that you won't have to empty every five minutes. Keep the wastebasket clean with a plastic garbage bag liner, and watch for spills and mold in the bottom. You can add a second wastebasket alongside to hold bottles, jars, and cans on the way to your recycling bins.

The worst is over. After the kitchen, you just coast down the smooth slope toward total organization. I think now would be a good time to take a break with a cup of tea in your cleaned-up, cooled-down kitchen and contemplate the sweet taste of organizing success.

Chapter 6

Sleep on This: Bedroom Bliss

*Q*uick — in what room of the house do you spend the most time? Even if you're a true couch potato commonly found glued to the tube in the TV room, a committed gourmet cook who can't stay out of the kitchen, or a perennial socialite spotted every night holding court in the living room, just about everyone but an insomniac spends most of their time at home in the bedroom catching up on sleep. Experts say we're *supposed* to sleep a third of our lives away, and everything you do in the room dedicated to relaxation can be extra sweet when you set it up as a personal and peaceful retreat.

To get started in bringing balance to your bedrooms, select where you want to begin: yours, the kids', or the guest bedroom. If you want, skim the headings of the following sections to target a problem area, or simply work your way through the chapter to put everything in its place. In fact, P-L-A-C-E sums up the steps that see you, start to finish, through the race.

✔ **Purge:** Donate or toss clothes, broken, unused, or outgrown toys, accessories, jewelry, and perfume you haven't worn or used in more than a year. Pitch kids' old artwork and papers. (Yes, you can save some! Read on.)

✔ **Like with like:** Organize clothes by type, style, and color. Group shoes, purses, scarves, and ties by color.

✔ **Access:** Stock your bedside table with everything you need to make it through the night. Move the clothes you wear most frequently to top drawers and the closest parts of the closet, using tiers to double the number of items within reach. Find a shoe organizer that works with your space. Move off-season clothes to another closet or storage, desk and papers to the office, extra books and tapes to the family room, extra toys and games to the playroom, and kids' papers that you want to keep to a memory box in the storage area.

✔ **Contain:** Put jewelry into jewelry boxes, men's accessories into valet trays, underwear and socks into drawer dividers, and shoes and accessories into organizers. Arrange books in bookcases and organize toys into crates, drawers, baskets, or containers with lids.

✔ **Evaluate:** Do you start to relax as soon as you walk through the bedroom door? Can you crawl into bed, enjoy your favorite relaxing pursuit, and sleep through the night without getting up? Do you wake up refreshed? Can you pull together great outfits and accessories — even in the dark? Do children sleep and play in their rooms happily and safely?

Master Bedroom

It's not just for sleeping anymore. Once considered a crash pad in which the bed was the primary focus, many adult bedrooms now double as a private place to relax, far from the blaring TV or boisterous kids. Organizing this room can send you to sleep more satisfied and calm, make opening your eyes each morning a pleasure, and provide sanctuary from the stress and strain of life.

Arranging your bedroom

With big items like beds and dressers to place and plenty of closets, doors, and windows to confuse the issue, arranging furniture for optimal bedroom function can be an architectural challenge. That's why you need a blueprint. Refer to Chapter 3 for blueprint basics, and then use these principles to bring order to your bedroom with the following steps:

1. **Sketch your bedroom to scale according to the instructions in Chapter 3.**

2. **Survey the possibilities of what to put in your bedroom.**

   Make sure you have the must-haves, and consider whether any additional options may suit your personal needs or help to streamline the room.

   Must have: Bed, one or two night tables, one or two lamps, one or two dressers, a mirror, and a closet or armoire.

   Optional: Built-in under-bed drawers, a headboard with a bookcase or cabinets, bookcase, media cabinet, reading chairs, and closet storage units and/or shelving.

3. **Measure the big stuff** — the bed, dressers, bookcase, media cabinet, armoire, and mirror and make the cutouts that I describe in Chapter 3.

4. Play with your layout.

Look for where you can optimize your space according to the principles of fingertip management and access. If you're part of a couple, think of drawing an invisible line down the middle of the bed like in *It Happened One Night* (strictly for the purpose of furniture placement!), and then arrange each partner's night table and dresser on his or her side.

Are two of you sharing a single bedside table, alarm clock, and reading lamp? Keep the peace with a pair of each situated on your respective sides. You'll both rest easier! (The same goes for your dresser too.)

5. Roll up your sleeves and put the furniture into place.

Finishing touches might include a full-length mirror on the back of the door, and a small wooden or wicker chest at the foot of the bed to contain extra blankets that don't fit in the linen or bedroom closet.

Do your best to keep the desk and paperwork out of the bedroom. How can you relax with all that work and worry staring you down? If there's no alternative, keep it as neat and contained as you can. Chapters 15 and 16 provide the full lowdown on organizing your desk and papers.

Making the great escape

Because bedrooms aren't just for sleeping anymore, why not turn yours into a personal escape that satisfies your every need? Check the following list for suggestions:

- ✔ Add a great reading chair with an overhead lamp and a small bookcase or end table to make the bedroom an anytime retreat. Insomniacs should skip reading in bed, so a nice recliner can provide a solution for the sleepless.

- ✔ Do you like to watch your favorite show all snuggled up? Does music play a part in your love life, relaxation routine, or morning wake-up? Add a small media unit to your bedroom and organize the equipment, tapes, and discs according to the principles in Chapter 9. Closed cabinets are better than open shelves for storing media in the bedroom, where you want the picture to be purely peaceful. Keep the remote controls in your bedside table drawer so you don't have to drag yourself out of bed to skip a track or flick off the power.

- ✔ Arrange your *boudoir* for *amour* by clearing out all the workaday distractions and setting the mood with some strategically placed scented candles. Have your favorite soft-and-sultry CD ready to go and and spray your pillows lightly with your favorite scent, unless somebody's allergic!

Stocking the amenities: Bedside table and dresser

Never does fingertip management seem as important as after you've crawled into bed, when a trip across the room for a pen takes on all the appeal of a trek to Siberia. For easy access, stock your bedside table with everything you need to get through the night so that you can sleep tight.

Start with a table that has drawers and/or shelves underneath to contain nightly necessities. On the tabletop go a reading lamp and alarm clock, and perhaps a radio or tape/CD player if you don't have a stereo in the room, a white noise machine if it helps you sleep, and a coaster for a mug of tea or glass of water. The top drawer or shelf can hold a book or magazine, remote controls, eyeglasses, eye pillow or shade, pen and paper, a flashlight, and a travel alarm clock in case the power goes out.

Additional shelves or drawers can hold books and audiovisual disks or tapes. Select only your bedroom favorites and keep the rest with your main media center and library.

Middle-of-the-night ideas can be brilliant, but they can also keep you up all night if you don't put them to rest. Keep a pen, small pad of paper, and flashlight in your night table so you can jot down anything from what your spouse should bring home from the store tomorrow to a quantum physics equation and get back to counting sheep. Some pens have built-in flashlights to assist your nighttime scribbling.

Main event: The dresser

Whether you call it a dresser, bureau, or chest of drawers, besides the bed, the dresser is the most important piece of furniture in the bedroom. How neat or messy it is governs how quickly, efficiently, and painlessly you can put yourself together on a groggy morning. The challenges with the dresser are twofold: Organizing everything you put in it and keeping the top clutter free. Like all surfaces, dresser tops too easily become storage areas. Don't let it happen; not in your personal haven! Here's what can stay out:

- ✔ Jewelry box(es)
- ✔ Perfume tray
- ✔ Valet tray
- ✔ One or two framed photos if you must, but why not hang them on the wall instead? Find homes for everything else in drawers.

Super-neatniks may like an armoire-style dresser that puts the top drawers or shelves behind closed doors.

Boxing it up: Jewelry

Dazzling diamonds or simple silver chains, your jewelry needs to be in its place so you can find the right pieces to polish off your look. Are you storing some of your jewelry in its original boxes? Much as you may like the feel of the ultra-suede or remembering that the bracelet came from Bloomingdales, individual boxes waste space and hide their contents from your hunting eye. Take out what's inside and toss the containers. *Exception:* You can keep jewelry in its original box for storage in a fireproof or safe deposit box.

Now, box on a bigger scale. Unless you buy one of those big, expensive jewelry chests, chances are you won't find one box that holds your entire jewelry collection, but two should do (three if you have a lot). Match the shape and size of each box to what you keep inside. For necklaces, look for one with a horizontal bar and sprockets for hanging. You'll also find circular sprockets for long chains and necklaces, either as a separate container or on the sides of a jewelry box with drawers. (Any jewelry box designers out there reading? Please, we need more hanging space!) If you don't have enough depth to hold bulky bracelets or earrings, buy a separate container for them.

If you're lucky enough to have the drawer space, you can get your jewelry off the dresser top by buying sectioned units that stack, sorting into the slots by like type and style, and keeping them inside drawers.

Don't let dust cloud the brilliance of your jewelry or perhaps increase the risk of infection in pierced ears. Skip the open-air ring displays and earring trees and contain everything inside a box or drawer.

Protect your most valuable jewelry from theft, fire, and disappearing down some mysterious crack by keeping it in a safe deposit box at the bank. Before you go, get your jewels appraised and add a rider to your home insurance policy to cover them against loss or theft. Keep a list of what's in the safe deposit box tucked into your jewelry box, and don't forget to get to the bank before any big affair! Most banks close by noon on Saturday.

Men's accessories: Tray chic

Men may wear fewer adornments on average than women, but that doesn't mean they don't need a place to put them. A valet tray, which can range from a simple flat tray to a more elaborate affair with a drawer, may not be as service-able as a real live Jeeves, but it's still a help in holding onto little things such as

- ✔ Tie bars
- ✔ Cuff links
- ✔ Watch
- ✔ Wallet
- ✔ Change
- ✔ Pins

✔ Pocket pen or pencil

✔ Pocket appointment book or electronic organizer

For infrequently worn items, choose a tray with a drawer to keep them out of the dust.

Now that you have the top all figured out and you're feeling a sense of accomplishment, take on the nitty-gritty of dresser usage and organization. What you put into the dresser is just as important as where you put it. Here is where organizing your wardrobe really begins! This piece of furniture is the place to keep the following items:

✔ Exercise clothes

✔ Nylons and tights

✔ Shorts

✔ Socks

✔ Sweaters (hanging them stretches the shoulders)

✔ Swimwear

✔ Thermal underwear

✔ T-shirts and tank tops

✔ Underwear and lingerie

Drawer management

Separate dressers are best if you share the bedroom. If you must share the bureau too, designate separate drawers for each person.

Allocate items among drawers by putting like things together and the least frequently accessed items in the bottom drawers. No, thermal underwear doesn't go with your slips just because you wear them both next to your skin. How often do you pull on long johns, and when do you ever add a slip on top? Put the thermals down below. Likewise, exercise hounds might want to keep their workout togs in a top drawer, but couch potatoes shouldn't bury them in the bottom as an excuse not to move!

Close to you: Innerwear

Your delicate items like to be handled with a soft touch, so start by dedicating one drawer to underwear and another to just nylons and slips. Next, add dividers so you can find the undergarment you need with ease. I prefer the soft, padded lingerie boxes pictured in Figure 6-1 to the thin, hard plastic kind. Another option is a drawer divider such as the one shown in Figure 6-2.

If you like to wear pantyhose under pants, keep a few pairs with inconspicuously placed runs. Use a permanent marker to write an "X" on the waistband and store them separately from your good ones.

Figure 6-1:
Keep lingerie straight and snag-free with soft, padded boxes.

Photo courtesy of Stacks and Stacks.

Matched pairs and lost mates: Socks

Often a mess and unmatched to boot, socks need some help staying straight in the drawer. Here are my favorite sock-it-to-'em strategies:

✔ **Fold and stack.** Fold each pair in half together and put them on top of each other in neat stacks.

✔ **Wrap and toss.** For a more free-form approach, wrap one sock around the other into a little ball and toss it in the drawer. Nifty as this trick is, it can also stretch out the outer sock.

✔ **Divide.** Install a drawer divider, either a system of snap-together flexible polymer strips that gives each pair its own slot, or parallel dividers that run from the front to the back of the drawer.

✔ **Color code.** Use the front-to-back dividers so that you have a single lane of socks, and then arrange it by contrasting color — black at one end, brown at the other, and white in the middle. Navy, gray, and green can go by the whites, or start a separate row if you have enough. With precise color placement, you can match socks to pants in the dark, or at least through a colorblind morning haze. Still, I recommend a final check before you walk out the door.

See Figure 6-2 for a view of these sock-taming techniques.

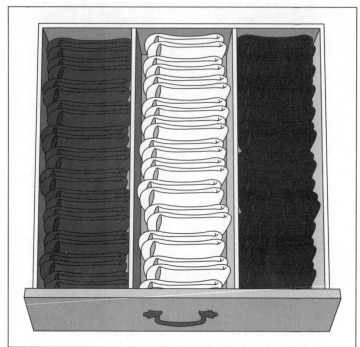

Figure 6-2:
Drawer
dividers
keep socks
in line.

Power coordinating: The closet

Take a deep breath. This may hurt a little bit, but the reward is that you'll finally open your closet door without fear and realize your wardrobe's full potential. Clean up your clothes with six steps that will change the way you dress for the better:

1. **Dress down your wardrobe.** Fashion changes each year, so go through every item in your closet, from shoes to suits and everything in between, and purge anything you haven't worn in the last 12 months or won't be able to squeeze into soon. This is a great opportunity to figure out what flatters you and jettison the deadweight. Grab a couple of friends and put on a fashion show, asking their honest but kindly couched opinion regarding what looks good and fits the current style.

2. **Move your off-season duds offsite.** Even if you live in a warm climate, you probably have at least a spring/summer and fall/winter wardrobe. Relocate your off-season clothes to a closet in the guest bedroom, attic, or basement, or into storage area boxes. See how much more space seasonal management provides?

3. **Double tier or layer.** If you have one closet rod and many short garments such as shirts, blouses, jackets, and skirts, adding a second rod underneath can double your storage space. Home improvement people can install rod number two directly into closet walls; those less inclined can opt for an add-a-rod that simply hangs from the one you have. Layering is another space expander if you have a long-hanging area. Here you hang a bar with holes for additional hangers from the rod. Keep a single color of garment on a bar so that you know just where to look for what. Consult Figure 6-3 to see how easy double-tiering or layering can be.

4. **Organize like with like. Think occasion first, and then type of garment.** Dressing for work is always a time-sensitive affair, so put all your professional clothes in the place most accessible when you open the door. You can delve deeper for casual clothes, when you have more time. If you're sharing a closet and have two double-tiered sections, each spouse takes one for short clothes and the rest of the closet can be split between the two. If there's only one tiered section, the taller person gets the higher rod. Devote this section to shirts — dress, and then casual. Within your work and casual categories, divide by garment type, and then style. See Table 6-1.

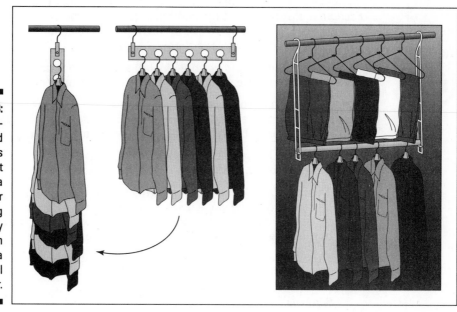

Figure 6-3:
An adjustable second rod doubles closet space in a snap — or try layering garments by tiering them down a vertical hanging bar.

Table 6-1		Great Garment Groupings
Type	*Styles*	*Notes*
Suits	Business	Keep men's suits together on a suit hanger that keeps the jacket in shape. Women's suits are more likely to be worn as mix and match and so can be split into skirts and jackets.
Skirts	Suits and separates	Use six-tiered hangers, separating by suit and other styles.
Pants	Dress, casual, jeans	Hang upside-down from the cuffs so the bulky waist is down near the floor. Forget the over-sized wooden pants hangers; compact little metal clip models will do.
Jackets, blazers	Suits and separates	Use jacket hangers to retain the shape.

5. **Light fades into dark.** Within each section, work from the lightest to darkest color for easy matching — white at one end, black at the other. *Exception:* Putting navy blue and black together invites chromatic confusion, so separate these two colors with the red/pink family, or put multi-colored garments in between them.

   If your closet lacks good lighting, install a battery-operated light so you can spare yourself the squint and get the right garment the first time.

6. **Stock the shelves.** The more shelves the merrier (or at least the more organized you can be), so if you have a walk-in closet short on shelves with room to spare, build them in! Here's what to put on them:

   • **Sweaters:** Hangers can ruin sweaters' shape, so fold them up and store them flat, grouped by color and season.

   • **T-shirts:** If you're short on hanging space. I prefer to hang T-shirts if there's room because it saves the work of folding them, keeps them easy to spot, and gives them a chance to dry if they come out of the dryer damp. In either case, sort them by color.

   • **Shoes:** Store them in boxes or directly on shelves.

   • **Purses**

   • **Scarves**

   • **Extra blankets, comforters, and pillows**

   • **Ladies' hats**

High, hard-to-reach shelves are a good place to store off-season items, such as blankets and sweaters during the summer and white shoes during the winter. You can also keep extra packages of nylons up here. (Buy in bulk on sale; they cost enough anyway!) Clamp dividers onto top shelves to section them off and keep things from falling over. See Figure 6-4 for this *bookending* trick.

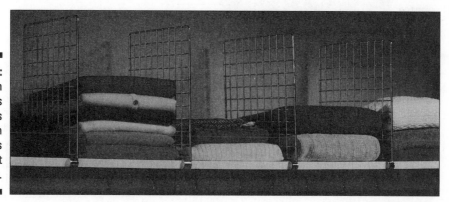

Figure 6-4: Clamp-on dividers keep things straight on top shelves without sides.

Photo courtesy of Lillian Vernon.

Keep a vented plastic laundry hamper in the closet to hold dirty clothes until washing day, when you can carry the whole thing directly to the machine.

Calling all fashionistas: Shoes

Do you really need so many shoes? Simplify your life by paring down your pairs. Every woman in the world should be able to get dressed with a pair each of heels and flats in black, brown, navy, white, and perhaps red, along with a pair or two of sandals, exercise shoes, and a few special items such as hiking boots or beach thongs.

The sheer number of shoe organizers available suggests what a time it is keeping pairs from spilling everywhere. The Container Store alone boasts 17 different types of shoe organizers in stock! They range from rounded hooks for hanging shoes to zippered cardboard shelves that protect the shoes from dust, but who wants to unzip every time you need a shoe? The best shoe organizer for you is the one that works with your shoes and your space. Here are a few tips you can peruse:

 ✔ If you have a free wall, use stackable units for vertical height. Wooden shelving is my top pick because it has flat surfaces for heels or flats. The metal units often require hanging heels over the back and so take a little more effort and time. Figure 6-5 illustrates the wooden kind.

 ✔ Pick number two: Open wooden cubes — still stackable; still work.

Figure 6-5:
Wooden
shoe
shelves.

Photo courtesy of Stacks & Stacks.

✔ A hanging rack or pockets on the back of the closet door can do the trick if you don't have sliding doors or more than a door's worth of shoes. Pockets don't hold heels well, though — they stick out at you like weapons.

✔ If you have shelf space available to store shoes, stack them in boxes. You can get clear plastic boxes that let you see your choices, but don't store suede shoes this way; the suede can stick to the plastic. A low-tech option is to leave shoes in their store boxes, clearly labeling the end — for instance, "black heels with bow" so you can pull the right black heels box. Another idea: Take a color picture and tape it to the box front.

✔ For those with floor space in the closet, you can get a rack that stacks flats on top and heels underneath. Lacking a rack, arrange your shoes in two to three rows, placing each pair heel-to-toe to save additional space.

✔ If you're very serious about your shoes, you may want a tilt-down shoe rack that holds 20 to 30 pairs. You can even get a shoe armoire that stands outside the closet!

No matter what storage system you use, arrange your shoes as you do your clothes: by color and moving from light to dark. (Sorting shoes by style is tricky, so stick to color to keep things simple.)

Do some of your shoes cramp your style or at least your toes? Stretch them out with a shoe tree. It's like getting a new pair without spending a penny! Prevent the too-small syndrome by wearing new shoes for a few hours on the carpet at home and taking them back if they don't feel good.

Accessories

Fashion experts tell us that accessories make the outfit. From bracelets to feather boas, belts to ties to baseball caps, accessories express your personal style. Unfortunately, the things that top off an outfit really tangle up the closet. Here's how to contain them and relieve accessory angst:

✔ **Ties and belts:** Racks are the rule for sorting out belts and ties, and you can find them in formats from flat to revolving. Measure your closet wall space before shopping. Again, sort by color, going by the main or background color in mixed-color ties.

✔ **Scarves:** If you have a free drawer or shelf, fold your scarves and lay them flat, layered ¼-inch apart so you can see the edge of each one. Angle the fold toward you so it's easy to pull. If you'd rather hang your scarves, drape them over a pants hanger or buy a special hanger with holes through which you thread each one. The sort criterion? Color!

✔ **Purses:** Start by considering: Do you really need more than a black, brown, navy, white, and dress purse? If so, store off-season purses as you do clothes and sort the rest by color. Arrange them on a shelf in the closet.

✔ **Caps:** If you've got just a few caps, put some self-adhesive hooks inside the closet door and hang them there. For a larger cap collection, see Figure 4-1 in Chapter 4 for a high-capacity rack to hang in your front or bedroom closet.

Trying to sneak some extra storage space for off-season items? When I was in college, we used to prop our beds up on cement bricks to make more room to stow stuff underneath. The grown-up version of this trick is bed risers that increase clearance for storage underneath (see Figure 6-6; don't those look better than blocks?). Use clear plastic boxes or rolling cabinets on wheels to take advantage of the extra space.

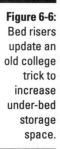
Figure 6-6:
Bed risers
update an
old college
trick to
increase
under-bed
storage
space.

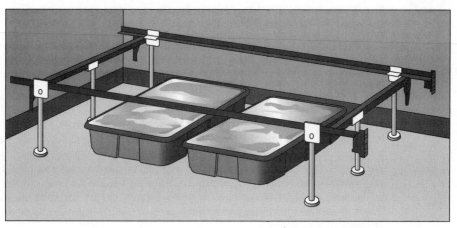

Children's Bedrooms

Kids' bedrooms are multipurpose spaces, sort of a small person's living room, family room, and office all wrapped up in one. Children may play, listen to music or watch TV, do homework, or entertain friends for hours on end in their rooms, so it's important to have a setup that serves all these purposes without ending up a mess. Hey, it doesn't hurt to dream!

Kid-friendly furniture

Children grow quickly, and many parents fail to plan far enough ahead when furnishing their bedrooms. Spare yourself replacing big pieces as often as you do overalls by keeping the future in mind. As toddlers move out of cribs and into a regular bed, bypass the cutesy options and invest in a nice bedroom set, including a desk and bookcase that will last through the teen years. Make sure the desk can accommodate a computer and printer, because kids seem to practically be using them in kindergarten these days and even if you don't anticipate such a purchase now, you don't want to have to buy a new desk too should you succumb somewhere down the line.

Wide open space is at the top of kids' priority lists, so line up beds and furniture along the walls to leave plenty of room to play. Some children outgrow this need and will want to rearrange the furniture for a different look later but my daughters, who have both loved to dance since they were 2, were still looking for central dance space when choosing college dorm rooms.

Bunk beds or trundle beds can maximize floor space in a shared room.

For dressers and night tables, apply the same general principles you used in the master bedroom. If two siblings share a room, it's best to have separate tables and dressers situated near their owner's bed.

Books and toys

I think every child's bedroom should include a bookcase. Not only does it help keep everything in its place, but books in the bedroom can make reading a daily habit from the get-go. Bookcase needs may expand as a child grows and goes from a small collection of picture books to popular series, novels, reference books, and texts. If you're planning ahead as I recommend, you may begin with a bigger bookcase than you need; just put current books on a lower shelf the child can easily access, and use the upper shelves for stuffed animals or knickknacks.

If there are so many toys in your child's bedroom that you have a hard time spotting the human being among them, it's time for a cleanup. Start with a purge of outgrown or redundant toys, which you may conduct in partnership with your child depending on age. Next, relocate what you can, using the playroom, if you have one, for primary toy storage and putting games with your family game center in the basement, hall closet, or family room. Then, contain what's left. See Chapter 10 for ideas on toy storage.

Is your child in toy overload? Explain that some kids aren't as lucky, and donating the extras to charity will make other children happy while still leaving plenty of fun things to play with. The section on toy garage sales in Chapter 24 provides additional housecleaning ideas.

Now, are you wrestling with 20 to 30 stuffed animals when dusting or making the bed? Tame the wild menagerie with a mesh net that drapes between two wall corners, or a plastic clip chain that hangs straight down from the ceiling. As you can see in Figure 6-7, the net needs a clear corner with no windows or closets in the way.

Figure 6-7:
One way
to tame
your stuffed
animal zoo.

Don't ever leave toys requiring adult supervision in the bedroom, whether it's crayons and markers for a 3-year-old or a chemistry set for a second-grader. See Chapter 10 for more about safely storing arts, crafts, and toys.

From gold stars to watercolors: Papers

Kids become papermaking machines much earlier than you may think, and you need to exercise the same vigilance with their artwork, compositions, and stories that you do with your own paper flood. My main point here is that children's papers should not be stored in their bedrooms so clear them out, and see Chapter 14 for a complete explanation of paper management — kid style.

One good place for papers in the bedroom is a bulletin board for junior high students on up. Juggling school calendars and snapshots of friends, kids can benefit from a bulletin board that serves as a personal information center and a place to put visual mementos of the moment. Don't use metal thumbtacks that can land tack up. The colored plastic ones always fall sideways and are easier to find on the floor. Office supply stores also sell jumbo tacks, 1-inch-plus, that you can spot a mile away. Get your children thinking clear early on by limiting bulletin board contents to what fits without overlapping. If you want to add something new, something old must come down!

Superhero and school clothes: Closet

Ah, for a grown-up size closet in a small fry's room! Closet space can get scarce outside the master bedroom of many homes, leaving the kids and their wardrobes no room to grow. Most children's closets are small, so make the best of the situation with smart systems such as the following:

- ✔ **Double tier.** If you want your children to learn to dress themselves before they're preteens, you need a half-height closet rod that they can reach. Refer to Figure 6-4 in the master bedroom for an add-a-rod that double-tiers without tears.

- ✔ **Group garments by like type and color.** Use the same system that I describe earlier in the chapter in the master bedroom section to make sense of children's clothes. Depending on your school's dress code and your child's style, it may be useful to start with two groups, school and play, and then subdivide from there.

- ✔ **Shelve.** If the closet has built-in shelves, use them to store toys and games for little kids, and then sweaters as the children grow up. Don't build shelves into a small closet, though; it's better to use freestanding shelves or a chest of drawers that can be removed as a child's clothes-hanging requirements grow.

Guest Bedroom

Having a guest bedroom is a hospitable gesture, but this room can be a waste of space if you don't put it to double duty. Set up right, the guest bedroom can make friends and family comfortable when they visit and serve other functions all the other days of the year. The guest bedroom closet may be storing your off-season clothes, but leave enough space for visitors to hang their things, too, and have some spare hangers at the ready. It's also thoughtful to provide a place to put nonhanging items such as underwear, pj's, and swimsuits. A small chest of drawers does the trick; leave the top two drawers empty and dedicate the rest to the room's other use. Another alternative to free up floor space is to place a stack of plastic drawers in the closet. Skip the cardboard type; they won't last long.

Additional uses for your guest bedroom might include

- Entertainment or reading room
- Playroom
- Exercise room
- Sewing room
- Hobby room
- Home office

If you're using the room in other ways, a sofa bed saves space and provides a nice place to sit. Make sure there's room to open up the bed without moving furniture. No heavy coffee tables in front, please! Here are a few other ways to use the guest room:

- **Entertainment or reading room**: Add a bookcase and/or media unit to make your spare room more stimulating. Keep it organized so you don't have to straighten up when guests come to stay. Closed cabinets can contain games and media, while a folding card table and chairs can accommodate gamers and be folded up into the closet when company comes. See Chapter 9 for more tips on organizing entertainment and media.

- **Playroom:** Use containers, along with shelves in the closet or closed cabinets, to organize toys and games. Chapter 10 provides more practical playroom tactics.

- **Exercise room**: The convenience of an exercise room right next to the bedrooms may be just the impetus you need to get moving! (You don't want to burn any extra calories walking downstairs, do you?) If you store equipment in here, arrange places to put it away when guests come, such as crates or shelves in the closet. Big equipment such as a treadmill, rower, or bike may or may not work depending upon your space and guest traffic. Weigh the room's best use against what you see on the scale. You can read more on setting up your exercise area in Chapter 12.

- **Sewing room:** A sewing machine with its own cabinet keeps itself out of sight and accessories besides; otherwise store the machine in the closet when not in use, along with containers for threads, needles, buttons, sewing scissors, and feet. Fabric and patterns can go into drawers, plastic containers in the closet, or a closed wicker basket placed neatly in a corner of the room. Clean up between sessions, especially if you have small children who could get into the scissors, needles, or sewing machine.

- **Hobby room:** There are a number of craft organizers available to store hobby supplies, from model glue to beads. Care and cleanup are key if you're getting into paint, ink, and other messy things. Wash up right after use, and put markers, knitting needles, ink pads, coin collections, stamp collections, small pieces, and dangerous or poisonous tools far away from curious little eyes and hands. Keeping the room clean can also motivate you to come in and pull out your latest project.

Expedite cleanup by skipping the carpet in this room, especially if you're using glue or paint.

✔ **Home office:** Save space by combining your desk and computer station into one with a specially designed piece or a desk with an extension. *Exception:* If you like to work on the computer while someone else is doing homework, a separate desk and computer table may be the way to go. Be sure you have some drawers in the desk to store things; add a file cabinet for papers and a bookcase for books. For more information on a home office and household information center, see Chapter 14.

With peace permeating your personal retreats, you should all be resting easy. Go take a breather. There's plenty more organizing ahead!

Chapter 7

Bathe and Beautify: Creating Functional Bathrooms

*T*alk about traffic! Some households should have stoplights installed to direct the flow of residents in and out of the bathrooms, and if you have teenagers, you may need a timer too. How can you keep order in a room so public, yet so intimate — the repository of personal care regimes for every member of the family?

Getting organized in the bathroom can make your mornings go faster and the nightly beeline for bed pick up speed and ease. Perfect your look by arranging all your toiletries within fingertip reach, and polish up your image with well-ordered facilities you can present to guests and visiting repair people without shame. With beautiful bathrooms, organization gets personal.

Where Order Meets Indulgence

Tackle the bathrooms one at a time. You may start with the master bath for inspiration; move on to the family bathroom, where you have your work cut out for you; and finish up with a finesse to the guest baths. In each room, select one section at a time — the countertop, cabinets, drawers, shower and bath, or linen closet and use the five-step P-L-A-C-E system to whip everything into shape and beautify your bathroom space.

✔ **Purge:** Toss odds and ends of soap and old, worn, or excess washcloths, towels, sheets, sponges, scrubbers, and loofahs. Eye shadow, lipstick, and blush more than 2 years old; foundation and powder more than 1 year old; and eyeliner or mascara more than 6 months old are neither hygienic nor high quality anymore. So throw them away, along with any personal care products that you haven't used in the last year. Check dates on medications and dispose of expired ones. Are you using all those travel products collected on your trips? If not, out they go. Old or extra magazines can move to the family room or the trash.

✔ **Like with like:** Organize personal-care items and supplies by type in your cabinet drawers, underneath the cabinet, or on linen closet shelves. Shower and bath items can be kept on standing or hanging racks by type or by person. Linen closet items may encompass towels, sheets, medicines, and cleaning supplies, all arranged into like groupings.

✔ **Access:** Place items close to where they're used but out of bathroom users' way, considering safety issues if children are in the house. Countertop items can move to the medicine cabinet, drawers, and under-sink cupboards. Medications need a cool, dry shelf out of the reach of small kids. Extra supplies belong in the linen closet, with the things you use most frequently stored on the middle shelves.

✔ **Contain:** Use baskets, drawers, and/or drawer dividers to contain items by like type: cosmetics, personal care products, medicines, hair accessories, nail supplies. Put anything that can spill in a leak-proof container. Label containers so it's easy to put things back from where they came.

✔ **Evaluate:** Can you find everything you need to get ready on the sleepiest morning and get to bed on a dog-tired night? Can you shave, style your hair, and apply makeup without taking a step? Is keeping the guest bathroom neat enough for strangers easy? Do you know just where to look when you run out of supplies? Are family members getting in and out of the bathroom fast enough to fit your schedule?

The Organizational Conundrum: Sink and Vanity

Though different people may frequent the master and family bathrooms, you can apply the same logic to both. As always, finish one room before moving on to the next.

If you have a nice, big counter alongside your sink, count yourself lucky and then count up how much stuff is cluttering the space. Things left on the countertop look messy, attract dust, and get in the way of your grooming routines. Here's what can stay out on your sink or countertop:

✔ Hand soap

✔ Drinking glasses

✔ Box of tissues

✔ Clock

✔ Radio

Keep a clock set five minutes fast in all the main bathrooms to get you moving in the morning. That you're in on the trick doesn't matter; the psychology works on sleepyheads.

For the rest of your countertop display, put everything away closest to where you usually access it. Elegant perfume bottles can grace a bureau in the bedroom. Shaving supplies go into a cabinet or drawer, along with cosmetics, hair products, and bath things. Slip the blow dryer down below, under the sink. Read on for more details about what goes where — then come back and clear.

If your bathroom scores low on drawers and you have a clear corner on the counter, get a set of small countertop drawers to keep your cosmetics and hair accessories neat and invisible. Figure 7-1 shows this sleight-of-hand. (Consider safety if children visit this bathroom.)

Figure 7-1:
Countertop drawers expand your options for cosmetic and accessory storage.

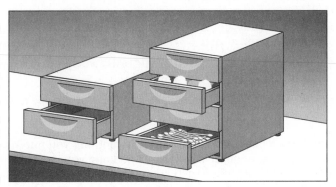

Photo courtesy of Get Organized!

Locate your wastebasket near the sink so tossing out tissues, cotton balls, and razor blades is easy. Plastic is best for bathroom trash bins; a bag lining keeps the wastebasket clean and protects it from corrosive agents such as nail polish remover.

Keep a couple of extra trash bags at the bottom of the wastebasket underneath the open one, so that a replacement is always ready to go.

Medicine cabinet: a misnomer

Whoever named the medicine cabinet must have had excellent health because the medicine cabinet is a terrible place to keep any kind of medication for three reasons:

- ✔ **Safety:** This cabinet is all too accessible to children so even if none live with you but some pass through now and then, keep small stomachs safe from the dangers of all medications, from aspirin to iodine, by storing them on high or locked shelves.

- ✔ **Spoilage:** Heat and humidity from the shower and bath can quickly dissipate the potency of drugs and dietary supplements. Head for drier, cooler ground.

- ✔ **Accessibility:** Many medications are meant to be taken with food. Unless you eat breakfast in the bathroom, that would put their closest use in the kitchen.

Now that you have the shelves cleared out, here's how to fill them up. Most medicine cabinets have three removable shelves that slide into slots of varying heights. If you have such adjustable architecture, match altitude to access by making the top shelf the highest to fit tall items. That leaves smaller things for the lower shelves, where you can easily spot them, and the shortest for the middle shelf. Here is an example:

- ✔ **Top shelf:** Hair spray, gel, mousse, shaving cream, aftershave, cologne, antiperspirant, mouthwash

- ✔ **Middle/shortest:** Toothpaste and toothbrushes, dental floss, razor and refill blades

- ✔ **Bottom/medium height:** Facial cleansers and lotions, makeup remover and pads, contact lens supplies, eye drops, nasal spray

Do you really want a day's worth of dust on something you put in your mouth? If not, skip the countertop display and hang your toothbrushes from slots in a medicine cabinet shelf instead. Get a different color brush for each bathroom user, and then write down the color code, noting the date the brush was put in service to remind you to replace it six months later. (Get a free one by scheduling a biannual checkup with the dentist.)

Dividing it up: Drawers

Divide your bathroom drawers for fingertip management of the snarl of items commonly found there. Dividers can range from 2-x-2-inch plastic trays and up to full-drawer sectioned trays. Special cosmetics dividers are designed to hold lipsticks, eye shadows, and so forth; others are sized to hold jewelry. Measure your drawers, count your categories, and shop.

Medications made simple and safe

Whether you pop a multivitamin once a day or take a complicated regime of pills by the hour, a well-managed medication system can make a big difference to your health.

✔ **Store safe and smart.** Keep all medications out of the reach of children, away from the heat and humidity of the bath, and closest to where you take them. This may mean that your daily dose goes into a kitchen cabinet for swallowing after meals, while allergy medicines are stored on the top shelf of the linen closet.

✔ **Group medications by like type.** Pain relievers, stomach remedies, sleep aids, and supplements may be located in different places according to the rule of access.

✔ **Stay up-to-date.** Check the expiration dates on both prescription and over-the-counter medications and pitch them when their time has come (usually a year).

✔ **Keep it straight.** If you take several medications each day, pill boxes with slots for each dose can make life much easier and prevent potentially dangerous mishaps.

✔ **911!** Keep a bottle of ipecac syrup in your first aid kit to induce vomiting in the event of poisoning or dangerous drug reactions. Post the number of your local emergency room on the fridge or close to the phone.

Marilyn's kids were always sick from allergies and colds, and she was afraid that in all the dispensing she'd give someone her blood-thinning medication instead of a decongestant. I recommended two baskets — a blue one for all the kids' needs that Marilyn can reach for when she hears a sneeze, and a pink basket labeled "Adult Medicine" where she can easily find her prescription.

If you have expensive jewelry, the bathroom is too public a place to store it. Keep your collection on the bedroom bureau or in a fireproof box to maintain peace of mind.

Got just one bathroom drawer? Unless you're a guy, this is probably the place for cosmetics and basic hair tools. Slip in hair accessories if they fit. A rolling cart of drawers is a great addition when you're short on built-ins. It works and it moves. See Table 7-1 for using bathroom drawer space effectively.

Table 7-1	Divine Bathroom Drawers
Drawer	*Items*
Cosmetic center	Foundation, blush, lipstick, eyeliner and shadow, mascara, sponges, brushes, tools
Hair care center	Comb, brush, headbands, barrettes, clips, hairpins, bobby pins, ponytail holders
Jewelry center	Earrings, necklaces, bracelets, watches, pins, jewelry cleaner, polishing cloth

Storing: Under-the-sink cabinets

The space under the sink is a primary storage area for most bathrooms but because shelves are rare in these cabinets, pandemonium is all too common. Solve this problem with space-expanding options:

- **Wire-coated shelves** are a quick, no-installation way to add a level to your cabinet. Buy the stackable or multitiered sort if you have lots of vertical space.

- **Pullout shelves** slide out of the cabinet to save you from having to reach inside.

- **Add a shelf** by buying a piece of wood to size and nailing it in. You may want to make your shelf half the cabinet's depth to leave room for tall things in front.

- **Hang a caddy** inside the cabinet door for hair dryers and curling irons. Check out Figure 7-2, and don't forget to account for clearance space.

Figure 7-2:
Cabinet door caddy for hair dryer, curling iron, detangler, and brushes.

Photo courtesy of Get Organized!

Next, group your items by like type to create under sink centers and contain them in clear containers or baskets. Table 7-2 shows you how.

Table 7-2	Under Sink Centers
Centers	*Items*
Hair care center	Dryer, curling iron, straightener
Nail care center	Manicure set, nail polish, polish remover, pads
Feminine hygiene center	Tampons, pads, freshness products
Sun protection center	Sunscreen, self-tanner, after-sun moisturizer (move to the linen closet for off-season storage)
Cleaning supply center (if no small children in the house)	Scouring powder, spray cleanser, glass cleaner, disinfectant, toilet bowl cleaner
Plumbing center	Plunger, drain unclogger

If your bathroom serves a large family, get each person a different colored basket to stow personal things in the under-sink cabinet.

Arrange items in the cabinet according to access — closest for use or daily need. That means the hair dryer should be on the side near the electrical outlet and hopefully, your plunger is used infrequently enough that it can go in the back.

Anything that overflows from your bathroom cabinet space can go in the linen closet, if you have one. Coming up short? Try the following:

- Try the various shelving or cabinet units that go above the toilet or stand freely on the floor. Some even have wheels for maximum mobility. Skip open-back shelves, which invite things to fall down behind.

- Open shelves look cluttered, so contain items when you can — including a toilet paper holder that conceals extra rolls while keeping them close at hand, and a container to hold the toilet brush.

- If you like to have reading material within reach, get a basket or magazine rack to hold up to half a dozen magazines. You don't need more here! Save space with containers designed to hold magazines on the bottom and extra toilet paper rolls on top.

Shower and Bath

Who knew keeping clean could be so complicated? If you have the same sort of array of personal care products in your bath or shower and piles of towels all around that I see in my clients' homes, you're well aware of the problem that cleanliness presents: more supplies than space.

Where to hang the towels

Install a towel bar for each person that can hold a washcloth, hand towel, and bath towel. Towel bars are easy to add to a bathroom and can keep towels off the floor and other people from snatching yours. One person can use the shower door bar if you don't have a bath mat hanging there; the back of the door provides another bar-hanging spot. For big families in small bathrooms, double up the hand and bath towel to squeeze two people onto one bar — if you absolutely must. Another space-saving option for a bathroom with four or more users is the towel bar that hangs on the door hinge pictured in Figure 7-3.

Put a pair of hooks on the back of the bathroom door to hold clothes and robes. Take down the clothes when you return the robe.

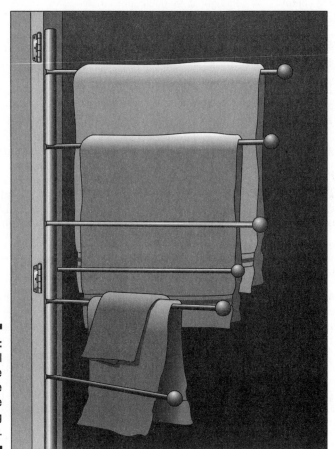

Figure 7-3:
This towel bar uses the door hinge for more hanging space.

Personal care products and bath toys

Every shower and bath needs storage systems to hold shampoo, conditioner, skin cleansers, brushes, scrubbers, loofahs, razors, and shaving cream. These can take the form of corner shelves, a rack that hangs from the showerhead, or a tension-rod pole that extends from the top of a bathtub to the ceiling and holds shelves made from wire racking or with holes to let the water drain through (skip the solid, water-collecting ones). Depending upon the size of your family, you can assign shelves by like products or by person.

Rather bathe than shower? You may want all your supplies on hand without standing up to reach the soap, so get a tray that fits across the width of the tub to hold bath essentials. Some come with a book holder, so you can relax and read without worrying about your best-seller getting wet, as you see in Figure 7-4.

Figure 7-4: Relax and read in a bubble bath.

Photo courtesy of Lillian Vernon.

Next take on the rubber duckies: Put kids' bath toys in a mesh bag and hang it from the faucet. If the bath toys don't fit, you have too many . . . *unless* you have a baby, whose toys are often super-size. Keep those in a dishpan that goes in the under-sink cabinet or floor of the linen closet between baths.

Hand washables solution: No wet stuff draped on the towels

Doing small hand-wash jobs in the bathroom may be more convenient than to trudge down to the laundry room, but lingerie draped all over is not an attractive sight. Get a closed, nontransparent hamper to hold hand-wash items until washing day, and then dry them on a wire grid rack that hangs over the showerhead, a horizontal rack that sits inside or across the bathtub (this rack is great for sweaters too), or an old-fashioned folding wooden drying rack.

Bathing suits and bras will last longer when washed by hand, particularly the elastic, which the dryer can leave lax and stretched. If you have too many items or too little time to hand-wash, use the delicate wash cycle on the machine and allow to air dry.

Safety and soft, dry landings: The bathroom floors and doors

The bathroom, with all its hard, head-cracking surfaces, is no place to take a spill. Put a no-slip mat or waterproof stickies on the tub or shower floor. Make sure that bath mats or area rugs placed directly on the floor have slip-proof backings (and are machine washable to make your life easier). If your shower doors are crystal clear, congratulations on your good cleaning habits; you may want to put up a couple of stickers to keep people from walking into them like dazed birds.

Don't skip the bath mat just because the bathroom floor is carpeted, because the regular soaking delivered by dripping bodies stepping out of the shower will shorten the life of your carpet. Do you shave your legs or wash your hair in the sink? Stand on a bathmat to keep splashes off the floor.

Closet of All Trades: The Linen Closet

Often viewed as the outfield of the bathroom, the linen closet can accumulate a strange assemblage of clutter but properly organized, this space can outperform its name to serve a variety of purposes. Whether your linen closet is in the bathroom or the hall outside, you should always be able to open the door and easily pull out a clean set of sheets or towels. This is also the place to look for backups of toilet paper or soap bought in bulk (and hopefully on sale!). And what a handy spot for a hammer, the shoe polish, the upstairs cleaning supplies. Everything is possible when you put everything in its place, as follows:

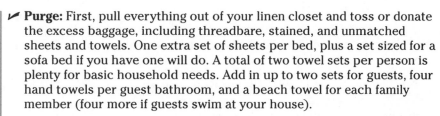

Linens and towels: Folding versus rolling

Here is a folding technique that guarantees neatness and visibility for bed linens. First, fold the top sheet lengthwise, then in half widthwise, and then in half again. Take the fitted bottom sheets and grab the pointed corners so the rounded corners fall inside. Fold it like the top sheet and add it to the stack. The pillowcase, folded in half twice, tops the pile. Place the stack on the shelf with the folds facing front and the open edges to the back so you can easily grab the full set. Proceed with the next set.

Fold your towels in half lengthwise first, and then in half again by width so they're ready to hang on the towel bar without reconfiguring. Like sheets, folded edges should face front and open edges back but stacking towels by the set is asking for a tumble. Make separate piles for bath towels, hand towels, and washcloths, keeping like colors together and in the same order from one stack to the next.

Rolling towels saves some space, but the price you pay is sloppy piles instead of neat stacks and a harder time telling different sizes apart. Have you ever noticed how rolls all look alike? Try it if your space is tight but roll at your own risk.

✔ **Purge:** First, pull everything out of your linen closet and toss or donate the excess baggage, including threadbare, stained, and unmatched sheets and towels. One extra set of sheets per bed, plus a set sized for a sofa bed if you have one will do. A total of two towel sets per person is plenty for basic household needs. Add in up to two sets for guests, four hand towels per guest bathroom, and a beach towel for each family member (four more if guests swim at your house).

Are you awash in minibottles of shampoo and conditioner mooched from hotels? They're not your brand, and the next hotel you visit will provide its own supply. Donate yours to a nursing home, and next time resist the urge to take them home!

✔ **Sort and sift:** Select the items that are best stored in the linen closet and group them by like type for easy access.

The linen closet may seem like an unlikely spot for tools but do you really want to run down to the basement every time you want to hang a picture or open a pipe? Keep a small toolkit in the linen closet for jobs in this part of the house.

✔ **Assign space:** Think high-low. Store items that are seldom used or dangerous to children on the highest shelves, small things that are hard to spot at eye level, and light but big items below. For higher-middle shelves, think personal care items, first aid kit, shoe care, cleaning supplies, toolbox. The middle-lower shelves can be used for bed and bath linens while the bottom shelves/floor can accommodate bath and facial tissue, extra blankets, trash bags, travel cosmetic/shaving kits, and a sick bucket.

First aid center: Safety first

A complete first aid center can be a quick, sometimes critical help for illnesses and injuries, but many of its contents can be poisonous or dangerous to small children. Prevent your own first aid emergency by keeping your kit on a high linen closet shelf.

The components of a well-stocked first aid center may include: adhesive bandages, gauze pads and adhesive tape, elastic bandage, arm sling, ice bag, heating pad, antibiotic ointment, muscle sprain cream, rubbing alcohol, hydrogen peroxide, calamine lotion, sunburn products, thermometer, scissors, tweezers, aspirin (ibuprofen/acetaminophen), antihistamines, loperamide, bismuth, liquid, syrup of ipecac, and prescription insect bite or food allergy kits.

✔ **Group and stack:** If jamming your clean sheets onto the shelf is something like pushing your way onto a New York subway car, it's time to clean up your act. The right folding technique can stack your sheets up neatly with an easy visual ID of what's what. There may not be as many ways to store a towel as there are shoes, but there are at least two: folding and rolling.

Next are personal care items and cleaning supplies: Contain items in clear or different colored baskets, grouped by like type, and make it easy (or difficult for kids) to access what you need. Pullout drawers that sit on the shelf can help. Add labels so that one look takes you to your target.

The best spot for extra blankets is in the bedroom, closest to their use. If you don't have room there, use a bottom shelf of the linen closet, because blankets are light and easy to lift.

If you travel frequently, keep a shaving or cosmetic kit always packed with sample-size products and ready to go. Replenish your supplies as you return from each trip.

The Half or Guest Bath

A half bath is really a half room (which luckily presents less of a logistical problem). Bath math dictates that you can have only half the stuff in a guest bath as in a main bathroom.

✔ **Sink and counter:** Maximize the aesthetics of the guest bath by keeping only what visitors may need out on the countertop. Sink and counter items may include a decorative pump-style bottle of liquid soap so that guests don't have to share germs, a box of tissues, a bottle of hand lotion, and some small paper cups, preferably in a wall-mounted dispenser.

✔ **Towel bar:** Hang at least two hand towels in the guest bath. If your family uses these frequently and you like things fancy, keep a separate stack of elegant towels on the sink for visitors.

✔ **Under-the-sink cabinet:** This is the spot for hiding away necessities and supplies, such as an extra package of toilet paper, box of tissues, bottle of hand soap, and feminine hygiene supplies. Some cleaning supplies to have here are sponges, scouring powder, spray cleanser, glass cleaner, toilet bowl cleaner, and a plunger.

✔ **Reading material:** Keep magazines neat with a small stand and don't overfill.

Now you're all cleaned up in your cleanup centers. Doesn't your bathroom feel beautifully pristine?

I'm out of _what?_

The most important item in any guest bathroom is toilet paper. While family members may be quick to pipe up when the roll runs out, guests usually won't, so spare everybody the embarassment by keeping some backup paper in plain sight. Simply place a spare roll on top of the tank, or go upscale with a decorative container designed to hold three to four rolls on the floor.

Chapter 8

Space for Gracious Living:
The Living and Dining Rooms

- -

In This Chapter

▶ Laying out your living room for sparkling conversation

▶ Striking the right balance between clear space and decorative display

▶ Grandma's fine china storage secrets

▶ Setting up your space to entertain like a pro and enjoy yourself as you go

- -

*T*he names say it all. Living. Dining. These are the rooms where you enjoy the good life, whether relaxing with friends or family or lingering over a meal. Formal or casual, grand in scale or apartment-size, these spaces can meld form with function to create a welcoming environment that pleases all the senses and soothes the body and mind. Here is where gracious living begins.

Whether the living and dining rooms are showpieces or the only place in your tiny pad where you can kick back and put your feet up, you want them to provide plenty of space for everyone in your life to live and breathe. Nowhere may more eyes appreciate your efforts to put everything in its place than here.

Creating Uncluttered Elegance in the Living Room

When you're ready to line up your living room, break down the project by the area: the furniture layout, tables, book and display cases, and the fireplace if you have one. P-L-A-C-E sums up the organizing process for your living room space. Here is how you apply it:

✔ **Purge:** Create an elegant, uncluttered look by eliminating any excess, outdated, or aesthetically questionable knickknacks, souvenirs, trinkets, and artwork. Clear out old magazines and catalogs.

✔ **Like with like:** Put books into bookcases by category. Group decorative displays into small, uncluttered clusters.

✔ **Access:** Arrange furniture into a conversation circle, moving bulky, casual, or worn pieces to the family room. Exercise equipment can go to the basement or extra bedroom. Remove excess pictures, photo albums, figurines, books, and CDs to the family/media room or into storage for rotation. Take papers to the office or information center, toys and games to the playroom or bedrooms, and the computer to the office or family room.

✔ **Contain:** Put figurines in a display case or on a bookcase or mantel. Contain photo albums, coasters, and extra ashtrays in drawers or closed shelves, and surplus coffee-table books in the bookcase.

✔ **Evaluate:** Can you present this room to guests with pride? Do visitors and family alike feel comfortable and at ease? Does conversation flow? Do you feel refreshed and renewed after spending time here?

A layout for living

Let's talk: The living room is the spot for the ancient art of conversation, and the perfect layout is conducive, first and foremost, to communication. Most people achieve this with a sofa plus a love seat or a few attractive armchairs, arranged in a semicircle so everyone can see each other and chat with ease. There may be a central focus to your circle — a piano, fireplace, painting, or picture window. In any case, the *plus* part of the sofa-plus equation is critical, because the straight line of a couch is bad conversational geometry. Still, you don't want to overdo it. Keep the room intimate yet open by stopping at two to three chairs arranged around the couch. When a crowd comes, you can bring in extra chairs from the dining room so everyone is sitting pretty.

You may need a coffee table to hold all those delicious accompaniments to sitting — coffee, cocktails, a slice of cake. Place the coffee table parallel to the couch with enough clearance to walk through but close enough so you don't have to reach to retrieve your cup.

End tables, true to their name, usually go on either end of the sofa (though they're equally comfortable alongside a chair). The strongest criteria for placement is where you need a spare surface or spot for a table lamp. Is the guest on one side of the sofa sitting in the dark? Do you sink into the armchair only to find you're stuck without a place to put your glass? Arrange your end tables (and lamps) accordingly.

Whatever your layout, remember that the living room is the place for your most beautiful things. Move the beloved but raggedy reading chair into the family room. Ditto the cuddly throw that clashes with your color scheme. Even if you only have a few nice things, let them shine by removing lesser distractions.

If your living room is large and you'd like additional seating, set up a separate area rather than cluttering your conversation circle — perhaps a place for reading with an armchair or two and end tables to go alongside.

Tables and smooth surfaces

Uncluttered elegance is the name of the game in the living room, so clear out the stacks of magazines and jumbled displays of figurines, photos, and knick-knacks. A coffee table covered with souvenirs from your last trip to Tijuana can't do the job. Too many photos in one place blur together and exhaust the eye. And be advised that the mantelpiece is not a mailroom.

If you're drowning in decorative items that crowd your view and make cleaning more difficult, pick your favorite ones to leave out and purge the rest. You can donate them directly to charity or to other family members, or place them in Halfway House storage as described in Chapter 3 for six months to a year to see if you miss them. If you decide to keep them, then replace some of your current display and continue to rotate your collection with the seasons or at midyear to create different looks and keep the room as fresh as it is clear and calm.

- ✔ **Coffee table:** Some people leave a coffee table absolutely empty to create a stunning effect. A single vase of flowers can also be beautiful. If you choose to display books, magazines, candy dishes, ashtrays, or other decorative items, do so sparingly and artfully, with plenty of clear space left over. If your table has a glass top, don't pile up books on the shelf below. Think display, not library.

- ✔ **End tables:** Showcasing a single lamp with enough room to park a drink alongside can put an end table to good effect. If you choose to add decorative pieces, one or two may do. Look for end tables and coffee tables with drawers or cabinets where you can store coasters, photo albums, cameras and film, cards and games, and anything that's currently cluttering up the room.

- ✔ **Bookcases:** Living room bookshelves can hold your household's main library or be strictly for show. Either way, make your bookshelves look great. Stand every book up straight with the spine out, and add shelves if you have more books than space. If you also use the bookcase to display knickknacks and photos, limit yourself to four items per shelf to prevent a cluttered appearance and make it easy to get the book you want. See Chapter 9 for tips on arranging books by category.

For a more formal look in the living room, contain your books in an armoire-style bookcase with doors. If the look of books is your bag, go ahead and let them show, but neatly.

✔ **Framed photos:** Whether on tables, bookshelves, the mantel, or atop the piano, framed photos are best displayed sparingly to highlight the special moments they represent. Cluster them in small groups, making sure you can see the entire frame of each picture, or go solo with single pictures here and there. Choose frames that work well with your décor and each other. If you have more photos than living room display space, you may want to make a collage to mount on a hallway wall or in the den.

✔ **Display case:** Display cases are meant for showing off your very best-things — but if they're jammed full, the effect is lost. Leave at least a few inches between pieces to provide a full view. Remove extra items and put them somewhere else or store them to rotate into the display later on. Save specific collections such as spoons, matches, stamps, coins, golf balls, and golf tees, for the family room, where the more informal atmosphere can showcase them better.

The bright fireplace

The warm glow of a fire in the hearth makes any gathering more festive. Fires can also make a big mess, like mounting a camping trip in the middle of your living room. Here are some hints to keep your home fires burning bright:

✔ Contain firewood in a solid-weave basket or attractive bin that keeps all the chips and bits of bark inside. Loose-weave baskets and flat wood carriers can leave your living room looking like the forest floor.

✔ Toss the miscellaneous spatulas or other improvised pokers and invest in a nice set of fireplace tools in a stand. These can be displayed next to the fireplace, or stored in a closet if you have children who might consider them toys.

✔ Get familiar with your flue. Know which handle position means *open* (generally the open position is flush against the chimney) and make sure it's that way before you light the first match! Write yourself a note and stash it in a drawer if you can't remember from one fire to the next.

✔ Extra-long fireplace matches make lighting easier. You can buy these in decorative canisters or get your own, and then keep them next to the tool stand or on the mantel.

✔ Clean the fireplace every time you use it, because ash is easily airborne and can soon migrate into the living room. Sweeping everything into the metal hatch in the fireplace floor is a good idea *if* you have a household member strong enough to lift the whole thing out when it's full. Otherwise, sweep the ashes into a dustpan and dump them directly into a garbage bag. (Carrying the dustpan across the room is asking for ash all over the carpet.) If you use the ashbin, empty it once a season or more if needed.

> ✔ Have the chimney professionally cleaned every year, or every other year if you don't use it often. Keep birds from flying in by placing a filter on top. The mantel is a natural display spot for trophies, clocks, and artwork. Don't put anything too small here, or it won't be seen. As with all living room surfaces, the look should be clean.

Old school or new: Entertainment options

I'm of the old school that believes the main entertainment in the living room should be people interacting with each other — so skip the TV unless you lack a family room. If you like to have background music, place a small stereo system on a bookshelf or run an extra set of speakers out from the media room.

Speaking of music, here's where I put in my plug for a piano in the living room. Not only may playing it improve the mechanics of your mind, but gathering around the piano to sing together is serious fun. Store sheet music inside the bench and keep any extras in coffee-table drawers. A piano light on top can illuminate the page when the room lights are low. Don't use the top for display if you have a grand piano that opens. Otherwise, keep it simple.

Keep the piano keyboard cover down to prevent dust buildup on the keys. If the piano is used often, tune it once a year; if not, every two years.

For a quick-reference summary of how to streamline the living room for sweet and elegant repose, see Table 8-1.

Table 8-1	Living Room Do's and Don'ts
Yes	**Nix**
A conversation circle composed of a sofa, love seat or chairs, and coffee table	Bulky or too-casual furniture
Beautiful art, sparingly arranged	Exercise equipment
A display case to show off decorative items in good order	Television (if you have a family room)
Tables with drawers and closed shelves to keep surfaces clear	Computer
	Crowded, jumbled displays
	Magazines and papers
	Toys and games

Good Food and Company: Dining Room

Whether you sit down here every night or reserve it for formal occasions, the dining room is a special part of the house. Yours may be a grand hall with a 12-foot table and candelabra that reaches for the sky or a small corner of your apartment marked only by a modest chandelier. No matter what its architecture, the ideal dining room is a serene place dedicated to the gift of good food and company.

The dining room is essentially an extension of the kitchen, so keep the pathway clear for easy serving and cleanup. Move anything that stands in the way between the stove and the dining table. If the distance is long, a rolling cart can be a great help in delivering dinner and clearing away plates afterward.

Many dining rooms look into the living room, which can be an advantage when you add tables and chairs for large groups. This setup also enhances the flow of a dinner party, facilitating movement from cocktails to dinner back out to coffee by the fire. If your home's blueprint opens the dining room into the living room, remember that you can always see one room from the other, and maintain strict standards for order and beauty in both.

Serenity in the dining room comes from clear views into other rooms and a pleasing, peaceful décor that feeds the spirit with no stacks of unpaid bills or schoolbooks. The dining room is not an office, and no matter what you do there during the day, you need systems in place to keep its original purpose sacred. P-L-A-C-E provides a quick reminder of these principles.

- ✔ **Purge:** Toss serving pieces and flatware that you haven't used in three years. You may want to give these to family members (make sure they want them); otherwise, donate to a good cause. Pitch unmatched napkins and placemats, and tablecloths you don't like or that don't fit your table.

- ✔ **Like:** Group china, stemware, and serving pieces by type in china and buffet cabinet shelves and drawers, and flatware by type in drawer dividers.

- ✔ **Access:** Arrange decorative pieces in the display area of the china cabinet. Keep spare table leaves and pads in a closet or the basement. Move extra dining chairs to the edge of the room. Remove papers, books, and anything unrelated to dining to other parts of the house.

- ✔ **Contain:** Use the china and buffet cabinets and drawers to hold serving pieces, stemware, flatware, tablecloths, and napkins. Put delicate china in storage sets with foam dividers to protect it from chips. Keep silverware in chests or wrapped in bags or cloths to keep it from tarnishing. Use plastic bags to keep serving pieces clean between uses.

- ✔ **Evaluate:** Can you easily pull out everything you need to serve a fancy or informal meal? After a party, does everything find its way back to its place without trying your patience? Do your meals here nourish at many levels?

Dining in style: The dining room table

The table is the *raison d'être* of the dining room, so why not go grand if you can? A nice, long table enables you to invite all your loved ones to share special occasions. To adjust for more intimate occasions, get a table with removable leaves.

The best spot to store spare table leaves and pads is *not* leaning against the dining room wall. A closet on the same floor is fine; can you tuck them behind the coats in the front hall? If space is short, the basement is the next stop.

Think singular for the table's centerpiece. More than one decoration can crowd your dinner and give you more to move at cleanup time.

Match the number of dining chairs to the size of your usual group. If you have more chairs than you need when your table is in small format, place them around the edge of the room. Keep extra folding chairs on hand for large gatherings. The wooden models available at import and furniture stores are much nicer than the metal kind.

As host, seat yourself at the end of the table with closest access to the kitchen to save you steps and from stumbling over guests as you serve and clear.

Display and storage: The china cabinet

In the dining room, the real dish display is on the table, so when purchasing a china cabinet think storage first. That means closed shelves alongside the exhibition area on top, and drawers and cabinets on the bottom. Put your prettiest pieces on the display shelf. Crystal looks nice under the lights, as do decorative plates, tea or liquor sets, candlesticks, and figurines. Don't crowd the display or you defeat the purpose.

Consider access when arranging your china cabinet. Contain good china in the closed shelves on top of the cabinet, along with stemware and barware. Reserve the bottom drawers for tablecloths, mats, and napkins, which are light and easy to lift out.

Six months after I had organized her, Carolyn called looking for her silver butter dish. I can't possibly remember where every client's things are kept, but by referring to P-L-A-C-E, I deduced that it should be in the first drawer under the china display cabinet with the other small serving pieces. There it was. Organizing just might make you psychic!

Now that's entertainment: The buffet cabinet

A buffet is a beautiful addition to the dining room, especially if you entertain often. With extra storage space underneath and a surface that you can use to serve up a family-style meal, a Thanksgiving feast, hors d'oeuvres, or an assortment of desserts, this piece solves problems and supports good times. Some of them even open up to reveal a special serving surface for hot and cold dishes.

Buffet drawers are a good place to keep your formal flatware, while the shelves can hold serving pieces, chafing dishes, and fondue pots.

Keep serving trays and bowls clean by containing them in plastic bags, so they're ready for action without washing even if you only use them once a season.

If you love candles, buy a supply that fits your décor and frequency of use (you don't need dozens if you only light them on holidays). Keep just enough candleholders to cover casual, fancy, and holiday occasions; five or so sets should fulfill every need. Store your year-round candle gear and a box of matches in the china cabinet or buffet. Keep holiday candles with other holiday supplies (see Chapter 12 on the basement and attic).

Handle with care: Storing china and stemware

Okay, maybe it makes you feel like your grandmother, but there's nothing like a quilted china storage set to protect your most delicate dishes. With different cases sized to hold plates, platters, coffee cups, and sugar bowls and creamers as well as foam to place between pieces, these sets protect your dishes from chipping and keep them dust free.

Storing china in sets is a bit of a spatial puzzle. First you have to figure out which dishes go into which containers; you may need to mix and match to maximize space. Next is fitting the containers into the cabinet in the most efficient way.

Then there's the question of finding what you need, which is easily answered by labeling each container with masking tape and pen or a label-maker — for instance, "12 salad plates, 2 soup bowls" or "Gram's creamer and sugar." Make putting dishes away easier by adding a cabinet location to the label, such as "top right in back."

Stemware can be arranged on shelves in columns of like type. If you have room, place them upside down to keep out dust. You can conserve space by turning every other piece right side up, but you may need to wash before you pour.

Go for the glow: Keeping silver shiny and bright

Air tarnishes silver, so if your silver or silverplate sits around marinating in oxygen most of the year, plan a polishing session before you need it. (That doesn't mean the night before. Think November 1 for Thanksgiving and the winter holidays, March 1 for springtime celebrations.) You can save yourself some elbow grease if you prevent tarnish in the first place by protecting your silver from air. Wrap pieces in cloth or purchase special antitarnish bags sized to hold single servings of flatware or larger serving pieces. Another alternative — and more expensive — is a special coating that blocks out air. You take your silver to a professional silverplater (check the Yellow Pages) and pay by the piece. The most effective way to keep the shine on your silverflatware is to store it in an antitarnish chest. Be sure to buy a chest large enough to accommodate your full set.

To help prevent tarnishing after meals, handwash silverware in warm, sudsy water — never in the dishwasher. Let the pieces soak while you clean up the rest of the dishes to loosen food and prevent contact with air. Be especially quick to clean silverware that has been used with salad dressings, vinegar, fruits, or salt, as these contain reactive molecules that start oxidizing before you're even done with dessert. After washing and towel drying, let silver air dry at least overnight, turning pieces over halfway to dry the other side. Don't put silverware away until it's completely dry.

Keep candles away from curtains and other flammable objects and blow them out when you leave the room. If children are present, place candles out of reach and accidental bumping range. A base or drip tray underneath keeps your table safe from falling wax. Candles that don't drip or jar or lantern-style holders are an even better bet.

Organizing and stocking the bar

If you have a bar area with shelves and possibly a cabinet, this is the spot for all your libation supplies. Resist the temptation to buy more glasses than you need just to fill the shelves. Arrange those you do in neat columns by type, turned upside down to keep out the dust. Other bar supplies to stock here include

- Liquor, grouped by type (clear, dark, sweet)
- Mixers, grouped by type
- Corkscrew
- Foil cutter
- Bottle opener

- Bottle stoppers or vacuum system
- Lemon zester
- Cocktail shaker
- Pitcher
- Decanter
- Ice bucket and tongs
- Cocktail napkins
- Special supplies — margarita salt, bitters, and so on

If your only bar accoutrement is a corkscrew you use once in a blue moon, store it with your kitchen utensils or above the refrigerator with party supplies. On the other hand, if you have a bunch of bar supplies but no bar, dedicate a spare dining room or pantry shelf to the cause.

Wine racks are best placed in a cool, dark spot of the basement or the coolest closet in the house to prevent oxidation of your wines. Arrange by varietal or appellation, with reds on one side and whites on another. Enthusiasts may want to check out catalogs for the many types of wine racks and home cellaring options available.

Keep track of an extensive wine cellar with special computer software, a database, or a word processing table listing vintage, brand, varietal, appellation, date bought, number of bottles, and price. If you like, add slots for tasting notes.

With your living and dining rooms done, you're ready to share your organizational victories with the world, so get those invitations issued!

Chapter 9

The Hangout Spot: Family and Media Room

Ah, home at last. You kick back on the couch, crank up the VCR, and prepare to lose yourself in your favorite film. But the tape in the box marked *Casablanca* seems to be projecting singing dinosaurs onto the screen — not at all the thing for your tension headache — the remote is nowhere to be found, and is that an old pizza box peeking out from under that pile of magazines?

The model family room is comfort defined, a casual place for letting it all hang out. But you can't relax among piles or while hunting for the remote control or digging through a stack of Rolling Stones CDs in search of some soothing Bach. Promote family harmony with a well-organized family room, and watch your recreation quotient rise.

How can you let everyone do their own thing in the family room, yet still have some semblance of order? Teach all the room's occupants the power of the principles of P-L-A-C-E.

✔ **Purge:** Toss any malfunctioning, obsolete, or duplicate equipment; videos you no longer watch, music nobody listens to anymore, and books you won't read again; and old magazines, including back issues you haven't read.

✔ **Like with like:** Arrange video- and audiotapes and discs by format and category, books by fiction/nonfiction and category, and photos by date in boxes or into albums or frames. Group remote controls together with a remote caddy.

✔ **Access:** Arrange furniture for conversation, watching television, and listening to music. Place home-entertainment equipment in a media unit designed to accommodate units and make connections easy. In the bookcase, place heavier books on lower shelves and lighter ones higher up.

✔ **Contain:** Store and contain tapes and discs in drawers, shelves, or storage units, books in the bookcase, current magazines in a rack, and games, toys, photos, and collections in closed shelves and drawers or the playroom or basement.

✔ **Evaluate:** Can you straggle into this room after a long, hard day and quickly access the recreation you crave? Is the room so comfortable and peaceful that you sometimes fall asleep in your chair? Do the members of your family get along, find what they need, and have fun when they're here?

Casually Neat Is Not a Contradiction

Though the family room is a great place to forget formality, that doesn't mean order can go out the window too. Neatness counts extra in this room because it's usually the most lived-in. The den's image permeates the consciousness of your home's inhabitants. Wouldn't you like that picture to be one of peace?

Furnish the family room with comfort in mind. Like to get lazy? Indulge in a reclining chair with a built-in or separate footstool. Or go overstuffed with big, comfy armchairs. A nice, long couch can accommodate the whole family at movie-watching time; point the couch toward the screen and angle chairs on either side so you can talk or watch. Add enough end tables to hold drinks, and double up their use with drawers and shelves underneath for photos, coin and stamp collections, games, and toys. Store some TV trays or lap trays in the closet if you're inclined to have snacks or casual meals here.

Fun or Frustrating: The Media Center

A media unit is a must to provide easy access to a full complement of equipment — television, VCR or DVD, and stereo system. Designed to shelve the various components of your system and accommodate all the connecting cables, media units also have drawers to store manuals, program guides, cleaning kits, extra cables, tapes, and CDs. Built-in units offer the best stability, but you can also buy a freestanding system. If you must make do with a bookcase, drill holes in the back for cables and cords. Use extra shelf space and shelf-top organizers to store CDs and tapes.

The media center is the focal point of many family rooms — and face it, it tends to be a mess. Some of my clients could be buried alive beneath their tapes and CDs, and if I had a dollar for every unlabeled videotape of a TV show or movie I'd be too rich to bother writing this book. Imagine settling back, thinking you were in for last night's late-night talk show only to have a horror movie come on instead. No wonder relaxing is so hard to do these days.

Some people call this the Information Age, but I suspect it's really the Equipment Age — and if you accumulated an epoch's worth of unused entertainment equipment, clear the stuff out. The eight-track tape deck? History! The skipping CD player you keep thinking you'll take in for service? Either do it or give it away. Your little tabletop TV is shamed by the new big-screen model you just installed. Move the smaller version to the kitchen or call a charity for pickup.

TV, VCR/DVD, and stereo equipment

Does your remote control like to play hide and seek between the couch cushions? Take control with a caddy that has a place for your remote unit and current program guide. You can even attach it to your favorite easy chair. See Figure 9-1 for ways to take control of your controls. If you have several remotes for the television, video player, and stereo system, a universal unit can combine them all into one.

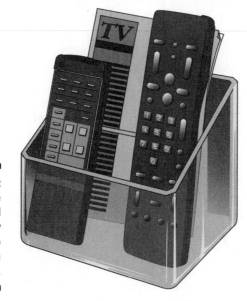

Figure 9-1:
Remote
control
caddy
stands keep
you in
command.

Fight media burnout with a scheme to make home entertainment easy again. Four easy steps can enlighten your entertainment collection and put hours of fun at your fingertips.

1. **Purge and sort.** Gather the family and go through all your tapes and discs, purging everything that no one's watched or listened to for a year. Cries of extreme sentimental value can be accommodated, but remember that you can always rent videos as well as borrow movies and music from the library. As you go, sort items by like format — videotapes, video discs, audiotapes, and audio discs.

   If your cast-off CDs still have popular appeal, take them to a used CD store for cash. You can also donate CDs and commercial videos and audiotapes to a library or school.

2. **Categorize.** Group like items by genre or category. Alphabetize titles within each category. Using the artist's or composer's name for audiotapes and the show name for videos is usually the easiest method.

   Audio categories may include classical, jazz, rock/pop, rhythm and blues/soul, rap/hip hop, blues, country, musicals/soundtracks, world/folk, children's, and books on tape. For video, consider categorizing by movies (subdivided into drama, comedy, musicals, and foreign if you have a lot), television shows, entertainment (concerts, magic shows), children's, sports, exercise, how-to, and home videos.

3. **Position for access and contain.**

   Devise your optimal storage strategy by comparing your space to the number of pieces you need to store in each format and identifying where you can most easily reach. Containing options for your audiovisual software include:

   • Drawers in the media unit, in a freestanding unit, or under tables. I like these options because they keep everything out of sight.

   • Bookcase or wall shelves. Shelf-top tape and CD holders keep everything in place, or you can use bookends to organize items by section and prevent tumbling tapes and discs. Wire shelves won't work here.

   • Spinning turntables.

   • Freestanding towers.

   Figure 9-2 illustrates one idea for media storage. Whatever you choose, make sure you can keep all the pieces in a given format together.

4. **Identify your media.** Make sure you have as much fun as your collection can offer with some basic media management:

   • Create a computer list — a database, spreadsheet, or even just a word-processing document — of everything in your collection by category. Keep an updated printout in a drawer of your media center as an easy-browsing menu.

- Label all video spines with program and length.

- Name, number, and date home videos. Protect them from getting erased by punching out the rerecord tabs.

- Keep one videotape for each family member for recording favorite shows over and over. Label the tape with the individual's name and the show if it's always the same.

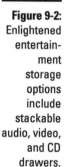
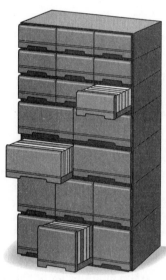

Figure 9-2: Enlightened entertainment storage options include stackable audio, video, and CD drawers.

Just the highlights: Home video editing

Improve the production values of your home videos by editing as you shoot or later. When we first got our video camera, we went crazy. We have two tapes of a Caribbean vacation and have rarely watched more than half an hour of either. Then there was our 6-month-old Mindy; now that she's 20, it's really not that fascinating to watch her bouncing in a seat for 10 minutes straight. Daughter number two got less footage, and Julie's tapes move along at a much more scintillating pace. Take your extra-long home videos to a professional studio and have them edited down to highlights. This is also a great opportunity to have your old 8 mm film and slides transferred to video so you can enjoy them more often. Just be sure to date, number, and log your originals before you let them out of your hands.

The Computer Equation

In homes without an office, the family room may be the only place to put a computer. The downside of this strategy is that one family member may want to watch a movie or listen to mind-numbing heavy metal music while another is trying to do homework or balance the checkbook on the computer. Rules may need to be set — such as homework assignments come first — and having a spare TV in another room can help ease their enforcement.

If you don't like the look of a computer in your family room, you can buy an armoire designed to keep it under cover. Refer to Part IV for a full discussion of cool computing.

Managing Your Precious Moments: Photographs

The cherished memories in your photo collection can become a clutter problem fast. Shutterbugs can benefit from a few friendly photo tips. First, purge the lemons: There's no prize for hanging on to bad pictures, so give them the boot. See? You *can* reinvent the past. After you've picked through and found all of the ones that are blurry, too far away, or where the subject's eyes are shut, you can manage the ones that are worth keeping efficiently by doing the following:

- ✔ **Label and date.** Match the moment to the memory by labeling and dating each envelope as you get it back from the developer. If your camera doesn't have a date stamp, date the backs of pictures too, and note the names of nonimmediate family members for when memory starts to fade. Never use markers, which can bleed; art stores sell special blue pencils for writing on the backs of photos.

- ✔ **Display.** What's the point of photos you never look at? Enjoy your pictures by putting them in frames or a photo album or scrapbook right away, or make a date with yourself to do it at least once a year (more if you're a frequent photographer). Some frames hold several pictures so that you can make your own collage. Have fun creating family history collages, and then hang them in the hall so everyone can remember where they came from.

- ✔ **Scrapbooks:** Assembling a scrapbook is a great family project. Choose a snowy or rainy day, or if your kids are in college, steal a few hours over break. Check out scrapbook stores chock full of things to jazz up your book, from funny quotes to fancy borders and stickers. If you prefer to seek professional help, there are specialists who teach design ideas and let you make multiple visits to their facility for advice and the camaraderie of other scrapbook creators.

- ✔ **Store safely.** Preserve your photos by keeping them in acid-free boxes or albums made with acid-free paper. Shoebox living can age photos fast.

A personal note for family shutterbugs

On a trip to Europe, I soon realized that postcards had better pictures than I could capture of the Eiffel Tower and other notable places — plus the postcards were already captioned. I hit the postcard stands for the famous views and kept my photos focused on my friends so I could see their faces and remember the times we shared. You can try this too.

For pictures you want to share, order double prints when you develop the film. If you want more than two copies — for instance, for a group picture — take multiple shots.

I remember how difficult splitting up the family photos was when my mother died — so when my girls were born, I started each one with her own album right away. I always take important shots twice and order double copies so I end up with four — one for me, one for each girl's album, and one for grandparents.

Books and Bookshelves: The Library

I know you're not a librarian, and it probably shows. You don't have to know the Dewey decimal system to bring order to your reading matter, though. Here's how to lighten up the library. Go through your books and purge all the dinosaurs, which include the following:

- ✔ Outdated or irrelevant reference books (such as the college guide if all of your kids have graduated)
- ✔ Novels you won't read again (Who reads anything twice anymore?)
- ✔ Outgrown children's books
- ✔ Old textbooks
- ✔ Anything you don't expect to open in the next year (unless it's a classic). Information is now easy to access and quick to change, so don't clutter your bookcase with yesterday's news.

Donate unwanted books to a library, school, or senior home, or sell your best titles to a used bookstore.

Arrange your books on the shelves by category, grouping like with like. For fiction, you can categorize by novels, short stories, plays, and children's books. Good nonfiction categories include reference (dictionaries, encyclopedias, thesaurus), biography, history, religion, English, arts, science, math, health/medicine, crafts/hobbies, travel, and photo albums, scrapbooks, and yearbooks. Within each category, alphabetize your books by author. Ease access and be kind to your case by keeping heavier books (think reference) on the bottom shelves and lighter ones (paperback novels) on top. Resist the urge to stack books two rows deep, as you may never see the ones in back.

If you purged and still have more books than shelf space, it's time for a new bookcase. Look for one with adjustable shelves so you can change the height to suit hard covers or paperbacks. Measure your space before shopping to be sure your dimensions match. Twelve inches depth is plenty of room for books, videos, or tapes.

Clutter or Current: Magazines

Magazines come out every week or month for a reason: You're supposed to read them now and move on. Keep only the current issues of magazines and purge the rest — yes, even if you haven't read them. If you later discover that you missed the only tell-all interview with your favorite movie star ever printed, you can find it at the library. (Schools sometimes use old magazines for various projects, if you'd rather donate than toss.) Assess your subscription portfolio. Do you really need everything you receive? Is there a magazine you haven't gotten to for the last three issues? Are you reading some of them online? Do you subscribe to a weekly news magazine simply because you think you should only to have it lie around unopened week after week? Are you tired of some of the titles you've been receiving for years? Call to cancel any superfluous subscriptions.

The whole magazine: Rack 'em

Contain your current magazine issues in a rack. As each new issue arrives, rack it up and discard the previous one. No doubling up.

You can use your magazine rack to store current catalogs too. The same rule applies: Toss out the old as you rack up the new. If you receive catalogs you don't want, call and ask to be removed from the mailing list.

Articles: File 'em

For good magazine management, mark the table of contents of each issue as you get it and tear out any articles you want to read. (If you're sharing with others or like to browse the ads, you can pull the articles when the time comes to throw the magazine away instead.) Staple each article together and place it in a To Read file that you can take along on commutes, to the doctor's office, and so on. See Chapter 16 for more on how to filter information flow.

Some people are prone to collect magazines that cover their profession or hobby to serve as a reference. If you're not referring to back issues more than once or twice a year, you're better off tossing them and looking up information at the library or on the Internet as needed. However, if you find yourself flipping through your old magazines a few times a month, they may qualify as a viable resource. You can retrieve information fastest by tearing out articles that interest you and filing them by subject, so when you want to know if you should use the wedge or the five iron to get out of a sand trap, you need only pull out the folder labeled "Golf — Sand Trap" rather than pore through three years of your favorite golf magazine indexes. If you must save whole magazines, keep no more than a few years' worth (after that the articles probably repeat) and store them in chronological order, grouped by year in magazine holders that sit on the bookshelf. Label each holder with the magazine title and issue dates.

Games, Toys, and Collections

A family that plays together stays together, but how do you keep your fun neat? Most families accumulate quite a few games, toys, and collections in the course of having fun. I'm all in favor of being fully equipped to play, and only ask that you give all your playthings a place.

Keeping games fun (and organized!)

If the family room is your prime game-playing area, buy a closed cabinet that can contain everything behind doors. A bookshelf is a less scenic alternative. Infrequent gamers or those just as likely to play in another room may put your gaming center in the playroom, basement, or hall closet, keeping just a couple of family favorites — cards, checkers — in a drawer in the den.

Keep electronic games by the TV on which they're played in clear storage boxes or special units designed to hold them, such as the one in Figure 9-3.

The toy crate

Toys need to be mobile when you have toddlers so that you can keep the kids amused as you herd them around the house under your watchful eye. While that's the case, keep a crate of toys in the family room so you don't have to chase up and down the stairs in search of a bear or truck. When the children are old enough to play in the playroom or their bedrooms without supervision, move the toys and eliminate the crate.

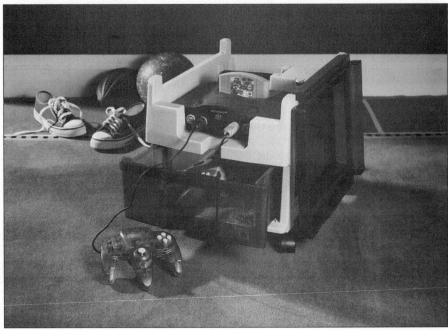

Figure 9-3:
Sleek
storage for
electronic
games.

Photo courtesy of Lillian Vernon.

Stamps, coins, shot glasses, and spoons: Collections

Collectors of coins, stamps, shot glasses and such tend to enjoy showing off, and the den is a good place for their displays. Whether you arrange your collection on a shelf, in a shadow box, or in a hanging wall display, make sure everything is easy to see — that is, well-spaced and at the right height. You don't want to hang your rare coins so high that no one can read the years. A glass enclosure can help preserve a valuable collection. Many collectors' clubs offer complete guidelines for storing and protecting your precious goods. If your collection is of less visual than personal interest, it may belong in a bedroom instead.

Now that you can actually find the movie you're looking for, I think everyone deserves two hours with their feet up and a gripping story on the screen. Doesn't your family feel more functional already?

Chapter 10

Organizing for Fun: The Playroom

In This Chapter

▶ Setting the stage for creativity

▶ Creating play centers for one-stop fun

▶ Purging the playroom without tears

▶ Advanced toy management

▶ Crafting art supply tricks

▶ Making a multigenerational playroom

*P*lay is important to people of all ages, but for children, amusement is a 24/7 job. The mess that can come from hard-core fun makes a separate room for play a great plan. Not only does a playroom keep toys, crafts, and games out from underfoot in the rest of the house, but a playroom also provides young minds with a special place to let their imaginations soar.

Children learn as they play. Show your kids how to keep the playroom clean and organized, and you'll give them a powerful tool for productivity and clear thinking that can last a lifetime. P-L-A-C-E provides the framework for your cleaned-up playroom. Here is how you employ it:

✔ **Purge:** Throw away or donate outgrown, unused, and broken toys, including games and puzzles with missing pieces. Pitch old or duplicate-color crayons, dried-out markers, paints, and glue.

✔ **Like with like:** Put items into play centers — toddlers, dress-up, playing school, and so on. Place game pieces and puzzles into resealable bags and onto shelves. Arrange books by category.

✔ **Access:** Put all large equipment, such as indoor slides or train displays, at one end of the room, and potentially dangerous or messy art and craft supplies in a childproof cabinet near their use. Keep small toys such as marbles and doll accessories higher up, out of the reach of smaller children who can choke on them.

✔ **Contain:** Place toys into containers by type and age group or individual. Add labels for quick identification and to help younger children learn to read. Put art and craft supplies into separate containers or rolling carts.

> ✔ **Evaluate:** Do children and adults feel free to play, create, and make believe in this room? Can children find and put away their own toys? Do games and puzzles always have all their pieces in place? Do you feel safe leaving your children here unsupervised? Is there a space for every sort of fun your family likes?

Positioning the Play Centers

The playroom can be conducive to creativity and to cleaning up afterward. Much of the action in this room takes place on the floor, so tackle that first and work your way up. A nice, soft carpet is great for ground-based games and play, but carpeting can also take a beating from art supplies and spills. My favorite solution is indoor/outdoor carpeting, which I initially installed with an eye toward a possible flood in our basement playroom, but quickly discovered two additional perks: Accidents can be vacuumed up or washed away with soap and water in a flash, and toys are easily pushed across the flat pile into piles for quick pickups. Genius!

Now for the fun part: Creating your worlds of play. You know how a grocery store stocks the pastas next to the sauces so you can pick up dinner all in one aisle? You can do the same in the playroom, setting up centers for various activities and age groups that make each spot a different adventure. Play centers are actually nothing more than an imaginative version of fingertip management and access, putting fun within easy reach.

One play center might include toddler toys, while another part of the room is set up to play school. The dress-up center can contain clothes and a mirror for showing them off; the building center could be stocked with builder sets; and the music center gathers together instruments, tapes and CDs, and players. If you have big equipment such as a slide or trampoline, establish an action center at one end of the room.

Your play center arrangements may need to change with your children's interests and ages. Freshening up the playroom with periodic repositioning keeps everyone interested in its organization, and provides an excellent opportunity to purge the cast-offs as you go.

How to Be a Senior Toy Manager

If you've been there, you know: Toy management is serious business. Those who do manage toys well ought to receive an honorable degree, acknowledging the advanced techniques required to keep order between fun-loving young souls and the adults who love to lavish them with gifts. The good news is that once you master the three key toy-management principles, you can keep your playroom and its players on track without panicking every time the grandparents show up with *presents*.

The three steps to advanced toy management are

1. **Purge:** In today's world, many kids are in total toy overload. To adults, toys can come to represent both love and money spent, and tossing toys may be even harder for mom than daughter. But as sentimental as each gift from loving parents, doting grandparents, and adoring aunts and uncles may be, kids outgrow toys quickly and can only play with so many current favorites at once. Keeping extra or obsolete toys encourages bad habits and wastes space — which itself is a critical part of the creativity equation. So take the plunge. Purge your playroom today.

   Depending upon your children's ages and the toys involved, you may choose to approach the task with each child individually, or do the whole family in one fell swoop. Sort toys and games by type, directing the cast-offs to trash, donation, and garage sale piles as you go.

   Purging your playroom can be approached gently. Never make children get rid of toys before they're ready, but do look for staged compromises that respect a child's feelings while also helping children form a healthy relationship with material things.

2. **Contain:** Enclosing toys in containers keeps them from becoming clutter and accustoms kids to looking for things in their place and putting their toys back in the appropriate container later. Match the container to the type of toy and age of the users. Colored open crates can hold large toys for small toddlers. Use a different color for each type of toy — blocks, cars, dolls, animals. Clear, pullout drawers suit smaller items and make seeing what's inside easy at play and cleanup time. Preschoolers love 'em. Closed wicker baskets or chests are an attractive way to house dolls and doll clothes. Containers with tight-fitting lids keep smaller children out of older children's toys, so that Judy can keep her beloved doll accessories in the playroom without worrying that little Phillip may stop by and swallow a tiny high-heeled shoe.

   Arrange your containers in cabinets or on wall shelves, keeping crayons, board games, and craft supplies up high and toddler-friendly toys closer to the floor.

   Go for closed: Look for full backs and sides on all of your playroom containers and shelving. Small toys and game and puzzle pieces have a way of slipping through cracks into irretrievable spots.

3. **Rotate:** Even after your purge, you'll probably have more toys than your children can play with at once. Absence makes the heart grow fonder, so prolong the appeal of toys and games by rotating your active stock. To establish a toy rotation, divide each toy type into a few different groups, so that the sum of one group from each type will leave your playroom well-stocked. Box up the remaining groups by set, label each "Toy rotation #___", and store in the basement or attic far from inquiring eyes.

   When your kids start to tire of the playroom repertoire, it's time for the big switcheroo. You can make a big deal of the switch, enlisting kids to pack up old toys before bringing on the new batch, or make the change yourself quietly one night. Surprise! Rotations also provide a good time to trim down the collection. Are all the toys you'll pack up still on the "A" list? Toss or donate the C's through Z's — but remember that a little time away can reestablish the luster of many a B.

No cutting corners: Storing games

One nice thing about games is that they come in their own box, but boy, do those boxes break fast, especially the corners. Mend breaks with masking tape applied to the inside of the box, which can keep the box looking nice and improve your chances of getting the game out and put away without pieces all over the floor.

The doll empire: What you can skim off the top

Perhaps the biggest toy disposal we ever pulled off was my daughters' extensive doll collection, and we didn't get it all the first time. We're talking about 15 to 20 dolls, a two-story house, a couple of canopy beds, complete dining and living room sets, a backyard barbecue, bathroom accessories, and tons of outfits — probably a thousand dollars' worth of merchandise when bought new. Though neither of the girls had played dolls in a year, one of them wasn't quite ready to let it all go. I helped her decide to keep one or two dolls and a few outfits apiece. This was fine with her, and a few years later the remaining dolls went too.

Our total garage sale take for the thousand-dollar doll empire? About $100, plus priceless space and the knowledge that we were making its new owners very happy. Garage sales won't make you rich, but they offer your children an education in commerce and provide some additional funds for fun. Why not use the proceeds for a family outing to a theme park, concert, or play? Investing them in the college fund may be thrifty, but won't provide an immediate reward to help show your kids that clutter-free living is good.

If you choose to donate, explain to your children that some kids aren't as lucky as they are, and giving extra toys to charity is a way of sharing happiness while still leaving plenty to play with. You're never too young to get in the habit of giving.

Learn to read while you play with labels

Even toy retrieval can become a reading experience when you label toy containers with their contents. Tommy may not know the word "cars" on sight, but show him that his toy hot rod goes in the drawer with those four letters on the front and watch his cognitive wheels start to turn.

Make the reading lesson easier by using both upper and lowercase letters in your labels.

Small letters, with their distinct shapes and heights, are easier to recognize than all caps. I recommend a label maker, which is relatively cheap (less than $50), for the job and the resulting labels look much better than masking tape or a curling computer label, and they're washable. With your help, your preschoolers may like punching out a label or two for themselves.

Speaking of pieces, protect your peace of mind by zipping them into resealable bags. This makes cleanup far easier when the box takes a tumble. Use the slide type of closure for easy access to younger kids' games and a pressure closure for those you might want to keep little ones out of.

Some games have paper books that are necessary to play the game. If the game's a family favorite, extend the life of the book by covering the pages with clear contact paper.

Getting it together: Puzzles

You can never put all the pieces of a puzzle together if some have gone missing, so use a system to keep them in their place:

- ✔ As soon as you bring a puzzle home, mark the back of each piece with the puzzle's name or a number, for example, "Farmhouse" or "23." If you use a number code, write the number on the puzzle box. Now if a piece pops up somewhere else, you know just where to put the piece back.

- ✔ Put puzzle pieces into a resealable bag inside the box to prevent spills.

- ✔ Devote a card or snack table to the puzzle for as long as you work on it. Place the table in a corner to keep it from getting knocked over or interfering with other activities.

The Reading Center: Children's Books

Playrooms are often freewheeling places — not the best environment for a reading center, so I generally recommend keeping most children's books in bedrooms or the library or family room. However, the playroom is the right room for activity, art, and craft books, and you may put the rest of your collection here if you don't have space elsewhere or if the playroom is your prime reading spot. Depending upon how many books you have, use a small freestanding bookcase or larger wall unit to put them into place. If you keep reading books here, put older children's books higher up so younger siblings won't access and destroy them, and devote the lower shelves to toddler favorites. Shelve books by like category: activity, reference, fiction or stories, fairy tales, religious books, and so on. See Chapter 9 for more on categorizing and shelving a library.

The Art of Organizing Arts 'n' Crafts

Setting up an arts and crafts area for kids is like arranging an adult workshop or hobby area, while accounting for safety issues and a lot more messes. See Chapter 12 for general organizational principles.

First, create the art center. Remind yourself that if there's a nice carpet on the floor, you may want to recarpet with indoor/outdoor material, use a drop cloth, or relegate activities involving clay, paints, markers, or glue to the kitchen. Keep all messy supplies in a childproof cabinet closest to their use.

Saving for a sentimental journey

Popular toys change at the speed of light. My girls grew up with toys that hadn't been invented in my day and contemporary kids can't even recognize. As a current mom of college students, I'm unfamiliar with today's toys. My point: Many toys are trendy, and it's generally best to get rid of them as they pass out of the spotlight.

Still, some toys are evergreens for educational or sentimental reasons, and to keep a few for the grandchildren is okay. I chose three boxes to hang onto from my children's younger days, filled with some dolls, a set of 2-inch-high animal families that's been off the market for years, and basic building blocks that can enable the construction of any dream, from houses to airports, fire stations, and entire towns. The dolls may be the most lasting reminder of my

limited skills as a seamstress. I labored over making them new outfits, and hoped that someday my grandchildren may enjoy playing with their mothers' dolls and laughing at their grandmother's stitches. As for the mini animals, when my girls were young there was a television show that taught life lessons through families of rabbits, bears, and raccoons. I made up a lot of stories voiced through the mouths of these guys, and plan to tell new ones the soonest chance I get.

So my sentimental savers are destined to be grandma's toys, a select and special few that meet my own needs while leaving my children the space to create their own memories with a new generation. When it comes to sentiment, selectivity is key.

If you don't have a mess-proof floor in the art center or want to double up your cooking with supervising an arts-and-craft session, set up your craft station in the kitchen, storing supplies in a high or locked cabinet and using the kitchen table for a worktable. You can knock off a stew or sauce while they stamp, paint, or glue, and everyone can have something to show at the end.

By the way, buy washable markers, paints, and glue while kids are young enough to consider the world and the walls their canvas. For a worktable in the playroom, a kitchen cast-off fills the bill. Laminated tops are easiest to clean up, while wood may get wrecked and stained by paints and crayons, but maybe you don't care.

Next, stock your supplies. As always, art supplies can be accessible close to the worktable, with like items together and everything contained in dividers or other containers in drawers or on shelves. An old dresser may be put to use for craft supply storage. Playrooms have lots of craft stuff and art supplies, so here are some ways to consolidate and store all of those supplies for those future creations:

- ✔ **Crayons:** Save new, intact boxes of crayons for school and collect the rest in a covered plastic box or metal tin at home. Metal won't get as marked up as plastic.

- ✔ **Pencils, pens, markers, scissors:** Use narrow plastic divider trays, preferably inside a drawer to prevent a spill.

- ✔ **Rubber stamps:** Store them in their original cases or spread on a piece of paper. Stamping the paper with the design can help you find the stamp you want.

- ✔ **Paints:** Stack watercolors in their own containers, organize others into plastic trays.

- ✔ **Glues:** Group together in a plastic tray.

- ✔ **Paper:** If you have several types (white, construction, drawing, and so on), use an office sort tray.

- ✔ **Beads:** Corral beads into containers specially designed to separate them by type.

Attention kids and parents everywhere: Crayons aren't used up just because you wore them down to the paper. Buy a crayon sharpener to keep a slim tip on your crayons and enjoy their full lifespan. Got more crayons than you can use? Day care centers are always happy for the donation.

Rec Room and Playroom Combo: All-Ages Fun!

We all need to play, and doubling up the playroom as a recreation and relaxation room for teenagers and adults can be a boon to family togetherness — if you have the space to let everyone do their thing. Keep centers in mind so that you can cohabitate playfully and peacefully. Add an adult sitting area with a couch, some comfy chairs, and perhaps a media center and/or library. Big games such as pool or ping-pong can go into their own game center away from the sitting area so the action doesn't detract from anyone's relaxation factor. Point the couch and chairs toward the kids' play areas, and you can keep a watchful eye while you enjoy your book or show.

Cleaning up your act

The playroom may be the space with the shortest organizational attention span in the house. Whatever the project or game, every session here needs to routinely end with cleanup time. From the moment your children can walk, show them not to walk out of the room until everything is put away. The payoff? Fun and easy play tomorrow, without a mess to wade through on the way.

Kid-friendly ways to clean up your act include:

✔ Clean up with them when the kids are young.

✔ Invite older children to think up better ways to straighten up and systematize the playroom. Throw down the gauntlet anew every year.

✔ Turn on special cleanup music and challenge everyone to be done by the time the song is over.

✔ Set a good example yourself in other areas of the house. Getting organized in the playroom can make fun come naturally for all — so forget your excuses and get playing with everything in its place!

Part III
Organizing Storage Spaces and Other Secret Places

The 5th Wave   By Rich Tennant

In this part . . .

The propensity for "Out of sight, out of mind," as the saying goes, is sure to drive you out of your mind when you're scouring the basement for a special holiday serving dish and company is on the way. Part III can help you put everything away in secret spaces, so storage is no longer synonymous with stress. You may even discover that storing more is sometimes less. So get busy in the basement! Get going in the garage! If you follow these guidelines, you may even have room for the car.

Chapter 11

Lightening Your Load: The Laundry and Utility Room

· ·

In This Chapter

▶ Preventing nothing-to-wear mornings

▶ Rising above piles with savvy sorting secrets

▶ How to shrink anything — or not

▶ Clutter-taming caddies and drying racks

▶ Setting up a mess-free mudroom

· ·

*A*ir the dirty laundry: You probably spend far more time than you like in an overheated room that smells like lint in a losing battle to keep your closets stocked with clean clothes. How can you ever win?

Weary washers of the world take heart. Getting organized in the laundry room can take a big load off your mind and lighten your burden of chores. Whether you have the luxury of your very own laundry room (bet you never thought of it that way), share a laundry room with fellow apartment dwellers, or lug your duds to the public Laundromat, a lean-and-mean approach to keeping your clothes clean can enhance both your look and your life.

The laundry room is a place for making things clean, so put everything into P-L-A-C-E by applying those five organizing principles.

✔ **Purge:** Toss out old laundry supplies; bent, misshapen, or excess hangers; worn or torn dust rags; and any dried-up or old craft or holiday supplies in your utility center. If you have return/repair items you haven't dealt with in a year, let them go now.

✔ **Like with like:** Put laundry supplies together by type above, next to, or between the machines, right where you use them.

✔ **Access:** Keep hampers in bedroom closets to collect dirty laundry at the source. In the laundry room, create a sorting center, drying center, ironing center, and utility center to complete each task in one spot.

> ✔ **Contain:** Keep laundry supplies in cabinets or shelving units near the machines. Place the ironing tools in an organizer on the wall or door. Put craft supplies in clear containers and label them for easy access.
>
> ✔ **Evaluate:** Do dirty clothes easily make their way into the right load? Can you reach all the laundry supplies while standing at the machine? Can you sort clean clothes without taking a step? Is getting dirty clothes in and clean clothes out of the laundry and helping with a weekly load easy for household members? Does working in this room make you feel like a paragon of efficiency, or an underpaid drudge?

Doing the Laundry Where You Live

Most of us don't have a choice in the matter, but if you do here's my maxim: Do the laundry where you live. Whoever thought of putting laundry rooms in the basement, two floors away from where we take off dirty clothes and put on clean ones, was clearly unacquainted with the principle of fingertip management. The closer you can locate the laundry to your bedrooms the better, so you who have first- or second-floor facilities can count yourselves blessed. The rest of you, whether descending to the basement or heading out of the house, can consider it extra calories burned or a social break.

No matter where you do your laundry, you can save time and steps by keeping a hamper for dirty clothes in each bedroom, where clothes can be deposited as each person undresses. Look for vented hampers that let clothes breathe, and if there's a lot of ground to cover between the closet and the washing machine, why not get one with wheels on the bottom so you can roll instead of carrying? Figure 11-1 shows this easy-handling hamper.

Hallway facilities

Hallway washer-dryer setups usually accommodate just the machines and a few cabinets or shelves above. Forget about spreading out a bunch of laundry baskets. At best you can stow baskets on top of the machines while the laundry is inside; at worst — if the machines themselves are stacked — the baskets must be stored in the bedroom at all times. You also have limited space for storing supplies, sorting, and air-drying — but read on for tips about facilitating each of these tasks.

If you can, enclosing hallway laundry facilities behind doors is best. Keep them closed so you don't have to look at the machines and think about your dirty laundry every time you walk by.

Photo courtesy of Get Organized!.

The laundry room

A dedicated laundry room provides the space you need to get the job done with ease, *if* you arrange the room well and refrain from filling it up with other stuff.

To give everyone easy access to supplies and key areas for doing laundry, divide the laundry area into the following centers:

- ✔ Sorting center for dirty and clean clothes
- ✔ Drying center
- ✔ Ironing center

If you have a laundry chute, put an 18-gallon garbage can underneath to catch clothes easily and prevent having to pick up the overflows and misses that shallow baskets can cause. You can use a low shelf or table to position the can as close to the chute as possible.

A well-stocked laundry room can conquer many a stain and ensure you always have the right product for the job. But a box of detergent you can't find has zero cleaning power, and shuffling through bottles when you have a big pile of dirty clothes staring you down can raise your irritation quotient fast. The right storage systems can help you whip your supplies into place and lose the laundry blues. The following can make laundry simple:

- ✔ **Built-in shelves above the machines:** A couple of midlevel shelves above your washer and dryer can contain your detergent and fabric softener at closest possible use. Solid shelving is better than wire racks because the smooth surface provides better balance to small containers and prevents any drips or leaks from oozing down behind the machines. The disadvantage of shelving is that you have to look at everything, which isn't as aesthetic as hiding things away.

   If you store cleaning or dusting rags on shelves, place them in a container so they don't ruin your view or fall through wire racks.

- ✔ **Built-in cabinets above the machines:** These offer the same ease of access as shelves. You do lose a little time opening the doors to locate and reach for an item or take inventory, but you have the added advantage of concealing the contents.

- ✔ **Freestanding shelves or cabinets above or next to the machines:** If you don't have built-ins and would rather not install cabinets yourself, you can purchase freestanding units that rise above the machines or stand along the wall.

- ✔ **Caddies next to or between machines:** From rolling wire rack shelves to slim towers that slip between the washer and dryer, there's a laundry caddy to suit every need. Look for one that works with your layout and can hold all your supplies in one place. Figure 11-2 presents a possibility.

Group supplies by type, so that all the detergents and bleaches go together close by the washing machine with stain treatments alongside. If you treat stains in a sink or on a worktable, then put your antistain products near there. The fabric softener can sit near the dryer, so everything has its own slot and retrieving and putting away is easy.

Apartment laundry rooms and public Laundromats

Organizing your laundry is all the more important if your residence has no laundry facilities. Designate a spot — under the kitchen or bathroom sink, in the linen closet, utility closet, or pantry, or in a back hall — to store all your supplies and a stash of quarters. Use a rolling hamper and portable supply caddy to ease transport.

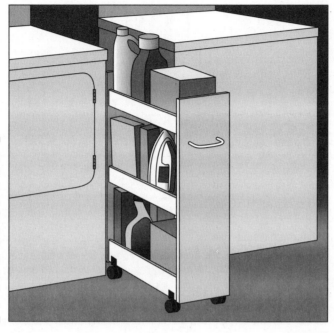

Figure 11-2:
If you're short on space, this skinny caddy helps keep laundry supplies in place between the machines.

Keep at least enough quarters on hand to wash and dry all the loads you typically do in a session. Whether you buy a roll of quarters at the bank or accumulate change in a jar, you can cut out hustling for coins from your chore.

Use your time at the Laundromat to catch up on reading by taking along your To Read File (see Chapter 16). This multitasking strategy has the added benefit of enabling you to remove loads as soon as they're done and keep other customers from acing you out of your machine.

The laundry list

The chemistry of cleaning is more advanced than ever, so stock up to bust stains and brighten clothes with laundry supply basics.

✔ **All-purpose detergent**. Liquids are less likely to leave residue on your clothes and can double as a quick spot treatment for food and greasy stains. Powdered detergent

mixed to a paste with water and applied directly to clothes can get out ground-in dirt.

✔ **Enzyme products** for tough jobs. Really dirty clothes and protein stains such as blood, grass, and chocolate require the power of enzymes, which you can find in presoak products and certain laundry detergents. Check the label and choose products with

(continued)

(continued)

enzymes for soaking, spot treating, or washing stubborn spots.

✔ **Spot stain removers.** Oily stains respond best to spot removers, which you can buy in stick, spray, or liquid form.

✔ **Fels Naphtha** for stains is a remedy handed down to me from my mother, who got it from hers. A bar of this strong soap from the personal bar soap section or the cleaning products shelf of supermarkets can work miracles. I've used this strong and inexpensive bar soap to take out spaghetti sauce, even blood.

✔ **Chlorine bleach** for whites and bleach-safe colors. Always dilute bleach with water and add it five minutes after the cycle begins to give detergent enzymes a head start and protect your clothes from bleach spots.

✔ **Nonchlorine bleach** to boost cleaning power for colored loads. You can add this right along with the detergent; in fact, *"brightening"* detergents already contain all-fabric bleach.

✔ **Fabric softener** to reduce static and wrinkling as well as soften and fluff your stuff.

If you use liquid laundry detergent, buy a small measuring cup so you don't have to put a messy cap back on the bottle. The first time, fill the cap to the line with water and pour it into the measuring cup to read how much you need. If you always use the same brand, use a permanent marker to indicate the level directly on the measuring cup. (An alternative is to save a cap from a previous bottle.) If you switch brands, you'll need to remeasure with each new bottle, and then write the cup measure amount on the current bottle.

Sorting Systems

Sorting, the first step to laundry success, can be as simple or as complicated as your clothes collection requires.

A well-organized sorting system can help you rise above those piles on the floor and keep each load neat and contained. Sorting solutions on the market include a set of canvas bags hanging from a frame with a hinge-top table above for folding (see Figure 11-3), sliding baskets set into a standing frame to maximize your vertical space, and the old-fashioned method of baskets set on a table.

To sort clothes the savvy way, do the following:

1. **The dry and the wet:** First filter out garments bound for the dry cleaners before garments go anywhere, preferably in the bedroom. Designate a separate hamper or hanging spot in the closet for items to take to the cleaners.

   The chemicals used in dry cleaning are tough on fabric, so the less often you take clothes to the cleaners, the longer they last. Once or twice a season is probably enough for all but the most-frequently worn items.

2. **The basic three:** Color is the key criterion for sorting laundry loads, and the basic three groups are whites, darks, and mixed. Separate along these color lines and you have an excellent chance of pulling clothes from the washer representing the same spot on the spectrum as they did when they went in. Cross the lines and all bets are off.

Red, black, and other dark colors can bleed, especially in hot water — so unless you're trying to dye your entire wardrobe pink or gray, sort these into a separate load and use cold water. If something does run, *don't* put the affected garments in the dryer, which will set the color. Rewash them, perhaps with a blast of bleach for whites or nonchlorine bleach for colors.

3. **The not-so-basic 11:** While the basic three categories can take care of singles, couples, and small young families, larger families and active kids can call for advanced sorting calculus that accounts for both volume — how much can fit in the machine at one time — and temperature. Leotards, shorts, and sport tops for gymnastics, cheerleading, and the health club need cold water, but all those plain white T-shirts can go gray if they don't get washed hot. If you're really down in the laundry trenches, your categories may look more like

Whites (no dark design)	Hot
Light mixed	Warm
Dark mixed	Cold
Sheets	Hot or warm
Towels	Hot or warm
White dress shirts and blouses	Warm or cold
Dark dress shirts and blouses	Cold
Knits	Cold
Jeans	Warm
Sweat clothes	Warm or cold
Pajamas	Warm

Here's a place where a little organization can pay off in spades: Treat stains right away. Your chances of saving the garment are higher the sooner you mount your counterattack. Keep a second set of stain-removal products in the master bathroom if the trip to the laundry room tends to delay your treatment efforts. Contain lingerie in mesh bags before washing, nylons in one and bras in another. Close up bra hooks to keep them from catching other clothes. Separate bags for each person make sorting easier when the wash is done. Finally, zip up all the zippers and turn printed T-shirts inside out to protect the design.

Figure 11-3:
A laundry
sorter with
star
performance.

Photo courtesy of Get Organized!.

Loadsful of laundry

I added it up: When both my girls were teenagers, I did 12 loads of laundry a week. That's nearly 50 loads each month! Most of us go through five outfits a week for work or school, maybe another five if you change when you get home, weekend clothes, workout gear, and something a little spiffier for going out in the evening. Add sheets, towels, and pj's, and it's no wonder we keep the machines and the long-suffering soul who runs them busy. Here are a few ways to handle laundry overload:

✔ Teach the rest of the family to do laundry and assign a weekly load to each person. Sheets and towels are an easy place to start. Type up a list of each load and the right dial settings for both washer and dryer, and then post it on the wall for easy reference.

You may turn to the reference list yourself when your mind is taking the day off.

✔ Tackle the problem at the source: your closets. Pare your wardrobe down to your favorites and most-frequently worn, and I promise you'll see the flow of laundry ease. (See Chapter 6 on the bedroom for wardrobe purging tips.)

Check for stains and dirty collars and cuffs as you sort loads, and give them a dose of the right product (see "The laundry list") before washing in the hottest water indicated for the garment. Check again before drying and rewash anything that hasn't come clean; the heat of the dry cycle can set stains for life.

Take oversized items such as comforters and bedspreads to a coin laundry with large-capacity machines. Large-sized washables can get cleaner and better rinsed, and won't test the limits of your own machines.

Drying without Crying

Just ask my kids: I can shrink anything. I'm afraid to say that even after two decades, operator error is probably to blame for all the wardrobe downsizing I've done. Shrinking clothes by mistake wastes the money you spent in the store and the time lost in the laundry room, so direct from the school of hard knocks I present these do's and don'ts for drying without crying:

- ✔ Remove dryer lint each time to optimize the machine's efficiency and prevent setting your clothes on fire. This, of course, will save you lots of time and trouble.

- ✔ Match the cycle setting to the load so that the temperature and timing are at least in the right ballpark. The rule of thumb is that the lighter the fabric, the lower the temperature should be. That puts delicates and permanent press at low, jeans and towels on high — get the picture?

- ✔ *Don't* count on the *automatic* setting to shut the machine off before your clothes have lost a size or two.

- ✔ Set the dryer's timer with a conservative eye. Most loads are done in 40 minutes or so (less for delicates). Schedule your trip back to the dryer accordingly and plan to pull shrink-sensitive items such as 100 percent cotton garments out while they're still slightly damp and then hang them up to air dry. Finish off the rest with an additional 10 to 15 minutes.

- ✔ *Don't* leave clothes sitting in the dryer after the cycle is done. Cooling in a heap can wrinkle clothes, while hanging or folding them hot will leave them smooth to save you ironing time.

Whether you're trying to outwit a wily dryer or air drying delicates straight from the washer, you need drying systems more advanced than. chair backs and doorknobs. Check out Figure 11-4 for a dandy drying idea.

The quickest way to get clean laundry back to where it belongs is to sort as you pull washing from the machines. Hanging is generally easier than folding, as anything that comes out damp has a chance to air dry, and you can easily sort by owner as you hang things on a clothes rod or rack or a wall-mounted wire shelf. Whether you're hanging items or folding them into piles, sort by person first; then, depending upon your space and the number of people you're dealing with, you can subsort by garment type — shirts, pants, socks and underwear, and so forth.

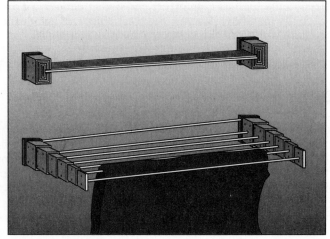

Figure 11-4:
A telescoping wire rack for draping small items does a lot of drying in little bit of space.

Do you find yourself trying to squeeze a dozen different piles of folded laundry onto the tops of two small machines? Simplify your life with a sorting table with space for all your piles. See Figure 11-3 for a double-duty model with sorting bags below.

Getting It Straight: Ironing

I hate to iron. Maybe it's genetic. My mother couldn't tackle the pile of wrinkly things without our weekly cleaning lady and me by her side. Against my will, I discovered that at least things went faster if you iron right.

Before you even start ironing, equip yourself with a reliable iron, ironing board, and cover. Using the kitchen table instead of a board only makes the job harder and puts you and your clothes at risk. If you're short on space, look for a board that hangs from a door that can be pulled down for use. Occasional ironers can also opt for a mini-board with folding legs that fits in a drawer. Though patterned ironing board covers might be pretty, solids make it easier to see the item you're ironing and get all the wrinkles the first time around.

An iron with automatic shut-off can prevent a safety hazard if you should go to answer the phone or stir the tomato sauce midjob.

Okay, here is your basic, no-frills, quick-and-efficient ironing strategy:

1. Start with garments that need the lowest heat setting, and then work your way up the dial. Otherwise, you're sitting around waiting for the iron to cool down between settings, or burning or melting something with your impatience.

2. Do the fussy parts first — collars, yokes, cuffs, and waistbands.

3. Once the small stuff is out of the way, do the sleeves. Then work from one end of the garment to the other without skipping around.

Never leave a hot iron with the plate flat. After use, pour out any water and stand it on its heel on top of the washer or dryer with the cord well away from the hot side. Don't return the iron to a plastic organizing caddy until it's completely cool, or you'll have a meltdown on your hands.

My favorite ironing tactic is preventive: permanent press. Why buy 100 percent cotton when there are so many great fabrics out there that come out of the dryer ready to wear?

Scheduling Your Laundry Day

Accustomed to doing laundry when you run out of clothes? There is a better way. There are two basic theories about how to schedule your wash: all on one day, or split into two. If you work every day, you may want to leave weekends free for errands, outings, and fun, in which case splitting up the job into one weeknight for linens and another for clothes would be best. On the other hand, if you have a young family, you may prefer to get the whole thing out of the way on Saturday or Sunday, when your spouse or a babysitter can take the kids or a play date can be arranged. Either way, if you find yourself frequently staring at an empty closet, your schedule needs refining.

Utility or Mudroom

The laundry room often doubles as a mudroom off the back or basement door, where everything from sandy beach towels to crusty boots can congregate. Your utility room may serve as an extra storage spot, or a place to do anything messy. The more hats your laundry room wears, the more you need to organize.

The mess-free mudroom

Though you may not think of the mudroom as wearing a public face, this is a primary point of entry to the house, and family and guests alike may troop through after swimming, picnicking, or playing. Make it nice and easy:

✔ Add a closed cabinet for beach towels, and bath towels and supplies if you have a shower and/or bathroom here. See Chapter 7 for more on setting up a beautiful and functional bath area.

✔ Use a closed cabinet or shoe rack for sports shoes and organize them by owner.

✔ Keep sports clothes neat with designated hanging space, baskets on shelves, or a stand-alone cabinet. Whether it's tae kwon do robes or tennis hats, these things have to go somewhere.

✔ Sports equipment can generally be relocated to the garage for easiest access. But if you're short on space there or this is the closest place to grab it as you walk out the door, use an organizing rack as described in Chapter 13 to keep equipment neat.

Utility unlimited

Utility means useful, which often translates as storage. If you have more space than you need to get the wash done, consider these additional storage uses for the laundry room:

✔ **Extra refrigerator and/or freezer.**

✔ **Holiday serving pieces and supplies.** Install shelves, or closed cabinets are better.

✔ **Hobby and craft supplies.** If you don't have a dedicated area and usually do your work close by — for instance, if the laundry room is on the first floor and you stage your craft sessions in the kitchen, then store crafts here. Shelving or cabinets are crucial here, and if there are small children in the house it should be high.

✔ **Patio cushions.** Though outdoor things generally go in the garage, storing cushions inside keeps them nice and clean for more dignified seating.

✔ **Return and repair center.** Pro: Storing your damaged goods in need of fixing or refunds here keeps them out of the way. Con: This room can be way out of mind, and you may never make the trip. Install open shelving that can both organize your return/repair items and make them more obvious.

Cleaning up the laundry room can leave you better dressed and less stressed. Don't get sidelined by stains or worried by wrinkles. Get organized!

Chapter 12

Where Clutter Clones Itself: The Basement and Attic

*W*hy do people love to hate their basements and attics? Because they give folks a place to stash their secret messes and in the process can cause a cycle of guilt that grows with the piles. You await the scientific studies to prove that the stuff in your attic and basement actually divides like single-cell organisms while you're not looking, but circumstantial evidence suggests that involuntary clutter breeding does occur. My recommendation to every client, from residents of tiny condos to homeowners with basements big enough to house a small nation, is to give these out-of-sight spaces a position front and center in your organized mind.

If the words *basement* and *moldy boxes* are synonymous in your mind and you turn a blind eye to the dusty debris on your uppermost floor — then ignore the obvious no more. Organize the storage spaces and activity places in your basement and attic, and stop clutter cloning in its tracks.

Lacking a basement or attic but still looking to store smart and organize tools and supplies for various household tasks? Read on for strategies that can be adapted to any area of the house.

Clutter doesn't stop clogging up your life just because you don't look at the mess every day. In fact, for some people hidden clutter is the biggest burden of all. So tackle your basement and attic with P-L-A-C-E and get more value from your real estate.

✔ **Purge:** Toss out any broken, torn, and worn items as well as return/repair items that have been out of use for a year or more. Duplicate tools; dried out glue, paint, and varnish; and old or excess workshop and hobby supplies get the heave-ho too.

✔ **Like with like:** Arrange all storage items by type — off-season clothing, entertaining supplies, rotating toys, and so on.

✔ **Access:** Establish storage, workshop, hobby/craft, exercise, and gift wrap centers. Keep flammable items away from the furnace and hot water heater.

✔ **Contain:** Keep large tools on a pegboard and parts in minidrawers. Hobby and craft supplies can go in divided drawers or cabinets (possibly childproof). Exercise equipment may be contained nicely in boxes, while gift-wrap supplies can go into plastic containers.

✔ **Evaluate:** Can you find storage items in a flash? Do you look forward to working in your workshop or hobby area? Can you easily exercise whenever the energy strikes? Are young children safe from dangerous equipment, tools, and supplies?

Down in the Depths: Functional Concerns

In the basement, clutter around equipment and machinery is inconvenient when you need service and dangerous if the jumble is flammable. A disorganized storage area makes finding and getting to items stored there difficult, sometimes impossible, so what's the point of holding onto them, anyway? A mess won't motivate anyone to get busy in the workshop or exercise center. And the whole thing can turn into a swamp of ruined stuff if a seemingly simple shower turns into a flood while you're at work or out to dinner and you're unprepared. The basement and its functions essentially boil down to three basic needs:

✔ A holding place for appliances that run the house — furnace, water heater, water softener, and so forth.

✔ Storage.

✔ Places for activity centers such as the laundry room, workshop, hobby or craft shop, exercise area, playroom, or family room.

The most important thing to do in the basement is to store all chemicals and valuable items on shelves or tables above flood level. Even if you don't live near water and no threat of serious flooding is present in your geographic location, water from especially heavy rain can make your basement a mud basin and a safety hazard. Being organized beforehand can lessen the degree of any such disaster.

Here are some additional precautions to keep the basement functional and friendly.

✔ Clear out the space around the furnace, water heater, other major appliances, pipes, and drains. Be particularly mindful of flammable and heat-sensitive items, as well as any valuables that may suffer beneath a burst pipe. Section off this area with a locked door if you have small children. To keep from fumbling for keys in the event of an emergency, a simple hook too high for a child to reach can do the job.

✔ Install a sump pump to fight floods.

✔ Install another sump pump — this one battery-operated for backup during power failures.

✔ Keep a large, battery-powered flashlight on hand to check equipment and the fuse box if the power should fail.

✔ Maintain critical equipment on a regular basis. Set up a schedule and post it on the wall.

Don't risk turning your basement into toxic soup by storing chemicals — for cleaning, garden care, household jobs, or hobbies — where floodwaters can reach them. Co-author Elizabeth witnessed the consequences of low-level storage while visiting her mother at her home in an Ohio valley. After an evening out during one of the season's first rains, they returned home to a full basement flood — and though Mom had resolved to move all the toxic supplies to higher ground before the rains began, she hadn't gotten to it yet. One glimpse of your mother stripped down to her slip, thigh-high in potentially poisonous water chasing bobbing cans of pesticide will convince you to store safe and high in the basement.

Storage Made Simple

Whether in the basement, the attic, or anywhere at all, storage can and should be simple, but many people miss the boat by storing things willy-nilly and without a plan. The complicated results tax the mind and make retrieving things hard, which defeats the purpose of storing them to begin with. There are two steps to simple storage: Decide what to keep, and then figure out where and how to keep it. W-A-S-T-E and P-L-A-C-E break these big questions down into bite-sized decisions.

Deciding what to keep

The five W-A-S-T-E questions (see Chapter 3) can help you zero in on what's worth keeping, and what's a waste of space and the time you spend dealing with it. Put each item to the W-A-S-T-E test before you put it into the box or onto the shelf.

✔ **Worthwhile?** Do I ever use this? Do I really need it? What if I just took a photo and filed it under "memories"? Items that you really want or need are probably worth storing, while those that are expendable or you haven't used in several years fail this test and should be tossed or donated. Holiday decorations may be worthwhile, but few people need to keep a collection of cardboard boxes.

✔ **Again?** Will I actually use this item again, or am I keeping it in case of some unlikely future or because I paid good money for it? Sure, this made a great decoration for my son's first birthday party but now he's in grade school and the moment's long gone. No matter how valuable something was to you in the past, if you won't use the item again, don't waste the storage space. Discard.

✔ **Somewhere else?** How many spare hair dryers does a family really need? Couldn't I borrow my neighbor's pasta machine if I should finally have that authentic Italian dinner party I've been thinking about for five years? If you can easily find an item somewhere else if and when the need arises, whether by borrowing or even buying a new one, don't store. Say goodbye instead.

✔ **Toss it?** Will my life change for the worse without my box of high school papers on hand? What happens if I haul this dusty old broken-down chair to the Dumpster? If you can imagine tossing an item without clear negative consequences, go ahead and do so.

✔ **Entire item?** Do you need the full set of luggage, or do you only use the carry-on? If you love the punch bowl but always serve in paper cups, why take up storage space with the unused cup set? Just because something came in a set doesn't mean you need to store every piece. Sort out the useful parts or pieces and throw or give away the rest.

Now that you ran the gauntlet, let me assure you that there's nothing wrong with storing things. Storing is an organizational basic: If you don't use something every day, storage is the way to keep it out of the way.

You can whip things in and out of storage more quickly if you can see what you're doing, so install enough lights to illuminate every nook and cranny your storage area.

Where and how to keep it: Basic storage principles

Though you use storage items less frequently than other things, some principles of P-L-A-C-E are still the guide for putting them away.

Like with like saves the day. Group all your storage items by category. Think like a calendar when organizing holiday items, devoting a separate container to each major celebration and arranging them chronologically. Smaller holidays for which you store less stuff — Valentine's Day, Fourth of July, and so on can be grouped together.

Store things close to where you use them, saving prime spots to access the most-frequently used items. For instance, if you break out your big coffee-maker every time company comes, keep it near the front of your storage area, but once-a-year holiday supplies can go farther back. If the basement has a door out to the garage, store sports equipment as close to the door as you can. Save the corner of the shelf closest to your work center to keep extra craft supplies. Get the picture?

Containing items makes them easier to group, find, move and stack, and also keeps them out of the dust. You have various enclosure options, each with its own best use:

- ✔ **Cases.** I love things that come already enclosed — golf clubs in a bag, a card table in a box. Keep storage items in their original containers, and then put them in a closet, on a shelf, or on the floor as befits their size.

  Though original boxes are great for storage, keeping empties is a waste of space. Do you need the box for the water glasses in your kitchen cupboard? Nope! There are two exceptions to the no-empties rule: Boxes for electronic equipment (computers, VCRs, CD players, and the like), which you'll need along with the foam packing inside if you ever have to pack or ship your components, and a few empty boxes for shipping gifts. Break shipping boxes down and put them with your gift wrap center.

- ✔ **Containers.** Clear plastic containers in a variety of sizes enable you to group like items and see them clearly. Label each one with its contents for even easier identification. If you have a large family and are storing individual possessions such as clothes or kids' papers, try transparent boxes in different colors. This trick is great for separating boys' and girls' hand-me-down clothes. Mark the sizes on the boxes.

- ✔ **Pullout drawers.** From large floor units to minis that sit on a shelf, drawers do the job too.

- ✔ **Coverings.** You can't fit card table chairs into a pullout drawer but you can store them dust-free by draping them with an old sheet. Even better are the clear plastic drop cloths they sell for covering furniture while painting, which enable you to see what's underneath and look less scary.

After you have everything neatly contained, you'll need a few places for those containers. Because the basement is an area for many diverse activities, you'll want to use wall space to keep stuff off of the floor. Keeping the floor clear also lessens the potential for any items to be lost to the threat of water damage. For your contained items, sturdy shelves are the next step. Metal shelves like the ones pictured in Figure 12-1 will withstand a flood and hold a lot of weight. Depending upon what you store and the earthquake activity in your area, you may want to secure freestanding shelves to the wall.

Cabinets, by hiding their contents away, make a nice alternative to shelves. Cabinets are suited for smaller items such as office and craft supplies, or chemicals and paints.

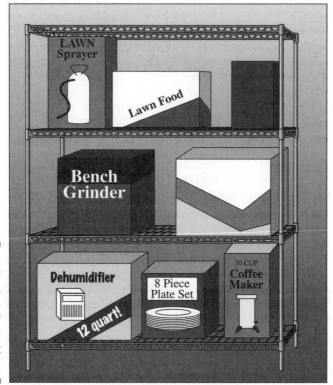

Figure 12-1: Metal shelf units can stand up to plenty of weight and basement weather.

Strategizing your storage solution

You've got basement storage principles down; now how can you put them into action? Here are some examples of how you can group items by category, contain them well, and position them for appropriate access in your basement storage area.

Save your back with a scooter

The crawl space, that bane of people with bad backs, gets a lot more accessible for storage with a little seated scooter like those you can get for working in the garden. When we were kids my father made his own by attaching wheels to a piece of wood. For him, the home-made dolly meant scooting instead of stooping; to us it was a free ride.

✔ **Luggage:** Keep only the pieces you use, with larger ones in back and smaller in front (don't nest them; you'll forget all about the inside pieces). Try under the stairs if you have space.

✔ **Home office:** Extra inventory and office supplies, on shelves and/or in clear containers.

✔ **Paperwork and memorabilia:** Tax records for the past seven years, real estate papers, wills, warranties, kids' memento boxes (see Chapter 14 on the work space). Keep on a high shelf to protect from floods and move indispensable items to a safe deposit box.

✔ **Hobby and craft supplies:** Extra inventory, stored in clear containers.

✔ **Picnic supplies:** Cooler, basket, portable dishes and utensils, grill, charcoal, blankets.

✔ **Holiday and party supplies:** Decorations, dishes, silverware, large coffeemaker, punch bowl, cups, card table, and chairs.

✔ **Bulk food and paper supplies:** Canned goods, drinks, and other non-perishable foods, bath tissue, napkins, and paper towels. Buy in bulk on sale or at warehouse stores, and shelve according to the pantry principles in Chapter 5.

✔ **Extra refrigerator and/or freezer:** Drinks, ice, party overflow, big-batch recipes. Put on a platform to protect from floods.

Items you're saving to donate can be collected in boxes or bags until it's time for a pickup or run to your local charity. See Chapter 3 for more on donating as a great clutter-busting technique.

See "The Attic" section later in this chapter for more storage ideas. If you don't have an attic, you can store attic items in the basement without losing any points in the organizing game.

Basement Activity Centers

Use the center concept to organize basement work and play by activity. Whether you have separate rooms or simply dedicated areas, sectioning off each center and stocking the space with the equipment and supplies you need gives you fingertip management of the task. You can find entire chapters in this book on the family room, playroom, and laundry room, so if any of these are in your basement, browse Chapter 9, 10, or 11, respectively, for how to set them up. Following is the lowdown on creating basement centers for the workshop, crafts and hobbies, exercise, and gift wrapping centers.

Home improvement: The workshop center

Happiness central for home improvement nuts but often a source of distress for those who don't know a wrench from a rivet (and would rather not), the workshop can become more useful to every household member with some simple organizational techniques.

Workshop floors often seem unfriendly, with cold, hard cement the default mode and messy activities such as sawing and painting defusing the motivation to improve. But take note: Tiling the workshop floor can warm up the room without making it any less washable. Another step up the comfort scale is indoor/outdoor carpet, which cleans up, lasts long, and doesn't mind getting wet.

Change your life: Get a wet-dry vacuum. Designed to suck up anything from wood shavings to spilled milk, this all-purpose appliance will serve you well in the workshop, kitchen, and car.

Tools

Do you use tools only when you can't get the maintenance man on the phone and there's no handy friend at hand? Then a single toolbox stocked with the basics will do. Here are the basics that everyone should own:

- Hammer
- Wrench
- Four screwdrivers: A big and small each of regular and Phillips
- Two pliers: Needle-nosed and regular
- Nails: All types
- Screws: Likewise
- Picture hangers: One size fits all

Power tools aren't just for experts and geeks. You can now get cordless, rechargeable, power-driven versions of everything from screwdrivers to drills that make short work of tasks that need tools.

On the other hand, more advanced handy people generally feel that accomplishing all jobs takes various sizes of tools, so the best way to organize the resulting proliferation is to hang them by similar type on a pegboard. From needle-nosed to supersized, put all the pliers together. Screwdrivers are a group, subdivided into regular and Phillips format and arranged by size. Visual types may like to spray paint the board with the tools in place for easy replacement, while the more lexically minded may prefer labels. If you go the stencil route, be sure to wrap each tool well with plastic before you spray.

Parts and other small stuff

Swamped with screws, nails, nuts and bolts, and mollies? Get as many sets of clear minidrawers as you need to give each part its place. Label the drawers to give the visual image written reinforcement.

You may be surprised to hear me say it, but: Never throw out an unidentified part. If a screw falls from somewhere and you can't find its source, hold onto it and you may locate the empty hole soon enough. Label one drawer "Lost Parts," put the current mystery pieces there, and purge them as they become old-timers.

Supplies: Glues, tape, paint, and light bulbs

There are as many sticky substances as there are things that need sticking together, running the gamut from airplane glue to glue guns. Do you really need them all? Probably not. You can fix most things with an adhesive trio: plastic glue, super glue, and cement glue. Go through your collection and toss anything else you haven't used in a year or that's clogged or dried out.

You also need masking tape, duct tape, and sealing tape for other sorts of sticking; paints and varnishes for surface improvements; and extra light bulbs to replace burnouts throughout the house. Store all these supplies in a cabinet, if you have one; otherwise, use a few containers on a shelf. Old shoeboxes are a look-cost alternative for containing tapes or glues; just be sure to label the outside with the contents so you know where to look. And don't forget to mark the paint cans to indicate which room and wall or ceiling they go with.

Yes, you can stick your fingers together with super glue, and yes, it's not fun. Prevent self-gluing disasters with a pair of thin rubber gloves.

The fun starts here: Hobby and craft center

Having a hobby is all about fun, so set up a shipshape center that makes every session a pleasure. If the hobby area shares a room with other activities, delineate a center that accommodates equipment, supplies, and work. Do you need wide open space far away from a window to practice your golf swing, or a dark room to develop photographs? A table to spread out your sewing, or a big piece of floor for a train track? Take space, lighting, and the comfort of your surroundings into account when designing your hobby center.

Next, designate space to store equipment and supplies. Closets, cabinets, or shelves can contain big stuff, such as a painting easel or sewing machine, while freestanding or shelf top drawers are good for smaller supplies. Storage containers can get quite specialized, so check associations, Web sites, catalogs, and stores dedicated to your hobby for systems targeted to your particular supplies.

There's a cardinal rule for keeping crafts and hobbies organized, one that adults often have an easier time teaching to their children than following themselves: Always, always clean up and put things away at the end of every session. Not only does this prolong the life of your paintbrushes and prevent a passing child or dog from taking a lick, but tidying up also makes coming back the next day a lot more fun. A work in progress is not a mess in progress. Leave your hobby center a clean slate and see your creativity shine.

Exercise center

The sheer weight of exercise equipment and bouncing bodies begs you to locate your workout center in the basement, close to the ground and far away from parts of the house that won't be enhanced by the scent of sweat. But make it nice. The model exercise area is a rejuvenating getaway, a place to leave your workaday worries behind and focus on the pleasures of feeling fit.

Not up for sit-ups on the cement floor? Carpeting can ease your crunches, as well as absorb the shock to your knees if you engage in high-impact activities. Carpet store remnants can be a cost-effective route to an exercise-friendly floor.

Arrange big equipment to account for the clearance you and any workout partners need for each activity. Folding equipment can create additional space for floor work when not in use. Store smaller equipment such as hand and leg weights, jump ropes, and resistance bands in a box or container sized to the job.

Finish off your exercise center with some entertainment. A minimedia center with a portable stereo and/or television can motivate and prolong your workouts, whether you cue up an exercise program, the news, your favorite tunes, or a book on tape. Check Chapter 9 for tips on setting up and organizing media equipment, tapes, and disks.

Keep exercise equipment that you use only outdoors, such as wrist weights for walking, in the closet closest to your exit door.

Gift wrap center

If wrapping a simple gift requires a trip to the attic for paper, a desk drawer for scissors, and the kitchen for tape, you can get back the joy of giving with a gift wrap center. A single location speeds up the job and also helps you keep inventory and restock supplies, so you're not running late for Sally's birthday party only to discover that there's not a sheet of wrapping paper in the house.

You can purchase specially designed plastic containers to hold flat and roll wrap, ribbon, bows, scissors, tape, gift cards, and pens as in Figure 12-2. A box about the size of a brown paper shopping bag is another option for standing rolls on end; put the remaining supplies on shelves or in drawers.

Stock your wrapping center with both birthday and all-occasion paper and trimmings. Holiday wraps can be stored with holiday supplies until the season draws near.

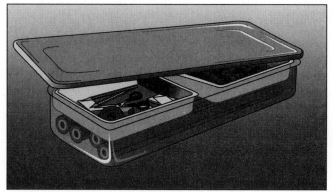

Figure 12-2:
Wrapping
containers
make gift-
giving easy.

The Attic

The word alone can conjure up images of cobwebs and junk. While a cluttered place crawling with spiders can quickly become household Siberia, a well-administered attic can serve as a powerful primary or adjunct storage area — so break out a broom and the five W-A-S-T-E questions and go clean it out.

Attic storage principles are essentially the same as in the basement, except that the place is likely to be hotter in the summer and colder in the winter, which makes the attic a bad choice for photos, tapes, books, and papers that could be ruined by extreme temperatures. Food doesn't fare well here either. However, clothes, toys, decorations, luggage, off-season sports equipment, memorabilia, and many other items do fine in the attic. Refer back to the section on storage earlier in this chapter and make full use of the space under the rafters. These items work well in the attic:

- ✔ **Clothes:** Off-season clothes, off-season coats, costumes, and hand-me-downs in waiting, sorted by category as described in Chapter 6.
- ✔ **Sports equipment:** Off-season or rarely used: skis, golf clubs, bikes, racquets and balls, bowling ball, volleyball net, sports shoes, and so on.

✔ **Toys:** To save for younger children or rotate back into active stock (see Chapter 10).

✔ **Baby (when expecting another):** Clothes, accessories, blankets, equipment (crib, playpen, carrier, swing), toys, books, CDs, and tapes.

✔ **Figurines and decorations:** Only those used in regular rotation as explained in Chapter 8.

Listen closely. Do you hear the silence? With everything in its place in the basement and attic, the clutter has finally stopped cloning itself. You can find what you need when you need it and sleep easy the rest of the time. Peace at last!

Chapter 13

Patrolling the Borderlands: The Garage, Patio, and Shed

*B*elieve it or not, garages were originally built to house cars. My work as a professional organizer has shown me that many people have forgotten this primary purpose, and some can't get a car into their garage if you pay them. Why do I find so much stuff jammed into garages, piled on patios, and spilling out of sheds and onto the lawn around? The good reason is that people love the great outdoors, and they tend to own an abundance of lawn and gardening equipment to enjoy and maintain their outside spaces. The less-admirable cause of all the clutter is that areas beyond the immediate living environment are easy to overlook.

Though you may be tempted to take a laissez-faire attitude to the outer limits, think about the face you present to the world with your household perimeters. Just because you can't see the junk piled high on your balcony from inside your apartment doesn't mean your neighbors don't. The fact that you forged a path from your car to the garage door doesn't prevent your passenger from observing the stuff on either side. Garden gear is in the yard; toys are strewn on the patio or porch; and garbage cans are forced outside because the garage and shed have no room. The result is an eyesore for you and the community alike.

When you clean up these spaces, you can get outside with everything you need to have a great time. Spruce up the grass. Throw dinner on the grill. P-L-A-C-E summarizes a plan to patrol your borderlands, putting everything in its place so that you can enter and exit the house with grace.

✔ **Purge:** Toss unused, outgrown, or broken sports equipment and toys, old supplies, and things too dirty or dusty to use.

✔ **Like with like:** Organize items into centers by like type: car accessories and supplies; tools; lawn, garden, and snow equipment and supplies; sports equipment and toys; pool supplies; patio furniture; and grill equipment.

✔ **Access:** Move inside toys back into the house. Keep car supplies on a high shelf out of the reach of children or enclose them in a cabinet. Put off-season sports equipment into indoor storage or the shed. Keep patio furniture and/or lawn and snow equipment in a shed. Put recycling bins near the garage door leading to the house.

✔ **Contain:** Use a cabinet or shelving in the garage for car supplies and a pegboard for tools. Hanging hooks can hold bicycles, lawn chairs, and ladders. Place sports gear into racks and balls and toys into baskets. Use a deck box to contain patio items, and if you've got a storage shed, house current lawn or snow equipment and pool supplies there.

✔ **Evaluate:** Can you drive in and out of the garage and park with ease? Is everything you need for outdoor activities here and nothing else? Do the patio furniture and grill set have off-season homes? Does your property appear neat and tidy all the way from the outside in?

Getting a Ground Plan: The Garage

The ground rule for what goes in the garage is that you currently use it there or outside. General storage and off-season equipment can be relocated into the house or storage shed, if you have one. Use W-A-S-T-E (see Chapter 3) to decide what's worth keeping and what's a waste of space.

Before you do anything, move the cars out of the garage, clear everything off the floor, and hose it down, starting at the back and working your way out the door. Sweeping does little more than rearrange dust in the garage. A hose with a good strong stream, on the other hand, can get dirt off the floor and down the driveway. The wet-cleaning method may also provide the motivation you need to keep the garage floor clear.

Next, park your cars in the garage, take a piece of chalk, and mark their width and length on the floor and their height on the wall. Open the doors and mark off their clearance curve. This is the space you need to keep clear as you consider where everything else goes.

Finish off your garage ground plan by figuring out what goes where. Move out the cars, survey the space, and see where you can install each of three options:

Garage safety guidelines

✔ **Shine a light for nighttime safety.** Install two exterior spotlights on either side of the garage door and a good overhead light inside. Motion detector lights are nice for automatic illumination as you pull in — or as a prowler noses around.

✔ **Computerize the garage door lock** so no one needs to worry about forgetting a key. Children can even go without one, as long as they can remember the code — so make it a word. Hide a house key in a designated spot in the garage so kids or forgetful adults can get in the door. Do keep the door leading from the garage into the house locked, unless you like to reward burglars who succeed in cracking the garage door code with an easy walk inside.

✔ **Regularly test the electronic block on the garage door opener,** which makes the door stop when it hits something, by putting a garbage can in its path and hitting *close*. Unblocked, a misfired close message may crush the hood of your car; in the worst case, the door may strike a child. Choosing aluminum for the door will make it lighter and therefore less lethal to things in its way, as well as save you the regular paint job.

✔ **Hanging hooks.** You can get bikes, big tools, sports equipment, lawn chairs, and ladders off the floor by hanging them on heavy-duty wall- or ceiling-mounted hooks. Put all items in easy reach and reserve the lowest altitudes for the heaviest items. Don't put up hooks haphazardly; measure what will hang there and leave clearance space accordingly.

✔ **Open shelving.** Whether mounted on the wall high enough to clear the cars or freestanding on the floor, shelves can hold and organize smaller items and supplies like car supplies.

✔ **Closed cabinets.** They may cost more than open shelves, but cabinets can save time and work by keeping their contents clean. With cars going in and out and circulating outdoor dirt, the garage will make unenclosed items grungy fast.

Think vertical in the garage. There's lots of wall space above automobile level just waiting to get used.

Dealing with Your Wheels: The Car Center

In today's mobile society, few investments yield such tangible benefits as a car. Often serving almost as a second home, cars take people to work and school, carry home the groceries, provide party transport, expedite errands, and enable trips near and far. With all these roles to play, cars can fall victim to wear and tear if not cared for and maintained. Protect your investment with organizational tactics that keep your vehicles in *drive*.

Parking without wrecking

How often do you hit a garbage can or level a bike when pulling in or out of the garage? Ease the parking process by purchasing a plastic parking guide like the one in Figure 13-1 that tells your tires just where to stop. More playful types may prefer to hang a tennis ball from the ceiling that taps your windshield to tell you that you went far enough. (Downside: A ball hanging from the garage ceiling can prove annoying to passersby.) Trick number three is a chalk or pencil mark on the wall. When your shoulder is even with the line, shift into park and power down.

Figure 13-1:
A parking guide helps you stop the car before hitting something else.

Photo courtesy of Lillian Vernon.

By the way, I recommend backing into your spot. Not only can this position the trunk closer to the door to the house for loading and unloading, but when you leave again you can exit the driveway with a full frontal view of kids playing and cars driving by.

If your passengers are prone to dinging car doors against the other car or garage walls, you can cushion the blow with bath mats hung from the ceiling overhead. Like the tennis ball, hanging bath mats may slice up your space more than you like, but those who prioritize their paint jobs may bite.

Supplies for a smooth ride

Unless you're a car wash junkie and mechanic's addict, you probably want some supplies on hand to keep your ride running and looking smooth. The list for the average motorist might include

- Antifreeze/coolant
- Windshield wiper fluid
- Motor oil
- Soap
- Bucket, sponges, and old towels
- Upholstery protector
- Fabric cleaner
- Whitewall tile cleaner
- Rubbing compound
- Wax
- Touch-up paint
- Squeegee
- Chamois cloth
- Extra windshield wipers
- Extra air filters (easy to change yourself)

Keep all these precious but poisonous supplies on a high shelf out of reach of passing children. If you wash your own car, you may want to contain your drying towels in two small garbage cans, one can for clean towels and one for dirty until you have enough to wash.

Maintenance is made easy by hanging a bulletin board on a garage wall to post a spreadsheet for each car. One glance can tell you when your car is due for an oil change or tune-up, or whether your mechanic is trying to resell you the same job he did last year.

If you like to look under the hood, get a flashlight with a hook designed to hang inside and leave your hands free to work.

Fixing It Neatly: The Tool Center

An avid carpenter or handyperson may prefer a workshop in the garage, where air and sunshine are plentiful and messes aren't a problem, to a basement location. If you're one of these and live in a moderate climate, set up your main workbench here. Otherwise, you could move your tools and supplies out to the garage during the summer, and then back into the basement as the temperature drops. See Chapter 12 for more on setting up a work center.

Part-timers can get by with a pegboard in the garage to hold tools for the car, bikes, and outdoor equipment, as well as a very long extension cord and an extra flashlight for everything from poking around under the hood to finding your way in a power outage.

Stock duplicates of tools you use in the garage and other parts of the house, so you don't have to traverse the property every time you need a screwdriver.

Keep a ladder or two in the garage for high-level jobs. A stepladder can cover most household tasks, while an extension ladder may be required for rooftop adventures. Both can hang on wall-mounted hooks, the stepladder vertically and the tall extension ladder horizontally.

The garage is also a good place to store your painting drop cloth — too big and messy to keep inside.

Maintaining the Great Outdoors: Lawn, Garden, and Snow Centers

Have you heard? Gardening can lower your blood pressure. If you feel yours rising as you go out to face the natural world, defuse the stress with a plan to make outdoor maintenance easy. By organizing the equipment, implements, and supplies you need to keep your lawn neat and green, the garden in bloom, and the winter snow out of the way, you can turn these tasks into stress-busting pastimes.

Start by showcasing this season's equipment. The lawn mower in the summer and the snowblower in the winter get front-and-center placement in the garage, while off-season equipment can be stored out of the way. Begin the season with an annual tune-up of lawn or snow equipment and end it by emptying out the gas. Got multiple gas cans? Label them so you know what fuel is for which machine.

After you have the equipment situation under control, organize your implements well. Group garden tools by like type and hang or contain them so they're easy to take out into the yard. Here are some guidelines:

- Rakes, lawn edgers, shovels, and other large tools can hang from hooks or special holders that grasp the handle with rollers. Put the tool head up rather than down to keep it out of the reach of kids. (This works well for snow shovels too.)

- Group smaller tools, trowels, spades, hand rakes, and so forth into a bucket that totes them out to the yard.

- Put planters, starting pots, and bulbs into boxes or plastic dishpans to keep them neat and mobile.

- Keep your garden seeds fresh in the refrigerator until you're ready to plant. A second fridge in the basement is an ideal home for your seed collection.

Contain your tastiest supplies. Bags of dirt, fertilizer, and plant food offer potential snacks to mice, rats, and chipmunks, and flimsy paper containers yield easily to rodents' teeth. Save yourself a mess by storing soil and fertilizer in sealed plastic containers or covered garbage cans.

Spare your back the strain of carrying a big bag of sod or fertilizer by adding a hand truck or wheelbarrow to your lawn and garden retinue. I won't mind if you use the wheelbarrow for your groceries too.

Keep a bucket of sand on hand to clean off dirty garden implements. Simply dunk the tool, work it up and down a few times, and put the tool away neat and clean. Replace the sand as necessary. If you choose to wash your tools with water instead, dry them well to prevent rust.

Winning Ways to Play: Sports and Game Center

Whether you live for tennis or you like to go by trike, playing outside is an all-ages pleasure, and the equipment involved can create all-ages clutter. Skis going every which way, balls underfoot, jumbles of toys, and bicycle traffic jams can clog the garage and make play a chore. Tackle your sports and recreational gear with organizing systems that can restore order to all your outdoor fun.

Sports racks are great no matter what your game is. From balls, bats, and rackets to bikes, golf clubs, snowboards, and skis, a rack can be found for every sport. You can be on the greens like greased lightning or head for the courts with a clear mind when you keep your equipment neat in an organizer designed for the job. Figure 13-2 shows you how to fast-track your game with an organizing rack.

For larger equipment, overhead hooks can stow your gear up and out of the way. Wall or ceiling hooks can hold bikes, sleds, and a variety of equipment. The trick is that high-hanging hooks are hard to reach, especially if the equipment is heavy, so consider swapping the location of bikes and sleds by the season.

And of course, you want to contain everything. Containers are great for those smaller pieces of equipment. Sort smaller equipment and toys into containers by type. A basket can hold balls and Frisbees, squirt guns could go into a bucket, and jump ropes can hang on a wall hook to keep them tangle-free.

Figure 13-2:
Rack up your sports equipment to get on the fast track to fun and games.

Buying your first swing set? Select one that can grow up with your children, with accessories that can easily be replaced as they move from fire poles to parallel bars. Save the one-horse pony swing for the park or you may find yourself tossing your purchase soon.

The Trash and Recycling Center

One of those facts of life that never goes away, taking out the trash can definitely get easier with the right organizational skills.

Trash management begins at the source, so start by compacting garbage as much as you can. Whether you use a mechanical trash compactor, your own hand around a soft metal can, or an old-fashioned downward push to waste-basket contents, you can save space and reduce the number of trash-toting trips by maximizing its density.

Keep a recycling container alongside the kitchen wastebasket for all your plastic, glass, and cans — an official bin or a more attractive trash can (make sure it looks different than the wastebasket so you don't get confused).

Contact your local waste disposal company to find out where and when to dispose of hazardous materials such as used motor oil, old cans of paint, and batteries. Some automotive stores will take your old car batteries for recycling.

Those who live in apartments without the luxury of a garage can still be eco-friendly. Keep two brown paper bags alongside the kitchen wastebasket to contain paper and other recyclables, respectively. As they fill up, take them down to your building's recycling center or to your car trunk to tote them yourself.

Ideally, garbage cans and recycling bins go right inside the garage, with the newspaper bin in the prime spot for daily pitching. Post a list of recycling rules on the wall to help you meet any sorting requirements.

You may not have given much thought to what makes a good garbage can, but I have. That's what they hire me for, right?

- ✔ Plastic cans are lightweight and easier to clean than metal.

- ✔ Locking lids can keep animals out of your trash in the garage and your garbage from going airborne at the curb. Having lived in the Windy City, I've seen trash all over the street before pickup, and loose lids blown halfway down the block afterward so go for cans with hinged lids that stay put even if the trash collectors don't bother to replace them. A close second are those with handles that pull up to lock the lid into place.

- ✔ Why lug when you can wheel? Garbage cans with wheels on the bottom require less muscle and accumulate less wear and tear as they smoothly glide to the curb. This is a great advantage when you have one fully loaded with heavy grass clippings.

- ✔ If you don't have wheels, match the size of the can to your strength. Only big, brawny people can carry big, brawny garbage cans.

If you do yard work, dedicate a separate can or two to lawn and garden trimmings and keep the garden cans in the yard closest to their use for the sake of convenience. If you have no out-of-the-way spot to place them, install a small decorative fence to block their view.

Staying Cool in the Hot Zone: The Pool Center

Pool owners well know that the right to swim on your own property comes at the price of precise maintenance. Here's how to organize this part of the perimeter.

- ✔ **Chemicals:** Keeping a swimming pool sparkling clear requires a potent chemical mix — and you wouldn't want a child or pet to ingest it, would you? Store pool chemicals on a high shelf in the garage or in a locked waterproof cabinet outside, keeping chlorine and acid well apart to prevent combustion. You can also buy specialized equipment that enables you to bypass the chemicals.

- ✔ **Maintenance tools:** You can purchase hooks to hang brushes and skimmers on the patio or in the garage. Spare filters and hoses should be stored in a shaded area such as a garage or pump house. In hot climates, a ventilated pump house can protect your pump, motor, filter, and pool equipment from sun damage.

- ✔ **Safety equipment:** Hang a long pole and a lifesaver ring near the pool in case you need to pull somebody out.

- ✔ **Swimming toys:** Put snakes, kickboards, resistance equipment, water wings, tubes, rafts, floating toys, goggles, and caps in a storage deck box by the pool (see Figure 13-3). Got more toys than that? Purge the excess! Move everything into basement or garage storage during winter months.

The Patio or Deck

Rarely does life seem as good as when sitting out on the deck on a beautiful day with a cup of steaming coffee, a cool drink, or a meal fresh off the grill. Don't mar the moment with patio clutter. Clear the deck!

First, move anything you're not using at least weekly to the garage, shed, or basement. Next, group like items together. These may include the following:

- ✔ Grill equipment and supplies, outdoor tableware
- ✔ Citronella candles, insecticides, insect repellants
- ✔ Patio furniture, cushions, and accessories

Finally, contain all the items in a deck storage box such as the one pictured in Figure 13-3. A deck box can keep everything you need in reach yet out of the elements: cushions, croquet set, outdoor tablecloth, and so on.

Figure 13-3:
Clear the
deck with a
storage box
for outdoor
toys, games,
cushions,
and dining
accessories.

Photo courtesy of Get Organized!.

Patio furniture

You want patio furniture to be comfortable, durable enough to weather out-door living, and easy enough to haul back into the garage or shed when winter approaches. Buy folding versions of chairs, tables, and lounges for easy off-season storage, heavy-duty weatherproof models for frequent use. Put the cushions away every night in the garage, storage area, or deck box to keep them clean and dry. To keep the patio area looking nice and free of spider webs, hose down furniture kept outside once a week. If you have portable chairs for picnics or the beach, store them on hooks in the garage or in the storage shed.

The grill center

Longing to light up the barbie? Start with the basics by choosing the grill right for you. If you use your grill less than once a week, look for one on wheels that you can move in and out of the garage or storage shed each time. A folding grill set saves off-season storage space and can also go to a tailgate party or picnic with ease.

Everyone can benefit from choosing a grill that has hooks for tongs, fork, and spatula, as well as a prep/holding surface off the heat. Although gas is less messy, some gourmet cooks insist upon the flavor of charcoal or wood flame.

When you decide on the right type of grill for you, next organize everything you need to get the fire started. Here are a few hot tips:

✔ If you have a gas grill and a source of gas in the house, consider installing a direct connection so you don't have to refill the tank.

✔ Contain charcoal in a covered plastic garbage can next to the grill. Use rubber gloves to handle charcoal without turning your hands black.

✔ Keep lighter materials on a high shelf in the garage. Starter cubes or electric lighters are more environmentally friendly than lighter fluid.

Don't ever light the grill inside the garage or house.

Once you set up your grill center, you want to keep your outdoor cooking environment clean. Consider all the insects and animals that live in or visit your yard, the dirt and dust that come with the outdoors, and the unique mix of soot, ash, and grease that grilling can generate, and you'll appreciate the importance of an organized approach to grill center maintenance.

Clean out the grill at the start of the season, checking tubes and vents for spider webs and debris that could turn into fire hazards. Before each time you light up, give the grill rack a scrub with a grill brush to remove any dirt that's landed there since the previous use. Repeat after you're done cooking and the fire has died down to clean off cooked-on food and grease. If you use charcoal, empty the ash after each cooking session to keep it from blowing all over the yard and to give you a clean start next time. Turn the faux briquettes in gas grills a few times a season to burn off the grease.

Use citronella candles, mesh food covers, or both to keep nasty flies off your food when you serve outside.

Apartment or condominium patios and balconies

In multiresident units, a small patio or balcony is often all the great outdoors you have. If so, the balcony may hold everything from a bicycle and beach chairs to a small potted garden to a barbecue grill and table. If you store things on your balcony, be aware of the view you present to your neighbors. If you wouldn't want to look at your mess, chances are the neighbors would rather not either. Try a deck storage box (Figure 13-3) to keep a few things out of sight.

Lightweight patio furniture that folds is easiest to take outside for a good cleaning under a hose or spigot. If moving furniture for cleaning is too cumbersome, try a spray cleanser and damp cloth. Another option is to use a bucket of soapy water and a second bucket of clean water for rinsing, just like washing your car.

The Storage Shed

So you've gotten this far and your gut reaction is, "Eileen, no matter how well I organize I'm never going to have enough room to get my car into the garage!" Well, don't just roll over and play dead: Get a shed.

A storage shed alongside the house is quite handy for keeping outside equipment such as the snowblower or lawn mower, garden tools and supplies, and even bikes if the structure is big enough. If you have one full of junk right now, go throw the stuff away and discover your garage annex.

Follow the principles of P-L-A-C-E in the storage shed, maximizing access by placing the most frequently used things in front and enclosing items in containers by like type. Install a shelf or two to contain small things and hooks for rakes and tools. Put all the hooks on one wall, so you aren't watching your head on both sides of the shed.

Great guns! The whole house is in shape, right down to the garage. With your space truly organized, inside and out, your entire environment is transformed. Home sweet home.

Using your garage like a basement

Many homes, particularly in the western part of the U.S., don't have basements, and their inhabitants have no choice but to shift basic basement functions to the garage. From storage to a (warm-weather) spot for hobbies, exercise, and play, a well-organized garage can act like a basement.

See Chapter 12 for the full story on setting up basement storage and activity centers. Make your double-duty garage go further by moving as many outdoor items to the storage shed as possible. Take a look up top too. Some garages have a little door leading to a mini-attic — usually no more than 2 feet high, but a great place to store off-season equipment such as sleds. You do need a ladder to get there, so you may think twice before trying to climb up with heavy equipment.

Part IV

Professionally Organized: Your Office

The 5th Wave

By Rich Tennant

"Giving a party has gotten so much easier since I bought an entertainment center."

In this part . . .

How would you like to work less and accomplish more? Would you like to impress the boss, improve client relations, influence colleagues, inspire staff, and finally see the surface of your desk? This part can help.

Getting organized on the job is one of the greatest boosts you can give your career — better than burning the midnight oil or going the extra mile when the finish line would have been one hundred yards back if only you'd been organized to begin with. Here are tips for everything from setting up your office for peak productivity to getting wired to the world with the right technology for the task. Your piles can turn into files. You'll clean up that endless e-mail queue and create a Take Action File so you always know just what you need to do. At the office, getting organized is dressing your space and your mind for success.

Chapter 14

Making Your Work Space Work

*Y*ou don't need to be an efficiency expert, interior designer, or *feng shui* master specializing in the Chinese art of placement to know that the right work space can set you up for success, while a *whatever* approach to your workplace layout can sap your time, energy, concentration, and creativity. Get organized to put your work space to work for you, and you may find time for an extra coffee break or two.

This chapter provides work space basics for employees, managers, and entrepreneurs alike. Whether you work in a corner office, a cubicle, a converted guest bedroom, or a basement — or are planning any of these spaces for your people — these principles promise to maximize productivity and minimize stress every day of the week. What more could you ask?

Do Less, Achieve More: The Zen of Organized Work

Fifteen years in office administration may not have provided me with a deep grounding in the philosophy of Zen, but my experience did prove the truth of Zen's premise: When you set things up to flow, they do so. Without flow, you may find that no matter how much you *do,* things rarely go your way. Organizing your work space is the first step to turning your tiny stream of effort into a mighty river of productivity. Rewards follow.

You work better when the layout and lighting are right, the view harmonious and free from distractions, and everything you need is within fingertip reach. A well-organized work space can increase your productivity to the tune of minutes or hours per day, days or weeks per year, while improving quality too. Do the math. How many dollars is that worth to you?

The subtle trick about this — one that I've seen trip up hardworking individuals and entire corporations — is that there's no one right way to organize a workplace. Needs vary between people and jobs and across careers. That's what keeps me paid . . . but I'm about to sign part of my paycheck over to you by clueing you in on the process. I don't know if that's Zen or not, but it's a zero-risk proposition.

Choose what you want to work on first. Your business office or home office? Furniture, equipment, or layout? P-L-A-C-E summarizes the secrets of transforming any workplace to the everything-in-its-place paradigm.

Focusing on Furniture and Equipment

The first step to organizing your workplace is deciding what you need. It sounds easy — especially when many companies try to decide for you — but in fact this can be a profound process that affects what you do every day. Remember that most corporations have a procedure for allocating resources, and it never hurts to ask for what you need.

Focusing on furniture and equipment can help you assemble the right resources for your job and jettison the clutter. Do you feel hemmed in by corporate policy or a small cubicle? Read on for tactics to free your mind.

Furniture: The basics

What do you need to furnish your space for good work? Use the following discussions to start your list, marking what you have, what you want, and what you don't need.

Finding the right desk

Working at the wrong desk is like wearing shoes that don't fit. Some even claim it can cause blisters to the brain. Reviewing architectural plans while taking notes on the computer, for instance, makes quite different demands on a desk than paying bills and balancing your checkbook, while writing a legal brief poses requirements of its own.

The right desk provides just enough surface area to get all your jobs done (more would be a waste of room space) and a layout that allows fingertip management of each task. Assess your needs in these two dimensions and choose between three desk formats:

✔ **Standard:** This is your basic rectangle, a space-efficient bet if you don't use a computer at your desk because you're blessed with an assistant, don't need a computer for your job, or have a separate computer workstation. If you conduct meetings in your office, a standard desk also leaves more space for a table and chairs.

✔ **L-shaped:** Add a perpendicular piece to a regular desk and you have an L shape, with the second side just right to hold a computer, to spread out papers 11-x-17 or larger, or to collate materials. If you currently get up to use a separate worktable for any of your regular tasks, get an L-shaped desk and gain fingertip management.

✔ **U-shaped:** Adding a third side to the desk allows you to easily toggle between a regular desktop, a computer station, and a clear space for big projects. You can also create a U shape with your layout as described later in the chapter, which, depending on your needs, may be a better way. Stay tuned.

No matter what shape desk you choose, look for two to four small drawers and one to two file drawers to keep everything in fingertip reach. You can find more on arranging, using, and stocking your desk in Chapter 15.

Computer workstation

A computer workstation can free up desktop space for phone and paperwork and give you room to spread out all the references you need while at the keyboard. A separate station is also the way to go in an office where employees share a computer, or in a home office where an adult may want to pay bills while a child or partner works at the computer.

Find out more about organizing and using your computer workstation in Chapter 15 on the desk, and see what cyberorganization can do for you in Chapter 17.

Ergonomically comfortable chairs

You spend a lot of time in your workplace chair, so find one that cares. A good ergonomic office chair with wheels will make your life easier and back happier. Put a plastic mat on the floor for smooth rolling from the desk to the computer, credenza, bookcase, or file cabinet. If you have a separate computer workstation that's shared or outside rolling range, get a second chair.

Guest chairs for an office are often more formal and less functional than work chairs, as people spend less time there. Be aware that placing guest chairs to face you as you sit at your desk establishes distance and puts you in the power position, which may be your intent in certain circumstances, but most meetings are more effective when conducted on an equal basis. Face your guest chairs toward each other in front of the desk and come out to sit with your visitor.

A couch is too casual for most professional settings, diluting the work attitude and encouraging colleagues to come in for a break. In a home office, a couch may serve as a constant signal to take a quick nap. Naps can be productivity tools, but you don't need to be thinking about sleep while you work.

Deciding whether you need a meeting table

Before you clutter up your office with a table, consider whether you need one here or could use a conference room instead. If you hold many small meetings (especially impromptu ones) where privacy or prestige is important, a table is called for. A round shape can put everyone present on equal footing, but a square or rectangle provides more space. Decide which matters more to you.

Credenza or bookcase?

A table and mini-bookshelf in one, a credenza can clear off your desk by holding the books or binders you need every day inside. Put a telephone, fax machine, printer, or small copier on top to get double duty from the piece and prevent piles of paper from forming there.

If your work requires many reference materials — you're a lawyer, human resources administrator, professor, or writer — then a bookcase is the way to get those stacks of books off the floor. The books are just temporary, you say? Until you finish this project? There will be another project afterward, and another stack to go with it.

Order an adjustable bookcase so that you can tailor the height of the shelves to the size of your materials. Place the heaviest items on the bottom shelves for ballast, things you use most frequently on middle shelves for easy access, and lighter items such as audiotape albums on the higher shelves. Organize your library by subject matter as described in Chapter 9.

Overhead bins for small-space dwellers

For offices or cubicles with limited floor space, overhead bins can ease the crunch by containing books, binders, stationery, computer paper, forms, and literature. Organize their contents by grouping like with like to establish mini-centers for different activities and putting things where you access them most — computer paper near the printer, for instance, and reference books close to the desk. Arrange books and binders by topic and paper products into flat stacking sort trays.

File and artwork cabinets

Stop! Before you buy a single file cabinet, skip to Chapter 16 and follow the file-purging instructions. See how your space and budget requirements downsize?

Next consider whether you should contain files in lateral or vertical cabinets. Vertical file cabinets, which pull out so the files are facing you, extend farther into the room in both closed and open position. Lateral cabinets, in which the files are perpendicular to you as you pull out the drawer, stick out less but take up more wall space. You may need to do your layout, as explained later in this chapter, before you make your decision.

From an efficiency standpoint, vertical files provide easier retrieval. If you need something in the front third of the drawer, you need only pull it out that far, grab your file, and go. To get any file from a lateral drawer you must pull the drawer out completely, and if what you want isn't in the half of the drawer you can see from the front, you have to walk around to the side, which is wasted time and effort. If your space allows, go vertical.

Designers, artists, engineers, architects, and anyone in charge of interfacing with such positions may need a metal cabinet with large flat drawers for storing blueprints, graphic designs, and artwork. Do you have just a few? Roll them up and slip them into poster tubes.

Literature rack

From my work in associations management, I know firsthand about fact sheets and brochures, collating and compiling, trying to pull the right pieces to make a membership packet. Whether you need to put together press kits for mailings or you work as a salesperson, insurance agent, or membership manager, you could use a literature rack.

The right rack for organizing literature holds stacks flat in different tiers so the paper doesn't bend and you can quickly find the pieces you want. Figure 14-1 provides a look.

Figure 14-1:
Make fast work of information packets with a literature rack.

Are you storing literature, stationery, or forms in vertical file holders? Don't be surprised to pull out bent pages that look sloppy and jam computer printers. Keep paper flat instead, so that the pages stay straight.

Equipping yourself

Many of us rely on a wide array of equipment, from low- to high-tech, to make our workday work. Few people, however, evaluate whether they really have the right equipment to meet their needs — no more, no less — and whether it's optimally placed for fingertip management.

A quick equipment evaluation can help you decide what you need, where, in your office layout. Are there items that you can easily use somewhere else, such as a copier? Do you need a fax machine at your desk to save frequent trips to the firm's central machine? After you decide what items you need in your office, jot down their dimensions for use in your layout.

For further discussion of how to select and use technology tools with twenty-first-century sense, see Chapter 17 on cyberorganization.

Peak Productivity Placement

Now is the time to put everything into place. Your goal? Fingertip management of everything you do. The way to get there? Blueprint your work space. You may not be an architect, but anyone can benefit from drawing up a floor plan to find the most productive office placement. You may discover a new way to face your desk for better concentration, hidden space for another file cabinet, or a nifty arrangement to put all your reference books within reach.

Drawing up the blueprint

Refer back to the section on blueprint basics in Chapter 3, and follow the instructions to draw your office to scale, mark the windows and doors, and create furniture cutouts. Add cutouts in a different color to represent equipment.

Start playing with placement of your cutouts on your floor plan to come up with one or more schemes that put each task within easy reach.

- **Purge:** Get rid of all unused or ill-suited furniture and equipment. Distracting artwork can be donated or go elsewhere. (Lots more on office purging is coming up in the following chapters.)

- **Like with like:** Line up your file cabinets. Find one spot for all your books. Create work centers for different activities by grouping together everything you need for a task.

✔ **Access:** Arrange your work space by placing furniture and equipment in a parallel, L-shape, or U-shape layout for better fingertip management.

- A parallel layout places furniture in two lines opposite each other — most frequently a desk and a computer workstation, credenza, bookcase, or file cabinet. Parallel layouts provide a space-efficient floor plan for jobs requiring a limited number of references and resources.

- For an L-shaped layout, furniture is arranged in two perpendicular lines to create a semi-enclosed space. Instead of turning a full 180 degrees from one side to the other as in the parallel layout, you swivel just 90 degrees from the desk to the bookcase, cabinet, credenza, or computer.

- U-shaped puts most resources within reach. You may have a desk and computer or drafting table parallel to each other, with a bookcase or file cabinet forming the base of the *U.* Don't need a computer station or worktable? Put a file cabinet parallel to the desk and a bookcase at the base.

The printer should be as near the computer as possible, while the fax may be farther away. Move infrequently used equipment, reference materials, and supplies to another room. Do you have extra supplies? Return them to the supply room or cabinet.

✔ **Contain:** Put files into file cabinets and books into bookcases or credenzas. Use overhead cubicle bins for binders, computer programs, or extra stationery. Under-desk drawers can keep supplies off the countertop. Finally, make sure you have a way to contain everything — for instance, add a credenza for the books and binders currently stacked on top of your workstation.

✔ **Evaluate:** How do you feel when you walk into your office in the morning? How does your flow go in the thick of a project or stressful situation? How do you feel when you leave your office at the end of the day?

Figure 14-2 pictures some peak productivity layouts.

Using space effectively

Here are some more tricks of the trade that you can use to fine-tune your space once you decide on the pieces of furniture you need and arrive at a basic layout.

Use the space beneath windows by placing a desk, short bookcase, or two-drawer file cabinet there. This is not the spot for a standard bookcase, a four-drawer file cabinet, or a tall computer workstation, unless you want to lose your view.

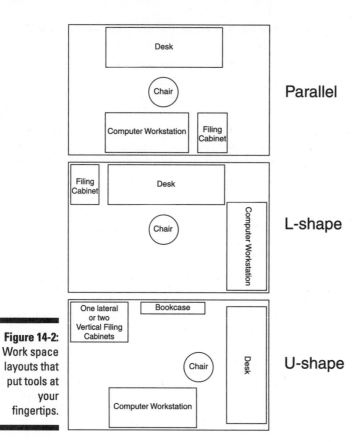

Figure 14-2: Work space layouts that put tools at your fingertips.

Windows aside, move the desk out toward the center of the room to slip a credenza, bookcase, or file cabinet behind it. However, don't face your desk to the wall. *Feng shui,* the ancient Asian philosophy of flow, and many a worker can vouch that this placement can *wall up* your thinking and make you susceptible to scares when people walk up behind you. Like you need more stress in your day?

Don't face your desk directly out the door. Suddenly every passerby is a pleasant distraction, and your thinking-into-space session becomes a major interruption when a colleague catches your eye and decides to tell you about her weekend tennis match. Place your desk perpendicular to the door, out of view of people passing by, for the right combination of concentration and control.

Take a ruler and measure your files from front to back to assess how many inches of storage space you need. Allow room (1 to 2 inches) for growth. With W-A-S-T-E techniques under your belt (see Chapter 16), you won't need much.

You should also allow clearance to pull out file cabinet drawers to double the cabinet's depth. Typical file cabinet dimensions are:

Tune up your workday with music

There's a fourth dimension to your ideal office layout: sound. Studies show that the right music can power your mind for peak productivity throughout the working day. When it's time to concentrate, slow, steady instrumental music can focus the mind and synchronize brain activity. On the other hand, you can fight fatigue on a slow day with your favorite fast and upbeat tune. Suffering from creative block? Cue up something new or unusual to force your brain cells to fire in different patterns.

- ✔ Vertical: 15 inches (letter) or 18 inches (legal) wide by 21 inches to 36 inches deep.
- ✔ Lateral: 36 inches (letter) or 42 inches (legal) wide by 18 inches deep.

Use four-drawer file cabinets to maximize your vertical space or two-drawer cabinets to provide an additional surface on which to put equipment or collate papers. The top drawer of a five-drawer model is basically only good for binders and books because the top drawer is too high to see files.

After you get your desk and file cabinets situated, add guest chairs and possibly a table to your layout, if appropriate.

Got a closet in a home office? A closet is a natural place to store supplies, especially if you add built-in or freestanding shelves. Remember to put your heaviest items — reams of paper and so forth — on lower shelves or the floor.

Natural light from windows provides a great mood boost, but can create glare when sunlight shines directly on a computer screen. Light placement is a particular concern if you work with art or design.

Give your interior design and the artwork on your walls the eye. Is the effect pleasant and harmonious, or distracting or distressing? A beautiful environment can bring out your best, but anything that your eye fixes on long or that you don't like can drag you down. Toss, donate, relocate, redo.

Cubes without Clutter

Your cube is small, square, not very private, and sometimes noisy. But millions of valued employees call the cubicle home, and organization is all the more important to staying on top of your game when working on such limited turf.

Start your cubicle makeover with the layout process just described. All the same principles apply, though you have less space to deal with and perhaps less flexibility in terms of what goes where. You can surmount the space problem with some cool cubicle tricks:

✔ Overhead bins to contain books, binders, and paper supplies off your desk

✔ A two-drawer file cabinet under the desk

✔ Under-desk drawers to hold a pullout computer keyboard, or pens, pencils and other small supplies

✔ A wall bar that attaches to the cubicle wall and supports shelves or sort trays (See Figure 14-3 for this cool cubicle tool.)

Figure 14-3:
Wall bars support everything from extra shelves to sort trays.

Work with your colleagues and office personnel to ensure convenient placement of such shared items as printers, copiers, and fax machines. These resources can be key variables in your productivity equation.

The Home Office

Everything I covered in this chapter pertains to any sort of office, but there are some special considerations when the office is at home. Your home office may be your primary workplace, or just a site for handling work you brought home from headquarters. In either case, making your home workplace work can provide professional results from everything you do there.

A basic principle for any workplace is that you want to minimize distractions. At home, you have to balance that priority with available space and your own personal style. Ask yourself a few questions to get started:

✔ How much space do you need to accomplish your tasks and store your supplies? (The layout process should provide the answer to this.)

✔ Do you prefer solitude and quiet, or do you need to know what's going on in the rest of the house?

✔ What temperature and lighting conditions make you most productive? Where can they be found?

In my experience as a home-based business owner and a consultant, the best solution is a dedicated room. Second best is an infrequently used room, such as a guest bedroom, that can be devoted to business 90 percent of the time. Last on the list, but sometimes the only alternative, is sharing space with a family/media room, kitchen, or bedroom. Don't worry. You can make the available room work!

Choose the best location for your home office by referring to the pros and cons listed in Table 14-1.

Table 14-1	Home Office Locations	
Place	*Pros*	*Cons*
Basement	Quiet and isolated for working and thinking.	Can be windowless, dark, and cold. You don't know whether the weather is right for a run to the office store or copy place, or if the kids are home from school.
Guest bedroom	All yours when guests aren't there. Most of the closet is free for storing supplies.	No work possible when you have guests. Need to compete for space with bedroom furniture, which may tempt you to take a few *zzz*s when you ought to be working.
Media room	Great double use of space for singles.	Other household members are likely to be blasting music or movies. You and your guests can't relax and watch a movie in your office.
Bedroom	Many apartment and condo dwellers have no choice. Leaves the living room uncluttered and restful.	Hard to sleep peacefully in your office with your desk staring you down. Your partner's sleep schedule may be interrupted. Space is limited.

(continued)

Table 14-1 *(continued)*

Place	Pros	Cons
Kitchen	Allows you to get basic household paperwork done while still watching the kids and staying in the thick of things.	Constant distractions on this stretch of household super highway. Forget about making client calls from here! Watch out for curious hands.

If your home office must share space with another function, create a visual and psychological divider with a tall bookcase or decorative trifold screen.

Household Information Center

Here's some food for thought: Your household information desk should function even better than the offices at Fortune 500 corporations. Why? Because you don't have a staff of thousands and sophisticated systems taking care of business. It's just you against the world and that stack of bills.

Your household information center may be located center stage at a built-in desk in the kitchen, in a room all its own, in a corner of the basement, or sharing quarters with a home office you use for business.

Choose your work space wisely . . . and change it when necessary

When I began my home-based business, I thought the basement would make a great space for my office. With a seldom-used sewing room already in place, the ground floor seemed like a natural double-up.

I lasted two, maybe three months. I didn't like the dark, the cold, or not knowing when my daughters came home from school. If my business was to survive, I needed a change, but what?

All the other rooms in the house were fully booked or so it seemed. The fourth bedroom served as a guest room, primarily accommodating our parents when they came to visit. That was just two weeks a year, so why not move the guest room down to the basement and let me emerge into the light?

My move upstairs changed my mood for the better and bolstered my business. There was sunlight. There was solitude when my kids were in school, a clear signal when they got home, and a door to close if I needed privacy.

Think twice before doubling your household information center with a home office. Are you asking for interruptions when somebody needs a pen or a birthday card while you try to concentrate or make a client call?

The household information desk

The desk is the heart of the household information center. If you make do with your old kitchen table, buy some freestanding drawers such as those pictured in Figure 15-2 in the chapter on desks. While there, stop and check out the principles for setting up a desk for success. Then tailor the desk to the task with a few additional household hints:

- ✔ **Split the pen/pencil center into two drawers if you have kids** to keep the younger generation out of yours. Remember that permanent markers can become permanent wall art in the hands of toddlers.

- ✔ **Personalize the stationery center.** Use boxes or dividers in the drawer to create separate categories: personal stationery; note and thank you cards; birthday and anniversary cards; and get well and sympathy cards.

    Buy greeting cards in bulk so you always have one when you need it. Don't forget a few baby and wedding cards too.

- ✔ **Create a money center drawer.** Put check refills, current bank statements, mortgage payment books, and a check box to hold current credit card receipts and statements here. If there's room, add a calculator to run the numbers. (Bank and credit card statements can be kept in a file folder if you don't have room here.)

- ✔ **Contain it.** Many built-in kitchen desks come with cabinets that can hold directories — telephone, personal, school, and membership — as well as the family camera and any stationery, cards, and envelopes that don't fit into drawers. You can substitute a wall or stand-alone cabinet or shelf if you don't have built-ins.

Household filing system

Create your home filing system according to the A-B-C principles discussed in Chapter 16 on information flow. Active files go in a cabinet in the information center, and inactive files should be boxed up for storage, here or somewhere else. You should be able to contain home files in about two file drawers (unless you have an extensive financial portfolio) plus a box for warranties. The most common household filing categories include

✔ **Auto:** Keep separate files for each car, including mileage logs, gas receipts if tax deductible, and maintenance and repair receipts, which can help the resale value.

✔ **Career:** Start a resume file with your first job and keep one copy of each version for reference, with one or two masters showing supervisor names and phone numbers and salary information. (You may think these facts are engraved in your brain forever but wait until you've worked another job or two and you'll see why you need to write it down!)

✔ **Education:** Save all degrees, continuing education units (CEUs), certifications, and transcripts. If you have children, keep a file for general information on their schools and year-end (not quarterly) report cards.

✔ **Financial:** Keep bank statements in a file. Let the bank store your checks and get a copy if necessary. Retain only the latest utility statements unless you're submitting them for free light bulbs or saving them to create a budget.

Keep current tax information in active files. After you finish your annual income tax return, purge anything you aren't required to save and move retained files into inactive storage. The minimum to keep past tax records is seven years, but many experts recommend holding on to returns for life.

Save records for capital gains and account tracking for stocks, bonds, funds, CDs, IRAs, Keoghs, and 401Ks. Toss monthly statements when you receive quarterly or annual reports. Some people prefer to use binders for investment documents.

✔ **Health:** If you currently follow an exercise or diet regime or a course of treatment for a particular condition, keep relevant information in this file. Throw away anything that doesn't pertain to your present condition, as such information changes fast.

✔ **Insurance:** Keep all receipts and insurance claim paperwork for one year unless the claim is still open.

✔ **Legal:** Marriage and birth certificates, divorce papers, adoption papers, car titles, passports, real estate closings, trusts, wills, leases, and so on. Keep copies in your files for reference and store the originals in a safe deposit box.

✔ **Medical:** At the end of the year, transfer medical information to one list per person, including major illnesses and injuries, date, doctor's diagnosis (with name and phone number), and treatment. You can create a computer spreadsheet or word-processing table to make tracking medical info easier.

✔ **Real estate:** Information on your home and improvements. Current home-improvement projects are filed in the active files. Put completed home improvements in the in active files.

✔ **Travel:** Toss information for any trip you're not planning to take this year. Your travel agent or the Internet will have updated the facts by the time you're ready to pack your bags.

Do you really need every card or letter you ever received? Save only a select few of the most special in a memory box in storage.

Warranties, receipts, and instructions

Maybe it's time to program the VCR or fax machine and the instructions are nowhere to be found, or the dishwasher has conked out two weeks after purchase and the receipt has gone missing. A good warranty file can help you get your money's worth out of what you buy and save the space taken up by storing outdated information.

Here's how to organize the information that can keep your appliances and devices running smoothly:

1. Get a plastic box with built-in rails for hanging files.

2. Make a hanging file and colored tab for each room of the house. Items that are used all over the house should be grouped into their own categories — TVs, VCRs, vacuum cleaners, and so forth. This simplifies the situation when the power goes out and you need to go around and reprogram, or you need to buy a new TV and you want to see what you paid for the past ones.

3. Use folders to create a few subdivisions within rooms — for instance, large and small appliances in the kitchen, or lawn, snow, and tools in the garage.

4. Staple the instruction book, warranty, and receipt for each item together and file.

5. Whenever you discard or donate a piece of equipment, pull the documentation from the file and send it along too.

Keep the special wrench for the garbage disposal in your warranty file box so it doesn't get mixed up with or mistaken for something else.

Children's papers and memories

Swamped by small masterpieces of art and literature? Nobody generates more paper than children in school, and viewing each one as a treasure is natural for the creators and their proud parents. Of course these creations are special but I can assure you, both as a parent and a professional organizer who's faced down this issue with many other parents too, that you really won't want or need these papers in the future. Still the instinct to save at least a few special things runs strong. The solution? A memory box.

To make a kid's memory box, purchase a file storage box with built-in handles, one for each child. Label it with the child's name. Inside goes one manila folder per year, labeled with the year and containing one drawing, poem, story, book, and writing sample. At the end of the school year, sit down with your child and have him or her pick out the best item in each category to save. There are three simple rules of the game:

✔ You can't keep anything that can crumble or break, which includes artwork with big clumps of paint.

✔ Food products such as the ever-favorite macaroni necklace are forbidden. Not only are they fragile, but food can bring on the bugs.

✔ A child's memento collection cannot outgrow the box. If the box gets full, some old things have to go to make way for the new.

Adding to the memory box makes a nice wrap-up to the school year and teaches the lesson that less is more. Now whisk that box off to a storage area for lesson number two: Living spaces aren't for archives.

Junior high and high school papers

Junior high and high school kids need a functional filing system to track their schoolwork and papers pertaining to activities. Give teens a head start on high achievement by teaching them to manage information flow from the get-go.

To set up a junior filing system, buy a sturdy container, such as a crate, with a built-in rack for hanging files. Use hanging file folders and tabs to create general categories for academics — math, science, social studies, history, foreign language, arts, and so on. Stick to generic names so you won't have to rename the category each year as the child segues from algebra to geometry. Add activity categories such as sports, clubs and groups, lessons, religion, and so forth, and one more for school information.

Show your child how to use the system to file current handouts, tests, reports, flyers, and other papers by category and class. Most files can be completely purged after final exams. As students get older, they may want to hold on to certain items such as the periodic table or algebraic formulas. Use a separate plastic box with built-in rails for hanging files to hold important papers over the long term.

A working work space doesn't just feel good — it delivers tangible rewards. Thoughts become actions and efforts become results, because everything is in its place according to your personal needs. Organize and watch your productivity rise.

Chapter 15

Command Central: The Desk

. . . .

In This Chapter

▶ Clearing off your desk with R-E-M-O-V-E

▶ Reaping the benefits of the right-now rule

▶ Cleaning and stocking desk drawers

▶ Cool computer workstation tips

. . . .

*T*he world turns on the work done at desks. Not to discount the efforts of workers in the fields, on store floors, or heading up the car pool, but eventually every product and service passes over somebody's desk. And from the look of some of the desktops I've seen, the fact that our economy still functions is a minor miracle.

The desk is the ultimate work center. Maximize desktop potential by putting everything in place, and your desk will drive your best efforts, facilitate your daily schedule, and set you up for success. Don't settle for less.

The Desk Is a Place to Do Work

Whether you look out over an expanse of burnished mahogany or pull up to an old kitchen table, the simple truth is the desk is a place to work.

In the hustle of daily life, you may forget what the desk is actually for. I've seen clients who turned their desks into a combination display case, dining table, bookshelf, and filing cabinet. No wonder they called me in for help.

This chapter is about restoring the original purpose to the most important piece of furniture in your office. Before you tackle the job, read over the previous chapter for tips on choosing and placing the right desk in your office. Now get down to what you do there.

What your desk says to the world

They say first impressions take six seconds, but your desk speaks even faster. What do you think when you see someone sitting among piles of papers, knickknacks, and supplies? Do the words *capable, professional, in control* spring to mind? Probably not. Your desk projects a powerful image to your colleagues, clients, staff, and superiors, and a mess sends the wrong message.

Even more important, the state of your desk speaks to you. Do you ever feel fatigued when you can't find your current project file in the pile, stressed when the message pad has disappeared with an important caller on the line, creatively blocked by a crowded view that leaves no room to think?

You can have control over what your desk says to you and the world. Make your desk say "success."

Clearing the desk

Over the course of curing many desktop disasters, I developed a simple system for clearing off the desk and setting up all your accessories and supplies for fingertip management of your job. Try the system and see if your work gets easier while your reputation improves. All you have to do is R-E-M-O-V-E.

Here's a rundown of the R-E-M-O-V-E process.

✔ **Reduce distractions:** Clear the desktop of anything that catches your eye or encourages people to visit such as in/out boxes, papers and files, photos, knickknacks, candy, or cookies. Keep your snacks inside your desk or credenza so you can work in peace. Move all your knickknacks to another surface and leave them for a day or two. After your trial separation, choose just a few to keep somewhere off the desk and pitch or donate the rest. Clear off photos by hanging them on the wall behind you or finding a display spot off your desk and outside your direct line of vision. Snowplow piles by using the right-now rule: If you're not using the paper or file right now, put it away.

As for that devilish distracter, the mail: Emergencies arrive by phone, fax, or overnight delivery, but whatever the U.S. Postal Service or interoffice mail brings can wait. Keep mail and its messengers out of your hair by posting two wall pockets outside your door or cubicle to serve as your in and out trays, as you see in Figure 15-1. If you can't get your mailbox out of your office, move it to a file cabinet or credenza far from your desk and as close to the entryway as possible.

Figure 15-1:
Pockets
hang on the
wall or over
the top of
cubicles to
keep your
mail off your
desk.

✔ **Everyday use?** Remove items that you don't use everyday. Consider sticky notes, the memo pad, staple remover, paper clips, binder clips, rubber bands, tape, scissors, ruler, highlighter, markers, calculator, and disk tray, and put away those that don't pass the everyday test. Staplers and calculators are questionable contenders. If they get daily use you can keep them on the desk, but if they don't and you have room in a drawer, off they go. And though you probably use pens and pencils every day, you may find that moving them from a desktop holder to a drawer makes them less likely to disappear. See Table 15-1 for an everyday use checklist.

✔ **Move to the preferred side.** For fingertip management, put everything you reach for on your preferred side: the hand you write with. Relocate pens, pencils, notepad, calculator, and disk tray to your writing side. The telephone is the big exception to the rule. Pick up the receiver with your preferred hand and you'll see why: With your writing hand busy, you can't take notes. Switching to the other ear leaves you with a phone cord strapped across your chest (or around your neck on really bad days). Move the phone to the opposite side.

If your computer is on your desk and you use it less than 50 percent of the day, you can move the monitor and keyboard to the preferred side too. Raise your computer up with a stand or computer arm and you have even more desk at your disposal, or get the space hog off the desk altogether with a separate computer stand. If you're on a desktop computer more than half the day, you probably want to keep the keyboard and monitor dead center.

✔ **Organize together.** Create mini-desktop work centers for the phone, computer, and time. The telephone center includes the phone, a message pad or log alongside, and the address and phone index slightly farther back. If you have an answering machine, that would be the item farthest to the back. Put disks next to your monitor to form a computer center, and group your calendar and clock (coming up) to create a time center.

✔ **View your time** with a desktop clock and calendar/organizer. Simple but effective, a clock on your desk saves you the extra motion of glancing at your watch and provides a constant time cue to cure a case of the lates. (Get a clock that displays the date and day, too, and one quick glance tells all.) Try viewing your time and see, literally, what I mean. Whatever written medium you use to track your appointments (see Chapter 18 on time management for more), I recommend keeping a calendar/organizer on your desk, open to today, to get you on your way. If you use a computer program to track your schedule, keeping your calendar in sight can be tough, which is why I don't recommend this method for visual folks and there *are* enough of you out there.

Learning experts recommend that you utilize all your senses. So if viewing your time doesn't keep you on schedule, buy a meeting reminder alarm at an office supply shop. You can set the alarm for multiple meetings in a day and the ringer goes off for each one. You can also use computer calendar or contact-management programs to set meeting alarms.

✔ **Empty the center** by moving the few items that remain to the perimeter. Remember math class? That means the edge, including all those empty corners. Now your desk is open for work, and *you're* open for business!

To help smooth your way through the R-E-M-O-V-E process, use Table 15-1 to help you decide what to keep on top of your desk. Things you use several times a day are the best qualified. Everyday items may be better in a drawer, and anything you use less than once a day definitely moves. Check off the appropriate column for each item, and then use the list to relocate excess desktop items.

Table 15-1	Desktop Decisions	
Item	*Use Every Day?*	*Several Times a Day?*
Pen and pencil holder		
Sticky notes		
Memo pad		
Phone message pad		
Stapler		
Staple remover		

Item	Use Every Day?	Several Times a Day?
Paper clips		
Binder clips		
Rubber bands		
Tape		
Scissors		
Ruler		
Highlighter		
Markers		
Calculator		
Disk tray		

If your drawers are too crowded to receive everything you try to get off the desktop, just put it aside onto a file cabinet or shelf for now and read on.

An answering machine, even if you use it several times a day, doesn't qualify for prime desktop real estate. All you need to do is view the flashing light and punch the buttons, so move the machine to the back of the desk, or off onto a nearby credenza or low file cabinet. To save space, purchase a shelf that will raise the telephone above the answering machine as pictured in Figure 15-2.

Figure 15-2:
Double up desktop space with a phone and answering machine shelf.

Photo courtesy of Lillian Vernon.

Check out Figure 15-3 for a desk set up with the R-E-M-O-V-E principles.

Downsizing your desk supplies

People can get a little giddy when it comes to office supplies, like on your first day of school when you can't have enough freshly sharpened pencils. But your desk is not a supply cabinet, so start by returning all duplicate items to the supply room or cabinet. Done that? Great. Now take a load off your desk by sending the following stuff to the trash:

- Dried out pens, markers, and highlighters
- Stubby little pencils
- Dried out correction fluid
- Dried out glue sticks
- Stretched out rubber bands and paper clips
- Small sections of staples that jam the stapler
- Promotional items you don't use

Finally, figure out whether you have the right supplies for peak performance. Are you always borrowing something from someone? Go get your own. Has a notepad or purple marker or set of binder tabs been sitting in your drawer unused for the last six months? Return anything that's still useful and toss the rest. Check out Table 15-2 for some of my top supply picks and one common office supply I *don't* recommend.

Table 15-2	Office Supply Secrets
Supply Item	*Secrets*
Correction fluid pen	For touching up small spots, especially cancelled meetings in your calendar or organizer.
Phone message pads	Think pink. Your messages will be easy to see. If you lose messages, a carbon pad keeps copies. A spiral notebook or phone log creates a permanent record and provides ample room to write. Downside: You can't rip out individual messages unless you start a new page for each contact.
Fax stickies	Skip the cover sheet and save trees.
Regular sticky notes	Just say no! I don't generally recommend sticky notes for anything other than faxes and flags (such as "sign here") and for plotting projects (see Chapter 18). Sticky notes fall off and get lost.
Paper clips	Separate small and large into two holders of different colors. The magnetized holders are great for fingertip access, but keep them far away from computer disks.
Stapler	Use a small one for standard jobs, a heavy-duty model for 20-225 pages, a long-reach stapler for booklets, and an electric stapler for multiple handouts. Keep only everyday staplers at your desk; specialty models can go elsewhere.
Glue	Try the liquid in a tube with a sponge tip applicator, which won't dry out like a glue stick. When you need a removable adhesive, as when laying out a room, the sticky note glue sticks are terrific.
Package or pocketknife	A retractable or folding knife makes for easy opening of any envelope or package.
Key tags	Clear up unknown key mysteries with little white disks that loop through the top of the key and give you a spot to write which file or drawer it opens.

Restock a supply just comfortably before you run out. When you load the last strip of staples into the stapler, that's the time to order the next box. If you're in charge of buying supplies, establish a *last* replacement policy — 1, 5, 25, and so on, depending upon how fast you go through things — to stay stocked without overspending.

Designating Your Drawers as Work Centers

Now that you know what you want on hand while you work, just where are you going to put it? Surprise! That's what your desk drawers are for. That's right — not for your shoe collection or the magazines you like to read at lunch, but for the things you need to do work.

Hopefully, you have two to four small drawers and one to two file drawers in your desk. No? Can you get another desk? Put a new desk with plenty of drawer space on your wish list and proceed.

Group like things together: staples and tape, mail supplies, and so forth. Next, achieve fingertip management by putting the things you need access to often in the drawer closest to you. Contain items with drawer dividers so everything stays in place. If you have no desk drawers — perhaps you're working at an old kitchen table in a home office — several options are available to remedy the situation:

- ✔ A pullout drawer that attaches under the desktop.

- ✔ A desktop drawer set. Refer to Figure 7-1 for an example, and get creative by placing the drawers on a file cabinet or credenza to keep your desktop clear.

- ✔ A rolling cart of drawers, as pictured in Figure 15-4.

- ✔ A two-drawer file cabinet under the desk or within reach behind or to the side of you.

Now turn each of your drawers into a work center:

- ✔ **The central drawer is the pen/pencil center:** Pens, pencils, ruler, scissors, markers, clips, tape, correction fluid, staples, staple remover, and so on.

- ✔ **The top small drawer becomes a mail and filing center:** Stamps, address labels, envelopes, business cards, hanging file tabs, file labels, and blank address cards.

- ✔ **The second small drawer turns into a stationery/paper center:** Letterhead, stationery, and note pads.

- ✔ **The file drawer is the project center:** Take Action File and current major project files.

Adapt placement of each item or of entire drawers according to frequency of use. Do you reach for letterhead more often than mailing supplies? Swap locations.

Figure 15-4:
Rolling carts
make up for
missing
built-in
drawers.

Containing the contents

With your drawer floor plan in place, the time to divvy up the space is upon you. Drawer divider options include

- ✔ **A sectioned flat tray,** usually designed to fill most of the pen and pencil drawer.

- ✔ **A deep drawer organizer,** which is the same as the flat tray but with higher sides for a deeper drawer. This is great to contain tall items, such as correction fluid, or if you're short of space and need to stack — paper clips on top of a box of staples, and so on.

- ✔ **Separate rectangular containers** — narrow for pens and pencils, wider for other supplies.

- ✔ **Built-in, movable vertical dividers.** You can also buy your own (see Figure 6-2 in Chapter 6).

Sturdy cardboard boxes and tops work just fine as drawer dividers. Try the top of a business card box to hold rubber bands.

Sort supplies into your drawer dividers by like type. Look at that — no more traffic jams on your way to the correction pen.

Personal possessions

Sure, you're a person, and you naturally need a few personal things at work. That doesn't mean your file drawer should store a shoe collection worthy of Imelda Marcos (believe me because I've seen it!), or a full cosmetic and manicure set. I recommend having the following on hand:

- Aspirin, ibuprofen, or acetaminophen. Where are you more likely to get a headache than at work?

- Ladies: A spare pair of nylons, and a pair of plain pumps if you wear street shoes to the office.

- Gentlemen: One neutral, go-with-everything tie in case yours takes a dip in the salad or soup. (I know, it wasn't your fault; you forgot your tie bar.)

- Parents: A school phone directory (you can use last year's) so you can call a parent if you're running late to pick up your child. Use different colored highlighters to mark each child's friends.

Keep your briefcase or computer bag under the desk in the spot farthest from your feet. Gym bags can also go here if space allows, or into a coat closet.

The Computer Workstation

In today's workplace, people at every level of all sorts of careers use the power of computer technology to leverage personal and team potential. Many let their cyberstuff get out of control in the process. More computer equipment and software isn't necessarily better. Like anything that takes up space and time, target your computer setup to the tasks you need to perform with any excess pared away.

Organizing your computer setup

If you have a dedicated computer workstation, reserve the area strictly for computer supplies and keep everything else at your desk. If you share functions, allocate computer supplies among your desktop, drawers, overhead bins, and/or bookshelves by grouping like items together and placing them for easy access.

When choosing a computer workstation, whether as part of a desk or a standalone unit, measure all your components — monitor, CPU tower, speakers, printer, scanner — then look for:

✔ Enough surface area to hold what you need on the desktop. This definitely includes your monitor and enough space to open up files, books, and reports to work from. You may also need room for a keyboard, printer, speakers, and disk holder.

✔ A pullout drawer to get the keyboard off the desktop.

✔ A drawer for pens and pencils.

✔ Shelves for reference books and/or disk trays.

✔ Another shelf for your printer or speakers. You can also use a pullout drawer in a cabinet below to hold the printer.

✔ A built-in disk holder if you need a lot of disks on hand.

✔ Floor space or a shelf for the CPU. Skip the closed cabinet, which is one more door to open every time you want to swap disks or reboot.

Organizing your computer supplies

A mess at your computer workstation can create such a mess in your mind that no amount of electronic intelligence can compensate. Use organizing principles to keep everything in its place as you work at the computer, and you can take full advantage of technology's awesome power.

Media

P-L-A-C-E is good news to computer users suffering from disk disorder. Rather than rummaging through CDs, diskettes, and DVDs trying to find something you know you have in there somewhere, set up a system for keeping them all organized once and for all. You not only save yourself time finding what you need; you also save yourself the stress of wondering whether you lost an electronic file. Here's how to make sense of your computer media:

✔ **Purge:** Remove all computer disks that you no longer need. If you sent those graphic files over to the production department and the newsletter is already in print, you no longer need to keep the originals. Toss or recycle the disk.

✔ **Like with like:** Use the color of disks and/or labels to categorize your media — perhaps graphics disks are yellow and financial are green, or corporate files go on blue and clients on red. See the next chapter for more on color-coding files and apply the same principles to your disks.

✔ **Access:** Keep your most active disks, backups, and program disks you use regularly, closest at hand. Old backups, programs you're not using, and installed programs you don't need to support by disk can be stored somewhere else, which may be off the workstation if space is tight.

✔ **Contain.** All disks can go into holders, with dividers or separate trays to distinguish between different types. Start by separating programs from backups, and then arrange by the categories established in the previous step. You can get a multimedia tray to keep different formats (floppy, CD, Zip, and so on) together. Some workstations have disk holders built in; make sure you have the right size.

Don't store your floppy disks or tape backups next to or on top of loud-speakers, computer monitors, CPUs, cellular phones, or even magnetic paper clip holders, all of which emit electromagnetic fields that could scramble or erase your data. Want to make your data even safer? If you have a CD writer, switch to compact discs as your storage medium. They remain unruffled in the face of magnetic force.

✔ **Evaluate.** Are you keeping too many disks? Would color help you distinguish graphics from word-processing or spreadsheet documents, or quickly spot client files or research information?

Reference shelf

Your workstation should have a shelf for reference materials, from . . .*For Dummies* books about programs to other books and binders specific to your project, and software and hardware documentation. No shelf? Position a bookcase close by and designate a shelf for computer materials.

If you have more than one booklet for any piece of hardware or software — printer, motherboard, programs — group them together in a resealable plastic bag. Add an empty print cartridge box to the bag for your printer. Even if you know the cartridge and printer model number, some office supply stores stock by their own numbers so having the box can help you spot and buy the right one fast.

Figure 15-5:
A computer paper holder is easy on your eyesight.

Paper holders

There are three ways to keep your paper in sight while working at the keyboard. An old-fashioned typing stand holds a piece of paper vertically. A newer, more compact version takes up just a few inches of desk space. Even better, clear the desk with a bar that clips right onto your monitor or laptop, as you see in Figure 15-5.

Do you see what I see? The surface of your desk! Whether the sight was long lost or just occasionally crowded out, now you know how to keep your desktop clear all the time. Your desk has become a place to do work. With everything at your fingertips, you get greater results for less effort. That's what I call a desk for success.

Chapter 16

Managing Your Information Flow

*Y*ou may have noticed that you're in the Information Age but most people's information management systems are stuck in the Stone Age. Whether you're a homemaker or a high-tech whiz, the ongoing assault of information can threaten to disorganize just about anything you do. The way to stay sane and productive amid all the noise is to use some simple techniques to put information to work for *you*.

This chapter gives you the tools you need to handle all the information that flows your way each day, file the keepers, and free yourself from yesterday's news. You *can* dig yourself out from under those piles of papers and prevent them from happening again. It's a bold promise, but once you discover how to put information in its place, the flow turns from an organizational foe into a very good friend.

The ABCs of Filing

Do you have a stack of papers, magazines, and other informational stuff sitting somewhere awaiting that elusive moment in which you decide where, if anywhere, they belong? Perhaps there are several stacks, strategically located — such as where you open your mail, on your desktop, or all over the dining room table.

If mounds and piles are your usual M.O., let me introduce you to a simple but elegant concept: files. I know that's a fighting word for some, but set your fear of filing aside. Done right, filing is as easy as A-B-C: activity level, basic tools, and classification and color. Be a filer, not a piler!

The info flow payoff

Studies have shown that people waste as much as 4.3 hours a week just searching for papers. That's 5.5 weeks a year. Do you really want to spend all that extra time at work? Wouldn't you rather stop staying late and working weekends by taking control of your information flow?

Then there's the matter of how much that lost time costs a company. Do the math for a ten-dollar-an-hour clerk:

4.3 hours/week	x $10/hour salary	= $43 a week lost
$43/week	x 52 weeks	= $2,236 a year lost
100 employees	x $2,236	= $223,600 wasted payroll

Now do the math for a manager's salary. How many dollars is smooth information flow worth to you?

Active versus inactive files

What's the difference between a current project file you pull out five times a day and one containing your tax returns from five years ago? Tons! Fingertip management dictates that only your active files should be taking up valuable space near your valuable self. Totally inactive files, such as old tax returns, belong in shadowy spaces where only auditors would dare to tread. Use Table 16-1 to sort out your active and inactive files and store them in the appropriate location.

Table 16-1	Match Files' Activity Level to Location	
Frequency of Use	*Examples*	*Location*
Daily to monthly = active	Take Action Files, current projects forms, reference	Desk/workstation, file cabinets, bookcases or shelves, literature rack. Salespeople may keep them in the car.
Quarterly or less =inactive	Past projects, records, and archives	Outside your main office space, the company's central filing system, a secondary file area in a home or small office, or off-site records company

Using W-A-S-T-E to filter information

Wait! Before you file a piece of paper, ask yourself if that paper is a W-A-S-T-E. All unevaluated information is a waste of time and space. That's why you need a system for assessing its value on the spot. What's important and worth saving? What can you let go?

When it comes to information inflow, W-A-S-T-E is a five-step filter that can save you countless hours and acres of space. For each piece of paper that comes your way, ask five simple questions to decide if it's a keeper or destined for the trash:

- ✔ **Is it Worthwhile?** Once you read or scan a piece of information, ask yourself, "Does this add real value to my work, home, or life?" The natural response is, "Well if someone gave or sent it to me, or if I looked up the facts or wrote the report myself, then the information must matter," but does it really?

    Keep: An incoming fax, minutes from a meeting you chaired.

    Toss: Incoming fax cover sheet (noting new contact info first), a coupon for a product you rarely use (don't even clip).

- ✔ **Will I use it Again?** This is the big question. No matter how worthwhile a piece of information may be right now, if you won't use it again, there's not a reason in the world to keep the excess paper. Read it and say goodbye.

    Keep: A memo outlining a new policy or procedure, the outline for a speech you'll give again.

    Toss: A fascinating article about a current political race (read it now or get tomorrow's update), vacation brochures about somewhere you've visited (info can change by your next visit), the program for a conference you attended (note follow-up items in Take Action File).

- ✔ **Can I easily find it Somewhere else?** Can your filing system compete with the contents of the Internet? Or the network of libraries connected by an international lending system that can bring you any book or journal you need in hours or days? Or your company's archives, your colleagues' files, or the many resources that are just a phone call away? It can't and it shouldn't. Information you can easily access somewhere else wastes space and should get the boot.

    Keep: The only plain-English description you've ever seen of how your office's phone system works, a glowing letter of recommendation.

    Toss: A carbon copy of a memo or report if you have no action to take, anything easily available in the library or on the Web (look there when you need it), a memo about a project that you assigned to one of your staff (forward the memo to that person and note any follow-ups in your Take Action File).

    The key word with this question is *easily.* If you expect to need this information in the future and it would be difficult to retrieve somewhere else, then file it. That's what files are for.

✔ **Will anything happen if I Toss it?** Imagine the worst. Would the sky fall down or your capabilities collapse if this paper or file was no longer in your possession? The answer is probably *yes* if you're solely responsible for the information, you need it for your daily activities, or it contains important tax or legal implications that someone else isn't handling. See the upcoming discussion of retention schedules and consult yours to help with the toss question. If the schedule doesn't require that you retain an item, toss it.

Keep: An easy and economical recipe your family adores, business thank you and recommendation letters you can use as references and testimonials.

Toss: A recipe you clipped a year ago and haven't tried yet (date recipes as you clip so you know when they should go), personal thank you notes (the gratitude won't go away with the paper it's written on), old catalogs and those you never ordered from.

✔ **Do I need the Entire item?** You can significantly streamline your files by only saving what you need — so break out the scissors and become a clipper. Toss out repetitive parts of old drafts. If you're interested in a sidebar from an article, save just that, and perhaps the title page for reference.

Keep: Articles from papers, magazines, and journals, portions of previous drafts that have changed.

Toss: The rest of the periodical, previous draft pages that stay the same, cover memo for the minutes from the meeting you chaired.

What should you put to the W-A-S-T-E test? Every piece of information that crosses your path. As you become proficient with the W-A-S-T-E process, the inflow of info will naturally direct itself to its proper place, in your filing system or in the trash.

Haven't seen a piece of paper in months, you say? Dealing strictly in e-mails and gigabytes? The W-A-S-T-E principles apply equally to electronic information. See Chapter 17 to learn more about cyberorganization.

The (false) paperless promise

Somebody said that the advent of computers would turn us into a paperless society. Have you noticed how the little devils have had the opposite effect?

Computers enable you to go through many different drafts of a document before reaching final form. A single push of a button prints out five or ten copies of a memo just to be sure everyone knows what's going on, whether they need to or not. Let's face it: The combination of people plus computers produces more paper.

People, however, decide whether to keep papers. Put every piece that comes into your possession to the W-A-S-T-E test.

Retaining and purging files

Purging is the most important step to a power file system. Papers don't go away on their own accord when they grow old and unimportant. Going through and clearing out the deadweight is up to you. I find that purging files is a formidable task for most people the first time around, but purging gets easier and easier as you polish up your information management skills. Whether you're starting from scratch or in maintenance mode, you can break the task into manageable chunks with the following steps:

1. **Get a records retention schedule.** Your company may have its own (check with your legal or accounting department). You can get entire books on record retention from the Association of Records Managers and Administrators' Web site (www.arma.org). Generally, personal files should be kept for three years and business and tax-related files for seven. Whatever your source, have your retention schedule close at hand as you purge.

2. **Start at the front of your first file drawer.** Pull out one file at a time and ask the five W-A-S-T-E questions of each piece of paper inside. Remember to consult your retention schedule at the toss question. Throw away everything that doesn't pass the test.

3. **Mark your quitting point.** When you run out of time or energy, grab a brightly colored piece of letter-size paper and place the paper vertically in the front of the file where you left off. Now you know just where to start next time — which better be soon.

Here's a hint to make future file maintenance easier: Each time that you use a filed paper, put a little check mark in the upper right-hand corner. Look for the check at purging time. No mark? If the file is 6 months old or more, chances are that you don't need this item.

Shred or rip through all documents containing your name and bank or credit card account numbers before throwing them away. Your company may also have a shredding policy for sensitive documents.

When to clean out files

Good times to clean out your files:

- ✔ At the close of a project.
- ✔ When you're on hold on the phone.
- ✔ Fifteen minutes a day.
- ✔ An hour a week.

Basic tools you need

If you're a carpenter, you need a hammer and nails, a stud finder, and a leveler. If you work with papers, your tools are binders, folders, hanging files and frames, labels and tabs, and suitable containers to put it all in. I've seen many would-be filers foiled simply because they didn't have the basics they needed to build their system. Assemble your tools before you start so you can file as you organize.

Loose-leaf books: Binders

Binders make the best holders for papers you refer to like a book: procedure and training manuals, computer information, logs, and reference material. Some binder bylaws to keep in mind:

- **Label the spine.** The spine is what you see when the binder sits on the shelf, so you want it to be clearly marked. Choices for labeling the spine range from laser-ready cardboard strips to slide down the spine panel to small self-adhesive spine pockets to making labels on a label maker.

- **Use dividers with replaceable colored tabs** to mark off different sections in the binder. Stay tuned for more on file classification and colors.

- **Clear sheet protectors** can keep pages you use frequently in good shape. Protectors can also hold brochures, business cards, and other odd-size papers. You need dividers wide enough to clear the protectors; look for those labeled *for sheet protectors* or *extra-wide*.

- **Pockets** inside the binder's front and back cover provide a convenient place to put items such as brochures or something you pull out frequently, such as a computer quick-reference card.

File your binders on a bookshelf by category, within fingertip reach of their use.

Keeping it together: File containers

Anything that doesn't get bound in a binder needs to be filed in a folder inside a hanging file. That's right — *a file that hangs from a frame*, not just folders jammed into a box or drawer so the front ones slide down and everything falls out, and retrieving and replacing files runs from hard to impossible. Places to hang files include:

- **File drawers** in a desk or filing cabinet. For drawers that come without built-in hanging rails, you can buy frames in letter or legal size. Beware the cheap two-drawer file cabinets available at many discount and some office supply stores. Fill them up with heavy files, and suddenly the drawers start to jump their tracks. Investing in quality for something so frequently used is worth your while.

✔ **Plastic file boxes.** These usually have built-in rails for hanging files, letter or legal, and come with a clear cover. Plastic file boxes may or may not have see-through sides. This is a great solution for semi-active home storage of items such as warranties that may be kept in an out-of-the-way place, but need to be easy to access. As pictured in Figure 16-1, plastic file boxes are also a productive investment for salespeople who need to keep a load of literature in the car. Note: While the carryall boxes with handles are fine for a few files, they won't hold much weight before the handle breaks.

✔ **Plastic file crates.** *Pro:* They have rails for hanging, and so are a big improvement over a generic cardboard box. *Con:* The contents get dusty and crates aren't nice to look at in the office or home.

✔ **Cardboard storage boxes.** A cost-effective option for inactive files, most cardboard storage boxes don't hold hanging files, which means your system organization can be lost and files are more difficult to retrieve and replace. One brand does have plastic rails that sit in the cardboard edge.

Figure 16-1:
Find the
right file
container
for the job.

Don't hang it just anywhere: Hanging files

With the frames in place, you need file folders to hang there, the ones with metal hooks extending from either side. These serve two purposes: to hold your files vertically and to divide them up by category. You have a few hanging file options, and here are the facts to help you choose.

✔ **Standard hanging files** are suitable for small file groups — about five folders or less.

✔ **Box bottom hanging files** have a piece of cardboard in the bottom to keep many files sitting flat, as in a box. Box bottoms come in 1-,2-, 3-, and 4-inch widths. Use two 2-inch files instead of a 4-inch file, which is just too awkward and bulky, but a three-inch is better than the sum of its parts, as hanging files do take up space.

✔ **Hanging file tabs** are the guides that turn a sea of files into a neatly cate-gorized system. Here, location is key. If you place the tab in back, the folders inside the file can block your view of the tab. Worse, it now takes two steps to find your file: Touch the tab on the back of the hanging file, then pull open the front to find the first folder inside. Instead, put the tab in the front of the hanging file to find your folder fast the first time.

Tough and durable: File folders

File folders are the foundation of your filing system, and, as you can see in Figure 16-2, file folders are not all created equal. Following are the details on the differences.

✔ **Two-ply, reinforced, or double top folders** (same concept, different brands) should replace all your standard models. Two-ply folders cost a little more, but the reinforced tab that runs across the top of the folder, right where you grab it, can keep folders in good shape longer, saving you the time and money of swapping them out when they bend or tear.

Have you ever noticed the parallel score marks that run along the bottom edge of file folders? This is where you're supposed to fold the folder to create a flat bottom as your file gets fat. Behold! The papers fit more comfortably in the folder and the front drops down to reveal the labeled tab in back.

✔ **File jackets** are manila folders with closed sides. Use these for small items that can fall out of regular folders, such as tickets or brochures.

✔ **File pockets/wallets** expand wider than jackets and serve well for stand-alone jobs such as a current project that may be toted to work at a meet-ing table or offsite. Wallets can also turn your open shelving units, where hanging files can't be used, into first-rate filing real estate. Slip some file folders inside to keep loose papers from catching in the folds. Note: Wallets don't fit well inside file cabinets, as their expandable sides can catch while you try to get them in or out. Buy plastic file wallets for longer use.

✔ **Classification or fastener folders** have metal prongs at the top or side to hold papers in order. Available in several sections per folder, classifica-tion folders are great when page order is important or you want to sepa-rate different types of information within a single file. For instance, my client in the mortgage department of a bank uses them to section off client information, correspondence, legal documents, and payment information for each loan.

✔ **File folder labels** are the finishing touch, and they're not optional. Labels generated by a computer or typewriter are much easier to read than your scrawl on a folder tab, especially for another staff member. Whether you're a doctor or just write like one, take pity on your col-leagues and use professionally produced file labels.

Checking out: Out guides

Anyone who shares files with others knows how they tend to disappear, usu-ally when you need a piece of crucial information while someone waits on the phone or your boss has firing on her mind. That's why every office should have an out guide, a sort of checkout system for files.

An old-fashioned out guide is like an interoffice envelope on a paper divider with a big red tab. You write the date, your name, and the name of the file you're absconding with on the next empty line and file it where the folder once was. There's a newer, sturdier version in red plastic that holds an index card in a pocket instead of a paper list. You can count on plastic to last longer.

Classification and color-coding

Remember that statistic about losing 4.3 hours a week looking for papers? You trimmed it down by getting your papers out of piles and into files, but here's the really critical step. When you classify and color-code your files, your fingers don't even have to do the walking — your eyes do the looking to find the file you need fast, and you're on your way to earning yourself an extra vacation. Tell your boss I said so!

Classifying by category

How to file your files? That is the question. Classification is the answer.

There are three steps to classifying your files: Choose the main categories, select a system for classifying the files within each category, and make a file index.

1. **Categorize:** Group your files by subject and give each category a noun for a name. If you have more than ten files in a category, repeat the process to create subcategories. For instance, *Insurance* files could

break down into *Disability, Health, Liability,* and *Workers Compensation.* An author may divide *Writing* files into *Books* and *Articles* and group *Public Relations* and *Competition* into *Marketing.*

The file categories and subcategories that support peak performance can vary by who you are and what you do. Here are a few examples:

- **CEO or small business owner:** Administrative, Clients, Financial, Insurance, Legal, Marketing, Organizations, Sales, Vendors

- **Government affairs manager at an insurance company:** Administrative, Government Affairs, Human Resources, Training

- **Financial analysis manager at a bank:** Asset-Based Lending, Bankwide, Commercial, Retail Banking, Treasury

- **Meeting planner for an association:** Category (one of several): Annual Meeting Subcategories: Advertising, Awards/Pins, Brochures, Entertainment, Financial, Gifts, Golf, Hotel, Registration, Signs, Speakers, Sponsors, Trade Shows, Travel

- **Personal:** Category (one of several): Financial Subcategories: Bank, Budget, Credit Cards, Investments, Loans, Subscriptions, Taxes

You heard about establishing boundaries? Make some in your filing system by keeping all business and personal files separate. Storing personal information at work, where the wrong eyes may run across private matter, is asking for trouble. If you work at home, a clear distinction between the two types can help you with everything from doing tax returns to pulling the right file when you have a client on the phone.

2. **Classify:** Files may be classified alphabetically, chronologically, geographically, numerically, or by subject. Choose from these five main classifications according to the contents of the files. The classifying system you choose also helps you create subcategories and name each individual file. Table 16-2 shows you how to match file types to the right classifying systems and establish order in any filing cabinet.

Table 16-2 Order in the Cabinet! Five File Classification Systems

Classification System	Order	Best Used For
Alphabetical	A, B, C, Aa-Ad, and so on	Files with proper names, clients, employees, vendors
Chronological	Years, months, days	Board minutes, annual reports, committee meetings
Geographical	Country, state, city, region, and so on	Territory files for sales, marketing

Classification System	Order	Best Used For
Numerical	0-100, 101-200, and so on	Numbered items: invoices, checks, legal filings
Subject	Follow the access rule to put the subjects you use most in the most convenient drawers	Everything not covered by the above methods

Choose a noun for a file name and ask not "What should I call it?" but "Under what name would I find it?" There's just one rule: No file may be called "Miscellaneous."

3. **Index:** Feel like you navigate your files without a clear path? A file index can point you to the information you need every time, fast. In a database, spreadsheet, or word processing table, make a list of all your files by category, subcategory, file name, and location. Put the index in your Take Action File (coming up) and update it as you add and purge files. Whether you're looking for something or wondering where to put a new piece of paper, you have a one-stop, easy-scan map of your system. Table 16-3 shows how simple your file index can be.

Table 16-3		File Index	
Category	*Subcategory*	*File Name*	*Location*
___	___	___	___
___	___	___	___
___	___	___	___

Attention executives: Are you friendly with your files? Get to know how your system works and where your file index is so that someone else's sick day, sudden promotion, or departure doesn't leave you lost. If you can't grasp it, it's too hard; call me!

Color coding

People from ancient sages to contemporary clothing designers say that color can affect your mood, even how you act, and it can definitely influence the behavior of your filing system. When used systematically, colored tabs, labels, and folders can provide quick identification in the drawer or on the desktop, making your mood much better than it would be after a bunch of fruitless browsing.

Color-coding matches the colors of your files to their contents, and it works best when there's a connection between the two. For instance, many people use green for Financial. Filing materials are most commonly available in red, blue, yellow, and green, so start your free association now.

Perfectionists or very visual types can order folders and labels in additional colors from office supply catalogs.

There are four places to use color in your filing system: hanging file tabs, file labels, and hanging and regular file folders. Here are the criteria for your color-coding choices:

- **Hanging file tabs** are the most critical place for color. As signals for your main file categories, these tabs need to be easy to see, and when left white become nearly invisible against manila files.

- **File labels** can also be colored for quick identification of the file itself. If you use manila file folders, do use colored labels for quick spotting in a manila sea. Match the color of the label to the hanging file tab.

- **Colored file folders** can be used together with or as an alternative to colored labels. Their advantage is that the big block of color is easier to pick out on your desk or in your briefcase than the thin strip of color on a manila file label.

    Another benefit of colored folders is that you can use white labels on all your files, so you can run full sheets through the printer and don't have to stock so many colors. The downside: Colored folders are more expensive.

- **Colored hanging folders** are fine, but because they never come out of the drawer they're really not necessary. Standard green will do.

Now that you know where color can go, use different hues to distinguish between categories. Whether you think of applying color as chromatic classification or a rainbow of responsibilities, color adds quick-look order to your files.

Though color is a powerful classifying tool, it can fragment your file system when overused. Choose a new color when a large group can be segmented from the rest of the files — say, more than half a drawer. Otherwise, unite on sight by sticking with a single shade.

Save yourself great grief by thinking all the way through your classification and color system before you start labeling. Having spent hours pulling off red labels and redoing them on blue when clients changed their minds midstream, I can assure you that you don't want this aggravation. Write a list with every category, subcategory, and corresponding color before you make your first label. If you're going to change your whole system, do one color, or even one category, at a time. Don't try to do it all in one day. (See more about scheduling chunks in Chapter 18.)

Mastering Your Mail

Repeat this mantra: *I am the master of my mail.* Many people allow the unpredictable arrival of information from the outside world to run and sometimes ruin their day. To counter this effect, I recommend a course of mail empowerment.

First understand that mail time is not when the mail comes — mail time is when you choose. The best strategy is to set an off-peak time for opening mail every day and stick to it as much as possible. Whether e-mail or snail mail, remember that the mail doesn't control you. You control the mail.

Smooth mail management calls for quickly sorting and whisking each item to the appropriate file or to the trash, and you can take your first pass without even opening an envelope. R-A-P-I-D is the road to a fast first response to the mail.

R-A-P-I-D response to incoming mail

First assemble your mail-processing tools: a letter opener (why risk paper cuts?), your calendar/organizer, a highlighter, and date stamp if you use one. Take your stack of unopened envelopes and sort your mail into the following five piles.

- **Read:** Newsletters, catalogs, reports.
- **Attend:** Notices for meetings, workshops, conferences, performances, events, store sales.
- **Pay:** Bills (window envelopes are a clue).
- **Important:** Memos, correspondence, and anything you can't identify (presume important until proven otherwise).
- **Dump:** Junk — ads, solicitations, political flyers, and so on. Don't even open these. Just toss.

If one of the pieces of mail is another invitation for a charge card you don't want, rip right through the unopened envelope before throwing it away. This prevents someone else from signing the form, saying you moved, and running up a tab on your dime.

When you complete your initial sort, open one pile at a time, highlighting important information and entering dates in your calendar as you go. Apply the five W-A-S-T-E questions to each piece and toss what doesn't pass the test. Finally take the survivors and a) delegate them to your staff, b) place in your Take Action File, or c) file in your permanent system.

See Chapter 17 for tips on handling e-mail — the same concept with a few cyber twists.

Reduce incoming mail by inviting less into your life: Pare down your subscriptions to the bare essentials. Tell companies not to sell your name. Delete yourself from existing lists by sending a request including your full name, in all its variations and spellings, and your address to: Mail Preference Service, Direct Marketing Association, P.O. Box 9008, Farmingdale, NY 11735-9008.

Outgoing mail

Thankfully, controlling the mail you send is easier than what you receive. Here are principles for dispatching the outgoing post:

- ✔ **Signed, sealed, delivered.** If you have a mailroom, the staff there can probably seal your envelopes by machine. Others will want a bottle or tube sponge moistener to seal envelopes without wearing out your tongue. Don't press too hard, or you can wash away the glue. If that happens, let the envelope dry, then seal it up with a glue stick.

- ✔ **Address for success.** Print a full page of address labels for each frequent mail recipient on your list.

- ✔ **Express for success.** Order airbills from your overnight carrier preprinted with your account information. Make an entry in your address card file or contact program with pick-up phone numbers, drop-off locations, and deadlines for express service.

- ✔ **Wrap it up.** Stock all the envelope sizes and types you need for normal mail traffic, including bubble wraps for breakables.

  One of the best delivery bargains going is the postal service's Priority Mail envelope, which invites you to stuff as much paper as you can fit into it and pay a flat rate for up to two pounds.

- ✔ **Pay postage without pain.** Why stand in line at the post office when you can buy stamps by mail and get a free USPS chart that breaks postal charges down by the ounce? A postal scale will give you a precise assessment if you stamp by hand; any business with much mail volume can buy a postal meter or use the electronic stamps available over the Internet.

The Take Action File: The Tickler Turns Proactive

So far I discussed files that sit around waiting to be used but there's another, more active kind. Tickler files are so named because they remind you, or tickle your memory, that you have to *do* something. Like being tickled, it's sort of fun for a minute — "oh yeah, glad I remembered *that*!" but you're also motivated to make it stop by completing the called-for task.

Traditional tickler files generally take the form of 7- or 31- day systems, both of them flawed. In the weekly setup, you have a file for each day of the week. The usual result is that you spend too much time moving Monday's unattended papers to Tuesday's file, Tuesday's to Wednesday, and so on until Saturday holds the whole week's worth. You've wasted valuable time transferring things and haven't gotten much done.

The monthly system contains 31 folders for the days of the month, plus another twelve for each month of the year. You file papers by the day for the current month and by the month for upcoming items. Here's the problem: On the fourth of the month, you file a memo in the 25th. On the tenth, somebody calls about a point on the memo, and you have to remember what day you filed it under. Chances are you'll end up searching all the way from the tenth to the 25th — 15 folders' worth — before you find the memo, wasting your time and your caller's.

The inefficiencies of popular tickler systems inspired me to create the Take Action File. A category-driven system that eliminates all that date-related shuffling and searching, the Take Action File groups tasks by like type and keeps everything you need to do within logical fingertip reach. Whether at work or at home, the system is designed to turn information flow into targeted actions.

The Take Action File system consists of twelve different categories, ten of which hold the current month's action items, with the eleventh for upcoming months and the twelfth for your File Index. Note that the category titles are verbs, not the nouns you use for other files, to keep action foremost in your mind. Take a look at Table 16-4 to get familiar with the Take Action File.

Table 16-4	The Take Action File System	
Category	*Contents*	*How To*
To Attend	Meeting notices, workshops, invitations	Enter dates in calendar (no details). File first in To Call or To Pay to make reservations, buy tickets, then in To Attend in chronological order.
To Call	Running list of calls/ phone messages	See Chapter 19 about time management for the phone.
To Copy	Originals to copy	Save copier trips by doing it in batches.
To Discuss	Memos and/or running list of discussion topics for meetings and phone calls (what and with whom)	Create separate files for each person who directly reports to you and your boss

(continued)

Table 16-4 *(continued)*

Category	Contents	How To
To Do	Running list and/or hard copies or papers	The catchall for anything not covered in other categories.
To Enter	Meeting notes, receipts, business cards, and so on	Whatever needs to be entered on the computer.
To Pay	Bills (and envelopes), bank statements to balance	Set up a schedule and pay as many as possible at a time.
To Buy	Shopping lists, catalog pages, and so on	Tear out page or make a running list.
To Read	Newsletters, memos, articles, and so on (pull out and toss the rest)	Group similar topics together. Carry file to meetings, appointments, anywhere you have to wait. For entire magazines, journals, and catalogs you haven't scanned yet, mark the month and year clearly in the upper right-hand corner and place them in a separate To Read magazine holder.
To Write	Correspondence, reports, memos, letters	Enter items and deadlines on Master List before filing (see Chapter 18).
12 Months	Action items for upcoming months	Label folders for each month and put them all in a hanging file. At month's end, sort items for the next month and file into preceding categories.
File Index	List of your current files	Use as a checklist to see if you already have a file made.

The great project file debate

You probably know what happens when To Do items turn into actual doing: some of them grow beyond a few pieces of paper and need their own project file. In theory, filing current project files in your permanent system under the appropriate category is most efficient, especially if you share them with others. However, some people work so frequently with current project files that keeping them in the drawer closest at hand makes sense. If that's the case for you, designate a project drawer within fingertip reach. Place your Take Action Files in front and your Project Files in a separate section behind. As projects are completed, purge the files for unnecessary papers, then transfer them to your permanent system.

Your Take Action files should get the most traffic of any in your system, so keep them in the front of your closest file drawer. If you're very visual, try a desktop holder such as the Decoflex (Figure 16-3) to keep your to-do items in view.

Those keeping score may have noticed that there's no *To Sign* or *To File* in the Take Action File system. Why? Items requiring your signature should be processed right away. If for some reason you run out of time, put them in your To Do File. And I'd like to eliminate the phrase "to file" from everyone's vocabulary. Just do it now! If you have an assistant who does your filing for you, use a special tray, located on your credenza or nearby surface, for this purpose only.

Figure 16-3:
The Decoflex keeps the Take Action File in easy reach.

In the Information Age, those who efficiently manage the abundance of communications and news are likely to emerge as the most productive and powerful. By putting information in its place, you can keep cutting-edge knowledge at your fingertips and clutter out of your life. Let it flow!

Chapter 17

Cyberorganization: The Next Frontier

• •

In This Chapter

▶ Choosing the right technology for the task

▶ Organizing the phone, fax, and features

▶ Keeping your computer cleaned up

▶ Managing electronic files and e-mail

▶ Making the most of your Internet connection

▶ How being wired can save you time and money

• •

*F*irst there was the telephone. Next came the computer. Then the two got together, and the information race was on. The world is wired, and systematic people are generally the winners in the technology steeplechase. Whatever your level of electronic expertise, when you organize your virtual life, you can find yourself wired for success.

This chapter is designed to help you handle everything that comes in and goes out over the wires. You can discover strategies to leverage technology at home, at the office, on the road — anywhere information flows in bits and bytes.

Choosing Your Communication Mode

With so many wired ways now available to converse, send and receive messages, transfer documents and data — to communicate — half the organizational battle is in choosing the most effective and efficient one for the circumstance. An e-mail may be cheaper than a long-distance telephone call but not if you spend too much valuable time writing out a delicate point that may be handled better live, or going back and forth to reach a decision. A fax is great for getting a document on somebody's desk fast, but not nearly as efficient as e-mailing the file if the recipient needs to edit it. Table 17-1 summarizes which wires are best for various types of tasks to help you choose your communicative mode fast.

Table 17-1	Which Wire?
Method	*Best Use*
Phone	Reaching a decision or making a plan
	Getting an immediate answer
	Delivering a quick message to voice mail when you know the recipient won't answer
	Reaching an individual
Video conference or broadcast	Sharing information and discussing issues among a group of people across distance
	Teaching/distance learning
Fax	Conveying technical information that is easier to read than hear
	Important communications requiring documentation
	Broadcasting a document to a group of recipients who don't all have e-mail
E-mail	Quick, paperless, one-way communications
	Broadcasting information to a group of recipients
	Sending a file that the user will edit or use electronically

Maximizing Wired Efficiency

Once you decide on the device, what can you connect it with? The type of your wired connections is becoming an increasingly important component of time management on the job and at home. *Bandwidth* is what tech-savvy people call the capacity of a line to transmit and receive data. Generally, the bigger the bandwidth of a line, the faster and more reliably information flows through it. There are specialists whose sole job is matching bandwidth to people's and systems' needs because bandwidth costs money. Fortunately, if you deal with less than a massive computer system, you can settle for deciding how many lines you need, and how big they can be.

Divide communication lines by the way that you use them. If you work for a corporation, someone else has taken care of this at the office. At home or in a small business setting, the wires you need may include

✔ Separate phone lines for business and personal use. No client or associate wants to talk to your 3-year-old.

✔ One to two more lines for fax and Internet use. You may double up Internet access with your phone or fax line if traffic on either is light. With Web-based services available to receive phone calls and faxes while you're online, you can multitask with a single wire and catch every contact as it comes. But beware: This may drive you crazy fast if you spend much of your time online and get many calls.

I don't recommend sharing the phone line with the fax unless you have a DSL connection, because there's no way to take a call while you send or receive a fax. If you only fax occasionally and don't care, get an answering machine or voice mail that can automatically route incoming faxes.

✔ A separate kids' line if you have some good talkers in the family.

Paper or Electronic: A File Is a File

Whether the file comes to you by snail mail or e-mail, pops out of your printer or sits on your hard drive, a file is a file, and should be evaluated and organized accordingly. Your electronic files — e-mail, word processing, graphics, sound clips, spreadsheets, checkbooks, all the files on your computer — should mirror the paper file system explained in Chapter 16. If you haven't read that chapter yet, I recommend you do so now. Following is a rundown of information flow principles as they pertain to electronic files.

Wasting not thy disk space

Computer files you don't need are just as detrimental to your performance and peace as piles of useless papers. Excess computer files crowd the screen, making it harder to find the file you want. They fool you into opening them thinking that they're something else. Worst of all, they waste disk space.

Nobody knows the value of bytes better than the administrators of corporate computer networks, whose job requires allocating scarce storage space among many network functions to achieve maximum companywide efficiency. You know the jokes you're storing? The ancient reports and memos? Multiply all the unnecessary files on your computer by the 100, 1,000, or 10,000 employees of your company, and the result represents a big chunk of costly resources going to waste.

Computer files can be archived much more space-efficiently than paper files — so when in doubt about whether to save something, simply move the file off your hard drive and onto a backup. Send anything you haven't used in a year to the trash.

Filtering file flow: Deciding what to save

Your decision whether to save or delete a file can help keep useful info at your fingertips or drag you and your computer down with stuff you don't need. To avoid the latter scenario later, you need to filter information by asking yourself some essential questions about the file in question. Apply the five W-A-S-T-E questions to every computer file you save, and stay as clear electronically as you aim to be in the hard-copy world. (See Chapter 16 for more on using W-A-S-T-E to decide what to keep and what to throw away.)

- ✔ **Is it worthwhile?** Keep an e-mail engaging your services and naming the terms. Toss an Internet joke. If you're going to forward it, do so right away and delete it before closing.

- ✔ **Will I use the file again?** Keep a handout for a presentation you may give again. Toss e-mail you answered. Note any follow-ups in your Take Action File; move the mail to the appropriate folder if you need it for official records.

- ✔ **Can I easily find it somewhere else?** Keep all essential computer documentation. Have you ever tried to get a major software maker on the phone? Save any information that can keep you out of the *hold* queue as well as paper and electronic copies of things you refer to on paper and update frequently — training programs, interoffice telephone lists, address lists, form letters, recipes, and so on. Toss Web site printouts. Bookmark the site so you can easily find it again. Do you have inactive files with printed copies? Decide whether you want to keep the file in paper or electronic form and toss the other one.

✔ **Will anything happen if I toss the file?** Keep e-mails with relevant information for a current project, and documents required by your retention schedule or that can be used again — form letters, templates, overhead presentations, and so on. Toss e-mails that have been handled, pertain to closed projects, or have no value, as well as previous drafts of a document after it's been submitted, approved, or published.

✔ **Do I need the entire item?** Keep e-mails with important information or documentation. (Move them to file folders in your system.) Toss unnecessary information from e-mails: headers, footers, signature lines, threads, a copy of your original e-mail, and unimportant portions of text.

Q: What's the best time to purge your e-mail? A: When you read it. Computer files provide a great clue at cleanup time — the date that shows when you last worked on them. If the file you face is more than a year old and your retention schedule allows, send the file to the trash.

We have a winner

Great! You filtered the files by using W-A-S-T-E and you have a few that passed the criteria that you really do need to save. Electronic files may be less physically tangible than paper, but they can still follow the ABC's of filing outlined in the previous chapter. To make sense of cyber files

✔ **Active: Distinguish between active and inactive files.** Use the criteria discussed in Chapter 16 to determine which of your electronic files are active. Inactive files can be moved to a backup medium or purged.

✔ **Basic: Know your basic tools.** The computer provides wonderful organizing tools in the form of filing systems you can manage with a click of the mouse: Explorer in Windows, the desktop for Mac users, and filing cabinets in many e-mail programs. In each of these, you can create folders and subfolders and use them just as you do hanging and file folders in your paper system.

✔ **Classify.** Follow the system in Chapter 16 to classify your electronic files, creating level one folders for main categories and subfolders inside to hold subcategories. Need to go to level three for a sub-subcategory? No problem. A computer loves a classification structure that works like an index.

Just as you file papers according to category rather than how they were produced, arrange your electronic files by subject regardless of what program they come from. For instance, in my . . .*For Dummies* folder I have word-processing, spreadsheet, and e-mail files for this book. Centralizing by subject makes it easier to find and open everything you need to work on a project, as well as to back up new information at the end of the day.

Unfortunately, computers don't currently provide a way to use color in your filing system. However, color is a great tool in word-processing and other documents, where you can use colored type or highlighting to call attention to key areas, edits, or questions. The *track changes* function employs color to show text that's been changed since the last version. Explore this option if you edit documents with others or like to track your own work.

Wired: Phone, Fax, and the Internet

With your electronic files all cleaned up, you're ready to get back to business. But before you pick up the phone, send a fax, or sign on to the Internet, stop to consider the many ways you can optimize your wired connections. Being organized in the wired world means choosing the right features for your phone. Programming your fax machine for efficient function and tidying up your transaction report tactics. Using the worldwide power of the Internet to save time and facilitate information flow. Following are some ways to a higher-wired IQ.

Old and new ways: The phone

One of the first shots fired in the communications revolution, the phone remains as popular as ever. (Do you doubt me? Take a look around at all the people chatting on their cell phones.) But is a telephone always your best connection? The phone's greatest strength can also be a time-wasting weakness: Calls take place in the present moment whether they work with your schedule and priority list or not. The goal is to take control. There are many means to get there.

- **Assistants/secretaries:** Nice if you can get one, an assistant can screen and prioritize calls, handle those that don't require your personal attention, and take messages. However, if you don't have many calls or extra administrative work for an assistant to do, managing and paying one may cost more time and money than it's worth.

- **Answering machines:** Available in many models with all sorts of features, answering machines enable you to screen incoming messages and don't cost anything after the initial purchase. Because calls can't roll over if you're on the line or someone else is leaving a message, a machine is generally not suitable for anything but the smallest of businesses, but an answering machine can certainly do the job at home. Phone-heavy families may want a machine with multiple mailboxes so you can route messages by recipient.

✔ **Computer voice mail programs:** Essentially an answering machine on your computer, this solution has several snags. The program only works when your computer is on, meaning you have to leave it powered up all night and when you travel to serve as your main message system. If you take messages instead of calls while working on an important project, each incoming call freezes your computer and interrupts your workflow. Some programs have low sampling rates and hence poor sound quality. If you also have an answering machine on the line and leave both on by mistake, they can cancel each other out.

The main advantage of these programs is that they usually include fax capabilities, which are discussed later in the chapter.

✔ **Voice mail:** Internal to the phone system, in your office or with your local carrier, voice mail can receive messages when you're on the line, away from the phone, or receiving another message, and it's the way to go if you don't want to miss a contact. The disadvantage is that you can't selectively pick up important or long-distance calls when you're busy or on another line. What if your boss or a key client from Singapore calls while you discuss tonight's dinner menu with your spouse?

✔ **Caller identification:** An electronic device that displays the phone number of incoming calls can help you decide what calls to take. If you're on the line, calls will flash on the display as they roll over to voice mail. Caller ID can be helpful if you have no other way to screen calls, but it's still an interruption and won't help you identify people calling from blocked numbers or phones other than their own.

✔ **Call waiting:** If you're on a call and another call comes in, an electronic beep notifies you of the second call. A tap to the receiver enables you to put the first call on hold and pick up call number two.

I consider call waiting an interruption that can decrease the productivity of a call, and it's rude. Instead of call waiting, let calls roll to voice mail when you're on the line, and then return them at your convenience. Get caller ID if you need to watch for important ones, so you're only rude when it counts. If you juggle business and personal calls, do not pass go: Get a second line.

✔ **Pagers:** A pager provides ultimate control over incoming calls, though using one means you have to call everyone back on your own dime. A pager/voice mail is the most powerful version, as the page notifies you of the caller's number the second the call comes in, and you can then check the message to see what the call's about. Many highly mobile people, such as sales reps and consultants, use a pager with voice mail and a cellular phone as their primary contact system.

✔ **Cordless phones:** Going cordless is great for phone-hounds who like to get things done while they gab. Though I don't recommend multitasking while doing business on the phone, why not repot a plant or pick up toys while talking with Mom? The hardcore may want a headset to free up your hands and get the crick out of your neck.

✔ **Cellular phones:** Answer honestly: Is your cell phone a tool or a toy? Mobile phones are appropriate for those who have frequent out-of-the-office engagements; for safety when driving at night or in bad weather; and for parents who want to be reachable for children's emergencies.

✔ **Speakerphones:** An often misused but potentially valuable tool, a speakerphone is key for phone meetings involving multiple people on that end of the line. However, the speaker can alienate people in one-on-one conversations and impinge upon privacy, so if you're looking for hands-free operation, use a headset instead.

Fill yourself in on how to use the phone most efficiently at work and in your life by flipping to Chapter 19 on time management.

Just the fax, please: Fax machines

The facsimile machine is an excellent way to get a piece of paper into someone else's view fast, or vice versa. From ordering products — why sit on hold or navigate the Internet when you can fax off an order sheet in seconds? — to transmitting business documents to receiving the e-ticket for the plane flight you just booked, the fax is such an efficient friend that it's not just for the office anymore.

Equipment options and extras

Most fax machines can make copies, which is a great convenience for the occasional page or two. Some can also double as scanners. Consider a fax with plain paper output if you receive many faxes, as heat-sensitive paper is fragile, crumples easily, and is difficult to run through the fax machine if you need to resend something you receive.

Fax programs for the computer are good if most of your outgoing faxes come from files on your computer. Sending them directly via a program that works over your modem can save lots of time and trees. You also get plain-paper output by printing faxes you receive on your computer printer. However, you have to have your computer on to send or receive anything, and you can only send paper by scanning it in — an extra, time-wasting step.

For heavy faxers, a stand-alone machine can keep the computer free for other uses and accommodate nonelectronic documents. You may still use a program to send electronic files. Set it up not to receive incoming faxes if you'd like those routed to the machine instead.

Programming your fax machine

Use the program function to enter your name or company name, fax, and phone number into the fax machine. This header will print on each page of your outgoing faxes and save the need to put a cover sheet on many. You can also program frequently faxed numbers and identify them by the recipient's name.

If programming a VCR is a challenge, entering data into a fax machine without the instruction manual requires a miracle, so make sure you always have the directions at hand.

Broadcasting

The ability to broadcast, or send the same information to a group of people, is one of the chief benefits of the Information Age, and your fax machine can broadcast for you. Use the option to create distribution lists for groups of people you routinely fax to, so you can send multiple transmissions with the push of one button. Don't abuse this ability by *spamming,* or broadcasting unsolicited faxes. Spamming is illegal in some states and annoying in all.

Did they get it?: Those darn reports!

Fax transmission can seem ephemeral — did it go? Did they get it? Transaction reports can provide a useful record. Reports also take time and paper every time they print, so you don't want to generate them pointlessly. I prefer to program the machine to print a report only when a fax doesn't go through, so I can take action on the errors and save sorting through the rest. There are times when a record of your outgoing fax is essential — to prove that you did submit a counteroffer on Thursday, for instance, or complied with a deadline. In these cases, print. You can also opt to print a list of the last 20 or 30 messages sent, to double-check against your To Do List or use as accounting to charge faxes to clients.

The Internet and e-mail

The Internet, the mother of all wires, has transformed the world. With the ability to transmit messages and data instantly, deliver information anytime, anywhere, and connect people in real time all around the globe, the Internet has the potential to be the modern age's greatest organizational asset. But if you have a mess of old e-mail in your incoming queue or piles of printouts on your desk; if you recently wasted an hour on an unsuccessful Web search, you know that the Internet can also eat time and cause physical and electronic clutter. Cyberspace demands advanced organizing systems.

Organizing your Internet use and using the Internet to get organized is a fun and fruitful effort for tech heads and newbies alike. With the reach of the World Wide Web and the portability of laptops and palm-held units, the computer has taken fingertip management to a whole new level. Here are some ways you may not have thought of to use the Internet to make your life easier and save time and money:

✔ Do your banking and pay bills online.

✔ Stay up-to-the-minute on financial news with online news services.

✔ Buy and sell stock with online brokers.

✔ Search for the best available prices on products from electronics to cars.

✔ Buy and print electronic stamps.

✔ Scan the card catalogs of the world's leading libraries.

✔ Sign on to the Web and send predesigned customizable cards for free. Use a reminder service to prompt you on birthdays and anniversaries.

✔ Put up a Web site for personal or business use. You can create a simple one yourself using shareware. Some Internet service providers host sites for free if you subscribe or allow them to post advertising.

✔ Chat online with long-distance family and friends to save yourself the phone bill.

✔ Compare airfares, buy tickets, make hotel and car reservations, and get travel and tourist information for destinations all over the world at online travel sites.

✔ Create and print a roadmap customized to your trip at many map sites on the Web.

✔ Create your own custom daily news report from the country's leading sources at various Web news sites.

Surfing: Some tips and tricks

The Internet contains countless resources for productive work, personal enrichment, and efficient shopping, but how on earth do you find them fast? Anyone who's been on a futile search, spent hours flipping through irrelevant sites, or simply been caught up in a chat or game knows that the Internet can waste time like crazy. Your organizing challenge: To use the technology to put time on your side. Here are the ways to do it:

✔ **Learn to navigate.** You wouldn't drive a car without learning how, so why surf the information superhighway without a license? A small amount of time invested in learning Internet skills can significantly increase the speed and decrease the stress of surfing the Net.

Explore different search engines and discover their relative strengths, which can vary considerably.

Discover search techniques, such as enclosing words in quotes to keep them in order, or using a plus sign between words to indicate they should all appear in a target document, to narrow your results.

See *The Internet for Dummies,* 7th Edition, by Levine, Levine-Young, and Baroudi (IDG Books Worldwide, Inc.) for a one-stop guide to surfing skills.

✔ **Bookmark the spot.** Use the bookmark function to store links to favorite or most frequently visited sites. These can often be organized into folders and subfolders, which you can set up by category such as any other filing system.

✔ **Surf at off-peak times** — midnight to 5 a.m. Pacific Standard Time — to speed your progress.

✔ **Set a time limit** before you sign on to keep you from surfing, shopping, or chatting longer than you intend. A desktop or watch alarm can alert you when your time is up.

Reading e-mail

Many people are now so e-mail reliant that they can't remember how they communicated before. The ability to send an instant message anywhere in the world for free (or almost) enables people to chat more than ever before. Need proof? Just look in your incoming queue.

E-mail is mail, and you need to manage notes delivered from cyberspace just as rigorously as the paper the postal carrier brings. Refer back to Chapter 16 for general mail-handling principles. Apply them, along with the following electronic refinements.

Read e-mail during off-peak times. If the beginning of the day counts as peak for you, scan the subject lines of new mail and read only those that pertain to important projects on today's To Do List. Leave the rest for later.

Junk mail is junk, whether it's the latest table of contents of a journal you don't care about or a joke from your beloved brother. To save yourself the time of reading junk mail, remove your name from mailing lists by following unsubscribe directions and politely asking friends, family, and colleagues to take you off their mass circulation lists. Toss the junk you do receive without stopping to open it.

Why not to save your Web site printouts

In the Information Age, knowledge gets stale quickly. Facts, figures, directions, and descriptions are constantly changing, and the Internet keeps updates close at hand. Today's economic statistics may be of interest today, but there will be a new set by tomorrow. Accumulating articles on the real estate market now is unnecessary if you're not planning to buy a home for another year. Use the right-now rule to access knowledge you need today, and bookmark the rest for later.

Move each e-mail and attachment you opt to keep (after it's passed the W-A-S-T-E test) out of the incoming queue and into the appropriate folder in your main filing system. *Exception:* Keep e-mails you'll respond to shortly and then delete in the incoming queue. There's no sense wasting time moving things that are going to be tossed. Items you only use online, such as instructions for listservs or a photo or poem you're saving to send on Mother's Day can also be kept by category in your e-mail filing cabinet.

Depending upon your programs, you can often directly open e-mail in your word-processing application. If you can't, cut and paste each e-mail you want to save into a word-processing document so you can open the document without toggling programs or signing on.

If you like to keep a few jokes or cartoons on hand to lighten your day, start a separate Humor/Inspiration folder — not random files on your desktop, but a folder all its own — in your computer filing system and limit its contents.

Writing e-mail

Dashing off a note is often faster than making a phone call, but how much time do you spend writing e-mails each day? It may be considerable, so make sure you're making best use of the time with some tips for writing e-mail that can zip you along at Internet speed.

- ✔ **Think first.** Before you spend precious time writing e-mail, ask yourself whether e-mail is actually the most efficient way to accomplish the task. The answer is probably yes if you only need to write a few lines to confirm a meeting, while setting one up from scratch may be better done by phone.

- ✔ **Auto-address.** Use an e-mail address book to store frequently used addresses and set up distribution groups. Some contact-management programs can interface with e-mail programs, enabling you to store all contact information in one place. If yours does this, use it.

- ✔ **Name it.** Use the subject line to provide your recipient with the same clues you'd want to receive while scanning your incoming queue. Change the subject heading for responses that vary significantly from the original topic.

- ✔ **Quote.** Use partial quotes to put responses in context. Receiving an e-mail that says "Okay" when you don't remember what you originally asked can be the ultimate senior moment. To quote key words in an incoming e-mail for inclusion in your response, highlight them before you hit the *Reply* button. Don't waste your reader's time and space by quoting the whole message if it's not completely relevant to your response.

✔ **Attach.** Use attachments to send long letters, working documents, or files from other applications. In the body of the e-mail, note the attachment and what it contains. Receiving unreadable attachments wastes everyone's time, so check that your recipient has the right program and version before sending. Most programs let you save your file as an earlier version if necessary. Some people can't open multiple attachments, so when in doubt, attach each file to a separate e-mail.

Be wary of opening attachments you're not expecting. Computer viruses lurk in unexpected attachments! Because people you know can pass them along unaware, keep up with current viruses and consult a knowledgeable Web site when in doubt.

✔ **Sign here.** Create signatures in your e-mail program to automatically insert your name and contact information at the bottom of each mail that you write. You can set up different signatures appropriate for various uses. You can even add a tag line to describe or promote your business.

✔ **Don't file.** If your e-mail program has an auto-file function that automatically saves a copy of every mail you send, turn the function off. Each time you send an e-mail, ask yourself whether you really need to keep a copy, and skip saving those you don't, which is probably most of the time.

See Chapter 20 on organizing your personal time and for more on using the Internet for cybershopping and services.

Learning Control: The Computer

Desktop, filing system, and mailbox all in one, the computer is one of the coolest tools around when you have it under control. Let the computer get the upper hand, however, and a twenty-first-century nightmare could follow. As an important component of your productivity equation, your computer is the place where getting organized can pay off in spades.

Electronic mail leaves a trail

Courts have ruled that electronic mail counts as legal evidence, so no matter how casual the context may seem, be careful what you say. Furthermore, many e-mails are archived on larger systems even after you delete them from your drive, and may be read by anyone from network administrators to your or the recipient's bosses. Treat this advanced communication mode with respect, and don't say anything you wouldn't say out loud, in the office, with co-workers looking on.

Maximizing your computer savvy

Whether you shop the Web, word process, or create a complex database, you can maximize the efficiency of all your computer work by following four basic steps: learn, save, back up, and clean up.

1. **Learn** the application or procedure you're using. How many hours have you spent pulling down toolbars looking for a function or trying to undo something you did wrong? Guesswork wastes time, so learn the task before you begin. Depending upon your resources and preferred learning style, try training manuals, tech support people, self-tutorials that come with programs, ...*For Dummies* books, courses at computer stores, schools, and colleges, or a personal tutor or trainer.

2. **Save** your work frequently. It sounds obvious, but though nobody ever sees a power blip or system crash coming, both can and do happen. Most programs allow you to set the time interval for automatic backup of open files. If you do an abundance of intense, important work, set this to be short. Discover how to recover automatic backups after a crash. Then save yourself the trouble by hitting the Save button more often.

Plug all your computer equipment into a high-quality surge protector. Unpredictable electrical events from power surges to a line getting struck by lightning (it happens!) can destroy your equipment and data forever.

3. **Back up** your data regularly. Total system failures, always a fact of cyber-life, are becoming increasingly common as the number of killer viruses multiplies. A nonrecoverable crash can be a complete disaster. If you work for a company with a networked system and a computer department, someone else is probably handling this for you. If not, here are the basics.

   • Choose your backup medium: floppy disk, CD, tape, or backup drive. Anyone with a floppy drive can use a diskette; the rest require more specialized hardware but offer more storage space.

   • Most people are best served to back up new data daily and make a master copy of the entire hard drive on a regular basis — usually weekly or monthly, depending upon the volume and critical nature of your work. Backup programs allow you to choose the frequency of archiving and whether to copy only new data or everything, and then the program does the back up automatically.

   • Keep four sets of backup: daily, current master, most recent past master, and a blank set for the next one. Rotate so that you can reuse your backup media.

   • Store a copy of your current master offsite — a safe deposit box, your sister's house in another state, or a records storage service — to protect against local disaster — fire, flood, theft, earthquake, and so on.

4. **Clean up** your computer, which makes messes you can't even see. From viruses to old programs to all the fragments of data created by editing files, a hard disk can get clogged quicker than a kitchen sink. Not to worry; cyberhelp is here in the form of programs and procedures designed to clean up your act.

- **Anti-virus.** With today's high-achieving hackers, you need an anti-virus program to keep your computer inoculated against infection. The best programs post upgrades on the Web to fight the latest scourge.

- **Scan and defrag.** Most operating systems come with two disk-maintenance programs. The *scan* program looks for and corrects disk errors, while the *defrag* program consists of rewriting all your edits on a file into a single location.

- **Uninstall.** When you're done with a program, don't just delete it; uninstall instead. Many programs have a multitude of leech-like attachments that can glom onto other system parts and gradually slow your computer down. Uninstalling cleans these out and helps keep you up to speed.

Other cool and quick tasks

What's the payoff of the savvy computer operations I just described? Quick, efficient work is one. A stress-free cyberexperience is another. And here are several other ideas for leveraging computer power in your daily life:

- Store and organize phone numbers and addresses in a database. Let your modem do the dialing and your printer do the labeling!

- Manage your time with calendar programs that offer daily to-do lists and meeting alarms.

- Manage personal or business finances, from tracking accounts payable and receivable to writing checks and invoices and exporting the data to a tax program at year's end, with an accounting-specific program.

- Do your taxes and file your tax returns by modem with programs suited to the job.

- Create grocery and other shopping lists in word processing.

- Make your own greeting cards with a graphics or photo program.

- Publish a newsletter, flyer, or announcement, complete with pro layout and graphics, with a desktop-publishing program. Send it directly by e-mail if you like.

✔ Make overhead slides simply by filling in the preexisting templates in presentation programs.

✔ Archive photos on CD or the Web, where you can give friends and family a code to view them. Use programs from word processing to graphics to specialized photo applications to place, play with, and touch up your photos in a variety of formats.

✔ Store, organize, and analyze your recipes with culinary programs, or toss all the old ones and search the Web for new recipes when you're ready to cook.

Making Data Management Easy

Everybody needs easy access to facts in many aspects of business and personal life. Facts are even more useful when you can store, sort, and use them efficiently, and these are just the sorts of tasks electronic technology does especially well. Data is your friend, and cyberorganization can tailor data to your needs.

Tables: Think like a grid

Tic, tac, toe — a table has the column-and-row format you know from the classic game, but you can go beyond three to display all the data you need to see. Easily created in a word-processing program, tables are great at-a-glance tools for categorizing and comparing information. You may use one while house-shopping to list features down the left side and the homes under consideration across the top; to decide what telephone system to purchase for the office; or to draw up a definitive list of laundry loads and settings as described in Chapter 11.

Tables can be sorted by simple criteria (usually alphabetical), but can't calculate numbers or create charts or other output, so stick to word-driven data.

Spreadsheets: Tables that act and do

A spreadsheet is essentially a table that reads numbers and performs operations, so if you want to add or subtract, multiply or divide, or even run a logarithm or employ if-then logic, this is the data-management method for you. With search, sort, and calculating capabilities, a spreadsheet can help you analyze profitability, compare credit card rates, compile statistical results, and more. Spreadsheets can also create graphs and charts from the data you put in them, which is useful for analysis, reports, and presentations.

Whatever your spreadsheet applications program, find out how to format and edit worksheets, create formulas, and search and sort, and you can have the basics in hand.

Databases: Information machines

At heart, a database is a table that performs certain functions on the data inside to produce lists, reports, and responses. A simple database lies behind some contact-management programs, while more complex and customized databases are used to run all aspects of business. Databases useful for daily organizing tasks include

- ✔ Build-your-own databases, from a simple address list to more complex applications for the computer-savvy, that allow you to define your own fields and generate custom reports. Associations use databases to maintain their membership lists, as do many subscription houses, while project managers may use one to track project time and costs. You can also use a database to create periodical indexes, customize customer service, or catalog your CD or wine collection.

- ✔ Contact-management programs that unite name, address, and phone functions with the ability to take notes, track correspondence, and generate meeting and follow-up reminders. Salespeople, lawyers, stockbrokers, accountants, and freelancers are among those well served by such features.

- ✔ Accounting programs that track income and expenses, create invoices, write checks, generate various financial reports, and even interface with tax programs that can figure and file your taxes.

Staying in touch: The concept of contact management

Most people know it's who you know, which is why a concise contact-management system is critical to being wired to the world. There are three primary formats for the classification and storage of contact information: the computer databases discussed here, card files, and address books. My experience has shown that different systems work better depending on how much you correspond by phone and/or mail, what these contacts are meant to accomplish, and your own individual style. The trick is to pick one system and stick with it. Keeping names and numbers in different locations turns every phone call into a mystery to solve. Leave the sleuthing to Sherlock Holmes and centralize!

- ✔ **Computer databases:** If your computer is on all day and you do a large volume of contact-based work, this is probably the way to go. Handheld computers are a variation on the same theme, and can synch up with the program on your main system to keep information current in both places.

- ✔ **Card files (such as Rolodex):** The original modular system is tough to beat for simplicity. Easy to move and toss as they change or become irrelevant, address cards also flip quickly and display all the information you need at a glance. It's easy to keep your file right next to your phone and find the number you need. A few hints:

    - Classify: File friends by name, clients by company, and vendors by subject — all delivery services under D.

    - Color code: Use colored sleeves to identify different groups, such as blue for business, pink for personal friends, and so forth.

    - Glue: Don't staple business cards to Rolodex cards; the staples can catch your fingertips as you flip and they take up extra space too. Use a glue stick instead.

- ✔ **Address book:** A book is handy if you need to take your contact information on the road and don't have a handheld computer or electronic organizer. Most paper organizers come with an address section. When buying yours, look for a three- or six-ring binder with plastic tabs. Don't write on the divider pages, because you can't replace them without replacing the whole book. Instead, stock up on refill pages and toss pages as they become outdated or too messy to read. Transfer any current addresses to a fresh page first.

Whatever your contact system, remember that you should enter information as soon as you receive it so you can throw the original piece of paper away.

If you don't have a database or aren't familiar with how to use one, you can achieve many of the functions you need for basic data management with a spreadsheet.

Balancing Personal or Business Finances

One of the most tangible payoffs of getting organized comes from bringing order to your financial affairs, whether personal or business. Balancing your budget and putting your money in the right place can help beef up your bank account, enhance your peace of mind, and ensure your future. Technology can keep track of the details and even do the math.

Get fiscally organized with four steps even a spendthrift or expense report dropout can follow:

1. **Track your receipts** to see what you spend. For one month, collect receipts for every transaction, from the grocery store to the gas station, restaurants, stores, airlines, utilities, insurance, lawyers, online vendors, office supplies — everything. Be sure to make a note of cash expenses when you don't obtain a receipt for things such as parking, fast food, or taxicabs.

2. **Assess your expenses.** Organize the outflow by creating two forms, monthly and annual — in a word-processing table, or in a spreadsheet or bookkeeping program that can crunch the numbers — to analyze and sum up your expenses. Across the top go categories (some broken down into subcategories), and down the left-hand side runs time — days of the month for a monthly report, or months of the year for an annual.

Budget Expense Categories (and Subcategories)	
Business	*Personal*
Office lease (straight expense or home office percentage)	Mortgage or rent
Utilities (straight expense or home office percentage)	Utilities (electric, gas, water, telephone, garbage)
Benefits (401K, pension, IRA, insurance)	Insurance (auto, life, health, dental, disability)
Payroll	Medical expenses
Taxes (federal, state, sales, payroll, Social Security)	Taxes (federal, state, property, capital gains)
Research and development	Loan and credit card payments
Marketing, advertising, public relations	Financial advisor, brokerage and bank fees
Professional services (accounting, legal)	Service people (lawn and garden, snow, housekeeping, and so on)
Education (CEUs, meetings, memberships)	Education (private, religious, clubs/organizations)
Car (gas, repair, parking)	Car (loan, gas, repair, parking)
Travel (plane, hotel, car/mileage, incidentals)	Travel (plane, hotel, car, incidentals)
Entertainment	Entertainment
Office supplies	Clothes
Equipment	Food
	Child care
	Child support

After you set up this form on the computer, use it for your expense report at work or for accounts payable or yearly expense forms, year-end taxes, or for a home-based business.

After entering your expenses on the form, you can throw away any receipts not needed for tax purposes, expense accounts, warranties, or returns. Home-based businesses, however, should save all receipts.

Remember that anything you buy can prove defective or fall apart. You can protect your purchases by holding on to receipts for three to six months in case of returns. Filing purchase receipts by the month in a small file box with tabbed dividers makes purging the old ones easy.

3. **Assess your income.** Create another form with the 12 months listed down the left-hand side and estimate all your revenues for each month: sales (business) or income (personal), investment earnings, child support, and so on. Use the previous year's tax bracket to estimate the percentage of gross revenues you'll pay in taxes, and subtract that amount from your annual total at the bottom.

4. **Compare the inflow with the outflow.** Subtract your annual expenses from your annual post-tax income. Hopefully the result is positive, leaving you some latitude to save, invest, pay down bills, buy new equipment, or even take a great vacation. If the result is negative, your budget is out of balance and you need to trim expenses, increase revenues, or both.

Keep enough money in savings or easily liquidated money funds to cover 3 to 12 months of expenses. Many people stake more than they realize on receiving their regular salary and anything from a market shift to an unexpected health problem can seriously downsize your income.

See *Personal Finance For Dummies,* 3rd Edition, by Eric Tyson (IDG Books Worldwide, Inc.) for more on balancing your budget and planning your financial future.

Organization is the heart and soul of information technology. The word *system,* from the Greek *set up,* was in the lexicon of organizers long before words came to describe the architecture of cyberspace. Whether you work with your kitchen cupboard or your computer files, systematic thinking can transform your life as radically as the Information Age has revolutionized society. Enjoy the ride!

Part V

Time Management Strategies for Home, Office, and Travel

The 5th Wave   By Rich Tennant

"I don't care how far you traveled, I'm not scheduled to meet with you until _next_ Tuesday."

In this part . . .

Whoever said that time is money was understating the case in the extreme. Time is a part of life itself, and Part V can help you make more of every moment.

No matter how smart or how rich you are, you never get more than twenty-four hours in a day. However, with the right time-management techniques, you can easily add some extra accomplishments or free time. Trim a week off an unwieldy project. Make a plan for five years out, then make your plan come true. The principles in this part can help you put time on your side at work and play to get the most living out of every day, not to mention arrive at meetings early, pick up your kids on time, and make it to the movies at the appointed hour.

Chapter 18

Planning Your Day and Your Life Like a Pro

• •

In This Chapter

▶ Planning for work, play, and personal agendas

▶ Assessing values and setting goals

▶ Keeping track of absolutely everything

▶ Working with your personal rhythms

▶ Rewarding yourself for a job well done

• •

*T*ime isn't money — time is the stuff of life itself. No amount of money in the world can buy a minute or an hour. Don't bother trying to cash in your mutual fund to recover a moment you missed, whether it's a kid's soccer game, a partner's spontaneous kiss, or a meeting that determined the promotions list. Planning means allocating one of life's precious commodities — time — unrecoverable and ever ticking by. Plan today to make tomorrow everything you hope and dream for, or at least to make sure you get the laundry done.

A plan is a road map to get you from here to there — from morning to night, from the beginning to the end of a project, from your first paycheck to a fat investment portfolio. Planning is the same process you go through when you drive to a new destination, though many plans are more important and so promise bigger payoffs than mapping your route across town.

Kevin, a highly skilled airline technician, told me he signed up for my time-management workshop because he worked such long days that his salary broke down to the minimum hourly wage he would earn at McDonalds. Whether you use time-management techniques to make more of your workplace skills, to free up time for fun, to run your household more smoothly, or simply to maximize the moment, the benefits of planning your day are cumulative, so you want to get started now. Planning may sound like work, but guess what? It's a lot less work than not planning. Furthermore, I make plotting your course easy with a four-step method to foresee the future. Just follow four steps with the aid of an easy-to-remember acronym—P-L-A-N— prepare, list, act, and notice.

Carpe diem: Seizing the day

Time management is a deep issue for me that goes beyond the sometimes superficial details of today's To Do List. I lost my mother to cancer when she was just 49 years old. She never heard anyone tease that she was over the hill. She never knew that I married, or met my daughters. She never went to Europe. All the things my mother didn't experience and the time we didn't share make every minute count for me.

Preparing for Your Future

Preparing for the future is the most critical step to time management. If you ever gave a speech unprepared, bolted out of bed remembering that an early morning meeting starts in 20 minutes, or tried to cook a fancy dinner without any forethought, you know that doing things on the fly is difficult, if not impossible. Even if you pull it off, the results are usually sub-par and the process stressful. Extend the implications to big issues such as plotting out your career, having a family, or retiring, and you can see that preparation is the point on which effective time management pivots.

Preparation is the part of planning in which you figure out what you're trying to accomplish and why, who will be involved, and where, when, and how you can do it. To help you through the heavy thinking are my high-performance prep questions, the Five W's plus How. Every time you need a plan, simply ask yourself: Why? What? When? Who? Where? How? The answers can map your path.

Assessing your values

Why? Every plan is driven by values. From deciding on a vacation destination to funding a capital renovation, from buying a home to building a skyscraper, knowing your purpose is the first step to preparing your plan.

Purpose is derived from values, whether held by an individual or an organization — so start your preparation by assessing your values or those of your team, family, or company. Your answer may be quite different depending on whether you're drawing up a five-year plan or starting a single project or job, whether you're deciding on the kids' activities for the year or whether to have kids at all, for instance. You may want to ask yourself some deep personal questions, such as: Is this a time to lead or serve others? Do you want power and the responsibility that comes with it, or would recognition for a job well done please you more? Does financial security take first priority, or is it time to take some creative risks? Take out a piece of paper and write down the top ten values guiding this plan, and then rank them by number. Here's a list to get you started.

- ✔ Accomplishment
- ✔ Adventure
- ✔ Caring
- ✔ Comfort
- ✔ Creativity
- ✔ Excellence
- ✔ Family
- ✔ Financial
- ✔ Friendship
- ✔ Fun
- ✔ Happiness
- ✔ Health
- ✔ Home
- ✔ Honesty
- ✔ Humility
- ✔ Independence
- ✔ Knowledge
- ✔ Leadership
- ✔ Love
- ✔ Loyalty
- ✔ Peace
- ✔ Power
- ✔ Recognition
- ✔ Religion
- ✔ Security
- ✔ Serving others
- ✔ Solitude

✔ Stability

✔ Structure

✔ Trust

✔ Wisdom

Once you understand your value structure, write a mission statement to point you to the plan you want to undertake.

Companies have long used mission statements to guide their strategic planning, and recent years have proven the benefits of clear mission statements for individuals and families too. Mission statements are value-based and answer the question *Why?* Here are a few examples:

✔ To enjoy some quality time with my mate or significant other.

✔ To move the company from a high-risk leadership position to a mid-tier provider with better profit margins.

✔ To have more relaxation time, entertain friends more often, and eat more healthily.

Discovering your goals

What? Now that you know why you're making a plan, what are you trying to accomplish? If values are the planning environment, goals are the product — the carrot, the target, the end result or outcome you're aiming for. Are you getting up and going to work every day without a goal? Your lack of direction may cause you to miss out on opportunities for promotion, personal growth, and a comfortable retirement. Trying to improve your tennis game? You may be much more motivated if you set a goal of having a smash serve by August.

Plain and simple, goals get you what you want. They are the concrete, material, and practical things that you actually do to accomplish the mission. For instance, if your mission is to have the most perfect lawn in the neighborhood, your goals may include planning a watering and fertilization schedule, consulting with lawn and gardening experts or books, and investing in high-quality lawn care tools. If your mission is to be healthier, dropping ten pounds may be on your list of goals. While your mission states your overall vision of how you want to live, your goals are the specific accomplishments that make the mission come true. Table 18-1 shows some goals to go with the mission statements made in the previous section.

Table 18-1	How a Mission Becomes a Goal
Mission	*Goal*
To enjoy some quality time with my mate.	One date night a week and a vacation mixing adventure with unstructured relaxation.
To move the company from a high-risk leadership position to a mid-tier provider with better margins.	Create a new organizational structure, sales initiative, and marketing retool that exploits existing strengths and minimizes risks.
To have more relaxation time in the evening, entertain friends more often, and eat more healthily.	Organize the kitchen setup, meal-planning process, shopping, and cooking.

Goals can be short or long term, and successful people establish both. Goals can come from you or from a parent, boss, or partner. Effective people balance self-generated with external goals. Setting goals enables actual desires to define the way we spend time — the ultimate empowerment.

Quiz question: What's your goal in reading this chapter? How does this chapter fit into a value-driven mission?

Setting goals by the clock

Timing is everything. Start too late on your goals and you won't have time to realize them. Set goals when you're overworked, overwhelmed, tired, or depressed, and chances are they won't represent your truest hopes or best potential. But set your goals when you feel good and can enthusiastically imagine feeling even better, and you're likely to aim high while still being realistic.

Although big goals are often set around New Year's, overindulgence in the dead of dreary winter weather doesn't bring out the best ideas. New Year's resolves are usually forgotten as people hunker down to the hard job of getting through the winter. The lazy, crazy days of summer can undo the best-laid plans just as well. Crisp fall breezes, however, enhance goal-setting; and spring, a time of renewal in nature, tends to get the juices flowing too. Why not renew yourself this spring with a goal-setting session inspired by the spirit of growth?

To set shorter-term goals, such as redoing the kitchen, organizing your desk, or developing an exercise program, choose a time when you feel good and you're not pressured by other projects. Many people like to plan at the end of the month for the next month, or every Sunday evening for the week ahead.

Going away to set your goals

Have you ever noticed how going away on a trip can put everything into perspective? How offsite meetings can spark good ideas and build consensus? Getting out of your usual environment can open up your mind to set goals and you don't have to fly to a beach in Mexico, but feel free if you have the budget!

If the weather's right, a park, forest preserve, or local beach makes a great place for thinking about goals. In a cold or rainy season, try a meditation center, cabin in the woods, library, or museum. Take a sturdy pad so you can perch anywhere, and perhaps a blanket or beach chair. Sit for a bit to clear your mind, and then let the ideas flow.

Nine types of goals

There are nine main areas to consider when thinking about your goals. If you're doing your annual goal session, you may want to cover them all. Working on a specific plan may keep you within a single category. If it's big goal-setting time, write each of the following as headers on separate sheets of paper:

Business

Family

Financial

Home

Mental

Personal

Physical

Social

Spiritual

Goal-setting techniques

Now how to decide on your goals? Choose from the following five techniques, or mix and match.

- **Six months left to live:** The doctor has just told you that you have six months left to live. What would you do with your remaining days? I know it's morbid, but imagining that your life is almost over is a powerful way to focus on what you want. Try to write down what you'd do in that limited time frame.

- **Write your own eulogy:** While you're at it, imagine what you'd like people to say about you after you're gone. Specifically, pick three people — a family member, a friend, and a business or community associate and write what you'd like to hear, with angel ears, at your own funeral. Compare this with what they may say today. The difference constitutes your goals.

✔ **Likes and strengths, dislikes and weaknesses**: A lighter approach to assessing where you are and what you want in life or a specific situation is to divide a piece of paper into four quadrants and answer the following questions:

What do I like/want to do? What do I dislike/not want to do?

What are my strengths? What are my weaknesses?

Things you like to do and strengths are goals or components of goals. Things you don't like to do and weaknesses are goals in a different way: How can you get these out of your life? For instance, if you like details but hate face-to-face meetings with people, you probably don't want to be a recruiter, salesperson, or publicist. Consider accounting, engineering, or research.

Weaknesses can also become goals themselves if you feel correcting them could help you get what you want.

✔ **Brainstorming:** To brainstorm your goals, take a piece of paper and write your mission statement on the top. Now, thinking of ideas as raindrops and letting them fall fast and hard, write down every thought that comes to mind, no matter how ridiculous or trivial it may seem. Let one idea lead to the next or make random leaps. Don't edit or judge. Just write.

After your brainstorming session, you may want to leave your list alone overnight to incubate. Come back the next day with a fresh perspective, review your list, and use it to write your goal or goals.

✔ **Mind mapping:** Similar to brainstorming, mind mapping is an exercise in free association, but here the emphasis is visual. To chart the terrain of your brain, take a piece of unruled paper and turn it sideways (landscape). In the center, write a keyword or phrase from your mission statement and draw a horizontal oval around it. As that idea sparks new ones, draw branches that are spokes radiating out from the central oval and write them down at the branches' ends. Continue branching from any thought that sparks a new one, letting your mind wander and your pen or pencil take you wherever the branches want to go, like a river flowing into tributaries and streams. You can add pictures or symbols if you like — whatever it takes to make your thoughts visible.

See Figure 18-1 for a picture of the mind map that helped me decide to become a professional organizer.

As with your brainstorming list, you may benefit from taking a night away from your mind map, and then coming back and using the map as a guide to writing down your goals.

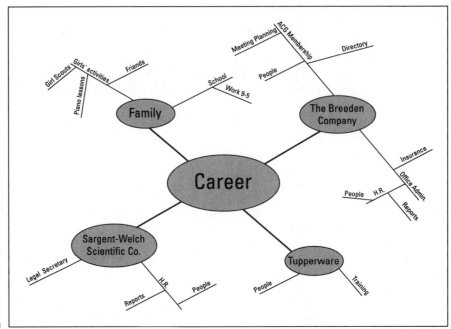

Figure 18-1:
The mind map that helped launch my career in professional organizing. Notice that organizing and people keep showing up in my favorite jobs.

Achieving your goals

How? Now that you know what you want and have considered the ways to get it, you're ready for the most challenging aspect of procuring your goals in the material world: The mental discipline. An optimistic outlook, keeping lists, remaining undeterred by setbacks, and aiming high all require perseverance and discipline. The rest of this chapter provides concrete tools for achieving your goals. You can prepare your mind to follow through on your plan with what I call the Three P's: putting it on paper, picturing the play, and pursuing the peak.

Putting it on paper

Studies have shown that people who write things down accomplish them. To Do lists and daily calendars are living proof of this principle. After completing the goal-setting exercises of your choice, write down the final results to complete your commitment and take a load off your mind.

Where you write your goals is less important than getting the writing done, but do choose a place that works for you. Some people like to use the goals section in their daily planner. Others prefer to devote a small notebook to their goals so they have a record over time. You can also write goals on regular sheets of paper and file them by the nine categories and/or date in a section of your filing system, or do the same thing on the computer. Consider how often you like to consult and add to your goals, and choose a format you can access accordingly.

Picturing the play

If you ever participated in a sport, you probably heard your coach say "picture the play." If a picture is worth a thousand words, visualizing the winning move can be worth its weight in gold.

Imagine yourself living your goal — in color. See the clothes you're wearing, the way the light falls, the people around you. If your goal is to ski down a mountain, include every inch of snow-covered slope, from the top over all the moguls to the final snowplow at the base. If visualizing from scratch leaves you staring at a blank screen, try clipping pictures from magazines that relate to your goals. You can paste them into a book or divide them into files by topic. If you visualize yourself as you want to be, you can ultimately stop seeing and start being.

Pursuing the peak

No one runs half a race, climbs half a mountain, or pulls their money out of a CD halfway to maturity, so never make a halfway goal. Aim for the top.

Sure, there may be failures and setbacks, obstacles to conquer and hurdles to clear as you work for your goal. The trick here is to see them coming. What can you do to get the information or training you need to succeed? Take a class? Read a book? Find a mentor or join a support group?

Remember that electricity wasn't discovered in a day and Abraham Lincoln lost eight political races before attaining the nation's highest office. Reach for the top and don't stop until you get there. The pursuit of the peak sets the winners apart from the losers.

You and your plan participants

Who? Every plan involves people. Who are the players in yours?

The first question is what role you play in relation to this plan. Are you acting as a parent, partner, employee, colleague, caretaker, manager, friend? We all play multiple roles. Your mission statement can guide you to yours.

Next consider whose cooperation and support you need to make this plan work. How can you get key players on your side, whether your mother-in-law, your boss, or the best caterer in town?

Finally, share your goal with someone — a co-worker, friend, or mate — anyone who will make you feel accountable for achieving it. They don't even have to ask you about your progress. Just knowing that they may, can impel you may help down your path. See Chapter 19 for more information on working with others and being accountable.

The planning time frame

When? Time is of the essence in any plan, and part of your preparation is assigning a deadline — one of the most powerful motivators your mind will ever face. Like the guy who runs the race, look for your finish line. Is the quarterly report due on the first of July? Do you need to book a plane ticket in time to take advantage of 30-day advance rates? Would you like to conquer the beginning ski slopes by January so you can move on to intermediate runs before the snow melts?

Once you set a deadline, another question crops up: What are the steps from here to there? That's the time to break down your goal into smaller pieces. You wouldn't eat a whole pie without slicing it up so break your goals into achievable steps, and then put them in order so you simply move from one small task to the next. (The next section on lists will help with this.) Slice your goals into bite-size pieces and succeed.

Breaking goals into subgoals is one of the few times I recommend using sticky notes. Write down each step between you and your goal on sticky notes, and then rearrange them on your desk or tabletop or computer screen until you get a time flow you can work with. You can also take a tip from Hollywood screenwriters and use index cards on a bulletin board to get the same effect.

Finding the right place for your plan

Where? Every plan takes place somewhere. Consider the best setting for yours. If you plan to go back to school, do you want to enroll in the local college so you can continue with your job or family life, or is there a better program somewhere else that offers a more valuable degree? Should your effort to expand your customer base focus on existing or new territories? Can scheduling the kids into summer activities close to home work best, or do you want to try sleepover camp or a visit to faraway relatives?

Keep an open mind as you decide where to pursue your plan. You don't have to vacation in the same place every year. Maybe your meeting would be more effective off-site than in a conference room. If you can't get going on your exercise program at home, a weekend at a spa or ski resort may give you just the jump start you need.

Lists You Can Live By

With your preparation in place, turn all those thoughts into lists to guide your actions. Lists are the primary tool for effective time management, and if you haven't discovered their true power, prepare to be pleasantly surprised.

The Master List

Start with your Master List, a comprehensive reference for everything you need to do, present and future, personal and business. There are three main Master List formats to choose from:

- A 3-x-5 spiral notebook
- The notes section of your paper organizer
- A computer (desktop, laptop, or handheld)

To pick the format that works best for you, consider how you like to arrange and add to your list. The basic concept is that as you think of something new to do, now or later, write it down. This could be a spontaneous thought, or an item you're placing in a Take Action File (see Chapter 16). Note that all Take Action items should go onto your Master List before they go into a file. That's how you ensure that you remember to go back and pull that piece of paper and do whatever it represents.

Some people keep their Master List in the order that things spring to mind. Others prefer to organize their list by category or project, starting a new page for each. Some prefer the portability and easy access of paper over the computer, while others like the power to move things around offered by a computer program. For instance, if you decide you want to plant roses but it's the middle of winter, you can easily create a new seasonal section right where you want it. If an upcoming conference starts out as one entry on your Master List but gradually accumulates additional items, you can move them all into one section to find them fast. Still, if your computer isn't on most of the time, are you really going to boot it up to record your midnight inspiration? If not, paper is preferred.

Whatever form your Master List may take, the important thing is that you write down everything that you need or want to do, in all aspects of your life. It doesn't really have to be organized. That comes next.

The To Do List

The To Do List puts your Master List into action on a daily basis. Again, you can keep this on paper or in a computer. Many organizers, both paper and electronic, have a separate spot for your To Do List. You may like to keep your To Do List there, or simply use your organizer for appointments and put your To Do List on a separate piece of paper. (See Chapter 16 for how the To Do List fits into the Take Action File system.)

Here are the four steps to creating and maintaining your To Do List:

1. **Create your To Do List from the Master List.**

   Today, take about five to ten items from the Master List that you need or want to accomplish tomorrow and write them on your To Do List. Some of these items may be due tomorrow, while others are intermediary steps or parts of longer-term projects. Don't schedule more than you can handle in a single day after you account for appointments. (There's more on choosing items for your To Do List coming up.)

2. **Rewrite your To Do List at the end of each day.**

   The To Do List, a daily tool, needs to be rewritten every day — not just copied over again. Go back to your Master List and see what's most important for tomorrow. Consider your meetings and errands. Keep your To Do List fresh and to the point.

3. **Set realistic time frames.**

   Most people tend to overestimate the time required to complete small jobs and underestimate large ones. With this in mind, set realistic time frames for each task on your list. If you did the job before, how long did it take? If it's a new job, jot down how long the task actually takes when you're done so that you know for next time.

4. **Allow for interruptions and overflow.**

   Things happen so even the most realistic time frames need a cushion to account for interruptions and the unexpected. Double or add a half hour to each task on your list to account for everything from emergencies to phone calls and cappuccino runs.

Acting with Rhythms and Routines

Congratulations! You now have your time-management system in place, but don't kick back and put up your feet. In order to realize the promise of your plan, you must act.

One of the fastest ways to burn up time is to act on impulse, doing whatever, whenever. The point of planning is to empower you to *act with rhythms and routines*.

Getting into the groove: Rhythms

You may have heard of *biorhythms,* the daily cycle of chemical secretions in the body that determines everything from mood to energy levels, alertness, body temperature, and your sleep patterns every single day. People are rhythmic animals but everyone is different. Combine individual biochemistry with personality and past experience, and you get infinite variations on daily peaks and valleys. The highest performers are those who work and live in synch with their own personal ebbs and flows. So get into the rhythm. Get in touch with the groove of your sleep, peak, and pace times.

Sleeping

Start with the basics: The only way to make the most of your waking hours is to get enough sleep. You may not have expected a book on getting organized to address your zzz's and dreams, but science has assessed the productivity price of sleep deprivation, and it is steep! Sleeping more can help you be better organized, while getting your act together can also leave more time for sleep. Ahh.

The problem is that we're so used to shortchanging ourselves on sleep that few people have any clue what their natural rhythms are. To discover yours, consider how you usually wake up in the morning — before the alarm, or only when it rings? If an alarm is required to wake you up, go to bed a half hour earlier tonight to see if you need more sleep. Keep pushing your bedtime back by half-hour intervals until you wake up before the buzzer goes off. If instead you usually awaken before the alarm, try setting it for a half hour earlier or going to bed a half hour later. Keep adjusting in 30-minute increments until you sleep through to the bell. In either case, you're now within a half hour of the amount of sleep you naturally need.

Feeling your best: Peak

Your peaks are the times you feel best during the day — energetic, creative, clear. If you tend to crawl out of bed and drag all morning long but perk up after lunch, you're an afternoon person. P.M. is your peak time. If, on the other hand, you get out of bed or arrive at the office raring to go, you have the rhythms of a morning or A.M. person. Many people have more than one peak. You may shine in both midmorning and late afternoon.

Identifying your peaks is important, because this is when you can really get stuff done. Your peak is the time to take on the hardest projects. Invent the better mousetrap. Make key sales calls, redesign the kitchen, or write the big report.

One of the best ways to leverage the power of peak time is to schedule a chunk of time each day, often known as *the quiet hour,* to devote to important projects. Clear your calendar of meetings and close the door. Forward the phones or have your assistant tell callers you're in a meeting. Alert your staff that you're unavailable for everything but fire alarms. Now go for the flow and see if you don't accomplish as much in an hour of peak quiet time as you do the rest of the day.

Analyzing your pace

Are you a tortoise or a hare? Everyone has different work speeds and though neither slow nor fast is better, knowing your natural pace can help you schedule your time for best performance.

- ✔ **The tortoise:** Moving ahead at a slow-and-steady pace, the tortoise is a highly focused person. You probably prefer to work on one project at a time and complete it before starting another. Multiple projects and too many close deadlines may stress you out. You have an awesome attention span.

- ✔ **The hare:** The hare runs in short bursts, taking breaks and jumping from one thing to another along the way. Enthusiastic, good under pressure, perhaps creative, the hare is a *chunk* person who needs to schedule plenty of changes of scenery for a productive day, and may need some structure and deadlines to stay on track and see things through to completion.

You know the fable about the race between the tortoise and the hare? In my version, they both reach the finish line at the same time because they work with their own natural rhythms.

Imagine two people, a tortoise-type and a hare-type, both have three projects to complete in their daily quiet hour. It's Monday, and all three projects are due on Thursday. Table 18-2 shows you how both people could best use their pace to reach their goal.

Table 18-2	The Tortoise and the Hare: Three Projects in Three Hours	
Day	**Tortoise**	**Hare**
Monday	Project A, 60 minutes	Project A, 20 minutes Project B, 20 minutes Project C, 20 minutes
Tuesday	Project B, 60 minutes	Project B, 20 minutes Project A, 20 minutes Project C, 20 minutes
Wednesday	Project C, 60 minutes	Project C, 20 minutes Project B, 20 minutes Project A, 20 minutes
Thursday	Submit Projects A, B, and C	Submit Projects A, B, and C

Both the hare and the tortoise reached the goal at the same time, but how they got there was totally different. The tortoise completed each project before tackling the next, while the hare broke them up into chunks and juggled the order so each quiet hour session was different. By knowing their rhythms, they used their own pace to get to the same place. Get to know your pace, and you can P-L-A-N accordingly.

- **The thoroughbred:** While you're in the animal kingdom, let me mention a master of pace: the thoroughbred racehorse. Trained to vary its pace depending upon its place and how much of the race has been run, a thoroughbred combines the best of focus and chunk performance styles. There's an animal to emulate!

- To tap the power of thoroughbred pacing for yourself, strive to adjust your pace to suit the current requirements of the project. Is this a time to work fast and furiously, or is slow and steady the way to go? During the long midstretch, try mixing the two performance styles. As a big deadline draws near, allot smaller chunks of time to other items on your To Do List and reserve peak time for this top priority. Remember that racehorses are highly trained — not just to run fast, but to match their pace to the needs of the race.

Routines

A routine is a standard sequence, a set of unchanging steps. Routines are an efficient way to accomplish repeated tasks, and the more you can standardize things you do over and over, from filing a certain report (create standard headings) to cooking dinner (do all your chopping first), the more time you can save. With the right routines, you can get more done while thinking about it less.

You don't need to think much when following a routine. So when do you suppose you should tackle routine tasks? That's right: off-peak time. To make the most of your rhythms, do routine jobs during those minutes or hours when your mind's on autopilot and your energy level has dropped through the floor. Before you know it, the simple reward of getting something done can wake you up and send you toward another peak.

Routines are relative. Everyone has different experience and skills, so while cooking dinner may be a routine for you, making a meal can be a new challenge for a kitchen neophyte. Table 18-3 lists some common repeated tasks, from daily to once or twice a year. Look over these tasks and assess whether they're routine for you and if you can improve upon your routine by streamlining the steps. If you make one small change now, the cumulative time-saving effect can be huge by the end of the month or year.

Table 18-3	The Routine Breakdown	
Daily	*Weekly*	*Seasonal/Annual*
Sort and read mail	Cleaning	Spring/fall clothes cleaning and rotation
Sort and read e-mail	Shopping	Wash windows
Make copies	Garbage removal	Polish silver
Send faxes	Laundry	Clean china cabinet/buffet
Phone calls		Clean upholstery and carpets
Data entry		Family portraits
Filling out forms		Purge toys
Everyday cooking		Car: wax, oil change, tune-up, rotate tires
Personal		

Cleaning up today's projects and creating tomorrow's To Do List are two important routines that you should complete at the end of every day. Just these two daily steps can help you maintain your organization for life.

Putting rhythms and routines to work: Priorities

After you have your rhythms and routines down, prioritize. A priority is a grade of importance plus urgency that determines when you tackle tasks. Here are two ways to assign priorities to your lists:

✔ **Numeric rank:** The most thorough prioritizing system is a numeric rank. You hardly want to rank every item on your Master List every night as you prepare tomorrow's To Do List. But if you already have a rough, priority-based idea of the five to ten items you want to accomplish, simply write them in priority order, ranked from number one to the end.

✔ **A-B-C:** If you prefer not to sweat the small distinctions between priorities, try the simpler A-B-C system for ordering tasks:

- **A:** High priority

- **B:** Medium priority

- **C:** Low priority (but it still needs doing or should get crossed off the list!)

The A-B-C system provides a nice code for your To Do List, so you can see at a glance the grade that you assigned to this task. Is it right for right now?

Priorities don't dictate the *order* in which you should tackle tasks, but they do determine *when*. You can probably guess that you don't just go one to ten, or A to C from the beginning to the end of the day. Match the priority to the productivity of the time slot, for example:

✔ **Peak time:** A's, possibly some B's, and number one to three priorities

✔ **Off-peak time:** B's, C's, and lower priorities such as eight to ten.

Crises can be often averted by the planning techniques discussed in this chapter. For unavoidable surprises — the delayed flight, the upper-management fight, the computer crash — you need a Plan B with options to cover things that may go wrong.

Calendars: Rhythms and routines meet lists

So you prioritized your To Do List according to your rhythms and routines. Now you have to juggle those tasks with commitments from meetings to mom-and-me groups, from doctor's appointments to dinner parties, from baseball games to business lunches. This is where your calendar comes in.

The rule of one

Use one planner/organizer to handle all your commitments, business and personal. Otherwise, you're likely to miss a morning meeting that's not at the office or arrive late at your daughter's afternoon tennis game.

Paper, electronic, or both?

Software products have revolutionized the idea of the electronic organizer by making planning programs mobile. Handheld organizers can stand alone or hot-sync with the calendar program on your desktop computer, and then slip into a purse or pocket for anytime access. Cool. In addition to search-and-sort capabilities, you can set these up to sound alarms, issue reminders, dial the phone, receive e-mail, or access the Internet, all from the palm of your hand. Brands such as Palm Pilot, Casio, Hewlett-Packard, Jornada, and Royal daVinci are on the market as this book goes to press. You get the same functionality but lose the portability by using one of the many computer calendar programs all by itself.

Still, old-fashioned paper has plenty of pluses when it comes to your calendar. First of all, if you're simply not tech-savvy, an electronic organizer can stand between you and your schedule instead of making you more efficient. Visual people often do better with paper, which allows you to see time and lists in a layout rather than as individual items. Paper also makes switching from week to week and month to month easier to plan activities in advance. For this reason, corporate VPs and CEOs who travel and do strategic planning may prefer paper so they can see an entire quarter or year at a time. Speakers, trainers, and meeting planners often need to book events months in advance and need to quickly check two or three dates to decide which one is best. Paper takes the cake here.

You can have the best of both worlds by using a computer program that offers all the advantages of technology but can also print out a paper copy to put in your organizer for portability or easy reference. The drawback is that you have to reprint every time you make a change on the computer, and any additions or changes you make on the paper copy have to be input into the program to keep it up-to-date. If paper is your primary reference point, an electronic-to-paper organizer can become double work fast.

Reading through the rest of this section, which further explores the possibilities of paper formats, may help you decide about the digital divide.

Matching the type to the traffic

Choose from a monthly, weekly, or daily planner depending upon how many commitments you juggle and how you like to view them.

✔ **Monthly** calendar may be just right if your dates are mostly occasional — doctor's appointments, lunch or dinner invites, birthday parties, holidays. Retirees and nonworking moms of young kids are examples of monthly calendar candidates.

✔ **Weekly** is what you want as things become regular — Scout meetings or staff meetings, client outreach, Friday night get-togethers with friends. Many sole proprietors or consultants like to use a weekly calendar because that's how they bid out and block their time.

✔ **Daily** is the bread-and-butter format for busy people. If you delegate or receive assignments, track the activities of several children with diverse interests, handle a daily roster of client calls, or drive your self-owned business forward on a daily basis, schedule one day at a time to facilitate 24-hour flow.

No matter what format you choose, you want to be able to see a month at a time to anticipate traffic jams and competing commitments. Add monthly pages to your calendar so you can take this bird's-eye view.

Exploring your options

These days, buying an organizer is nearly as complicated as buying a car. Decide on the features that can bring you up to speed. This overview of organizer options can help.

✔ **Size:** Just as a compact car maneuvers easily and can park in the tiniest of spaces, a small, pocket-size organizer provides a portability advantage that allows you to tote it anywhere without hassle. But if you have a big family, you know it takes a van or SUV to hold everything you need, and so it goes with planners. If you have many appointments or use the extra sections and features, 8½-x-11 may be the size for you. There are several sizes in between too.

✔ **Fillers and sections:** Add-ons are available such as address/telephone, year-at-a-glance, telephone log, expense record, project planner, notes, goals, maps, reference information, and various clear pockets sized and divided to hold business cards, stamps, and so on. Choose what you can really use, but remember that the more you put in your planner, the bigger and bulkier the results.

✔ **Spiral or rings:** I recommend rings over spiral binding for your organizer so that you can add or remove things as you need them or they become outdated. Do you really need to be toting around last January's calendar in June? Many ring models also contain a moveable ruler that extends past the top of the page to mark the current day. You simply snap the ruler into today's spot so you can immediately open to the right page with a single flip. And who knows when you may want to measure something!

> If you need to see previous appointments, keep your old monthly calendars in your planner and remove the daily pages.
>
> ✔ **To zip or not to zip:** Zippered organizers do hold more and so all too often encourage you to stuff them full of miscellaneous papers that don't belong there. This is an organizer, not a filing system. If you like the zipper and don't mind taking the extra time to unzip every time you open your planner, the rule is that you can keep a pen, pencil, and calculator inside, and no other extras.

How much is your organizer worth to you? How much time would you spend re-creating it? How much money or reputation would you lose by missing the meetings or losing the contact information inside? Put a note in red at the front that says "REWARD: $50 for the return of this organizer" or whatever it's worth to you. Make the amount worth the finder's while, and I bet you'll get it back with a smile.

Using your planner well

All of your decision-making over what planner to use may amount to little unless you find out how to use it to your benefit. Here are the techniques you need.

Four types of time

Many people only think to mark specific things they must do or attend in their calendar but remember, this is a planning tool for your whole life. Use your planner to plot out *all* your time, not just your appointments, meetings, and parties.

There are four types of time to enter on your calendar. Write the items in order by type as you plan your day, week, or month:

> ✔ Specific appointments, meetings, events, deadlines, trips, visitors, and so on
>
> ✔ Quiet time
>
> ✔ Family time
>
> ✔ Personal time

Include other people's commitments if they affect yours — the kids (got to pick them up), your boss, colleagues, or staff (if you need to cover for them), your spouse (when you have to take over carpooling duty, find another escort for an event), or roommates.

Schedules change all the time so keep yours looking neat by using a correction pen to white out cancelled or changed entries. It looks much better than scratch marks and frees up the space to write something in its place. I recommend saving your pencil for other purposes, as lead can smudge and become unreadable on the calendar page.

Marking your time in space

Take advantage of your calendar's visual layout to position events in time. If an appointment or meeting falls in the morning, put it toward the top of the day's box. If you plan to go to the gym after work, write it after all of your workday obligations. The idea is to see the flow of your day, week, or month visually.

Depending upon the format of your planner, you may have hours printed on the page. Use these as a guide, even if you approximate (it may not matter exactly what time you get to the gym, unless you're taking a class). Write or circle precise times.

Color-coding your calendar

Color can help you navigate your filing system (see Chapter 16), and make sense of your schedule in a single glance. Choosing a color for each type of event in your calendar can guide your eye to what you're looking for and help you see how well you're balancing the way you choose to spend time. In Table 18-4 is a suggested color scheme.

Table 18-4	A Color Code for Your Calendar	
Color Pen	**Type of Event**	**How To/Why**
Blue or black	Business (household business if a homemaker)	Think "B" for blue or black and business.
Red	Important events or projects	Quarterly report due date for management, end of contest for a salesperson.
Pink, green, purple, brown, and so on	Personal	Your favorite color! Match it to your Personal file color. Use a different color for each child.

You don't need to carry ten different pens everywhere you go to use color in your calendar. Most personal and children's items can be entered at home, so keep those pens there. If you need to add something while you're out, use your standard blue or black, and then circle it in the right color when you get home. You can also keep a rainbow at your fingertips by carrying a four- or ten-color pen.

Using your To Do List as your planner

If you work primarily on projects, at home or at the office, and don't need to plan a dozen meetings or appointments, this simple To Do List may be all you need besides a monthly appointment calendar. Here are the six categories to make up your list:

- ✔ **To write:** All correspondence, reports, proposals, and so on.
- ✔ **To call:** All your outgoing calls for the day, including phone numbers, so you can simply dial one after the other.
- ✔ **To do:** Everything else that doesn't fall under one of the other five categories.
- ✔ **To attend:** Meetings, appointments, performances, games, including the time.
- ✔ **To go:** Errands such as the grocery store or dry cleaner, the library, a sick friend's house, the copy center, and so forth.
- ✔ **To purchase:** Enter the item and the name of the store so you know just where to go and what to look for when you get there.

Keep the categories in this order on a steno pad or something about 6 inches x 8 inches. Here's what goes under each heading. As always, rewrite your To Do List daily, accounting for new priorities and progress down your path. Table 18-5 provides a picture of using your To Do List as a planner.

Table 18-5	To Do List as Planner
Communication	*Activities*
To Write	To Attend
To Call	To Go (errands)
To Do	To Purchase

Statistics say some days are better than others

Do you ever find yourself saying, "It's just not my day"? If it's a Monday or Friday, statistics are on your side. A staffing firm did a study of productivity by the workday and found that Tuesday took the prize for getting things done, followed by Wednesday, Thursday, and then Monday. Friday, of course, was the least productive, as most people's minds are already out the door by week's end. Monday suffers from an overload of weekend mail and calls from clients or customers, as well as reentry shock. So think *sandwich* when planning your week, and put the meaty stuff in the middle.

Noticing and Rewarding Your Accomplishments

Look at this: You followed a plan (to read this chapter) and achieved your goal (to find out how to plan your day and your life). What now? Do you just go on to the next chapter or get to work on your report or jump to your household chores? No! You need to notice and reward your accomplishment. Smile — it's payback time!

Rewarding your accomplishments can get you to your goals faster, now and in the future. Each time the pleasure center in your brain registers a tangible treat for a job well done, you become more conditioned to tackle your tasks with gusto the next time around.

Reading the comics or doing the crossword may be your reward for a small task. A day at the beach, special dinner out, or new outfit can be called for at the close of a project. Did you just land a major promotion or contract, finish off a huge or hard project, or do something really amazing for somebody else? Think vacation or the art class you've been eyeing in the college extension catalog.

Conditioned as we are to rush from one achievement to the next, never feeling good enough, never feeling done, it can be surprisingly hard to notice and reward your accomplishments. Make it easy by coming up with your own dream list of rewards. Keep it on file. Add to it whenever you discover something new. Use your reward list to spur a lifetime of achievement and well-deserved pleasure.

Chapter 19

Scheduling Skills for Maximum Productivity

"**D**o not squander time, that is the stuff life is made of," Benjamin Franklin said. So imagine you're in traffic, trying to get from here to there. What one thing squanders the most time of your trip? The red light.

Red lights are all around you in life, making you stop and wait as the minutes tick by, adding time to every task that could have been saved if only you were driving in synch with optimal traffic flow.

Time management is the way to green-light your day, eliminating obstacles and time wasters to give you the *go* signal every step of the way. You already discovered how to make and execute a plan. (If you haven't, skip back to the previous chapter. I promise that the how-to of plan execution will pay off.) But because even the best laid plans can go awry, you need green-light techniques to put your plans into action without the sudden stops that can come between you and your goals. Think green . . . and become a time-maximizing machine.

Going with the Flow: The Time Log

Flow is in, and for good reason. Whether you're driving a car or playing basketball, churning out a report or researching torts, the ability to get in the groove so that you're working with time instead of against it is key to peak productivity. Psychologists call this transcendent marriage between time and the mind *flow,* and when you get flow, you're good to go.

To find flow, you have to take control of your time and eliminate the interruptions and time wasters so common to the average day.

The first step is to find out how you actually spend your time by keeping a Time Log. A record of all the time you spend on every little thing, from the moment you rise in the morning until you put your head down on the pillow at night, the Time Log is a powerful tool for discovering how you allocate the minutes and hours of your life. Be prepared for good news and bad. I'll give you the bad news first: Unless you're practicing good time management or are a very exceptional person, you probably waste a fair amount of time. The good news is that once you find that time, you can reclaim it. The extra minutes and hours are a free gift from me to you, no strings attached.

To start your Time Log, take a sheet of ruled paper. In the left-hand margin, note the time you change activities, and on the line to the right list exactly what you're doing: getting ready for work or bed, commuting, doing projects or paperwork, making calls, talking to visitors, attending meetings, reading mail, making or eating meals, walking the dog, watching TV, and so on. Also note who else was involved so you can later determine how relevant each activity was to your goals and who tends to take up your time the most.

If you'd like to try a different method, you can create a spreadsheet on the computer, making each row on the sheet represent a 15-minute time block. Many people find this easier because the blocks remind them to log what they were doing. Accounting for time accurately on the computer spreadsheet can be harder, however, because not all activities neatly fall into 15-minute blocks.

Whether you go manual or electronic, keep your Time Log for at least several days in a row, and optimally for a whole week including a weekend to provide a complete picture of how different days go. I know logging your activities and the time taken is somewhat of a hassle, but hey — just pretend you're a high-paid lawyer. Attorneys always log their time.

Fixing Your Flow: The Busters

When your log is complete, take a good look to see where the time went. Total up your time by activity type, both for each day and for the whole week. Are you spending time on things according to your priorities? Does anything stand out? Too much time on the phone? Too little time for yourself or with your family or friends or on your current key project?

How much time did you spend procrastinating? How many interruptions did you have? What kind? Who were they with? Are there things you shouldn't have been doing, because the activities could have been delegated or you simply should have said, "No"?

Can you bundle certain activities together? Are you going out to run errands twice in one day when they can be consolidated into one trip? Could you get all your paperwork out of the way at once? Can you set aside a morning to take care of client calls?

Take a red pen and circle anything that was, in light of your values and goals, a waste of time, even a meeting with your boss or a phone call to a friend. How can you get these time wasters out of your day?

Procrastination busters: Read this now

You can't get flow without getting started, and starting is often the hardest part. For most people, procrastination isn't a result of laziness or lack of resolve. Procrastination can be a deep psychological situation involving fear of failure or success, or a natural result of overload. Sometimes you simply don't know where to start.

Procrastination is such a widespread problem that I make a point of providing excellent ways to beat it in my workshops and training. First, consider whether you tend to do better when working with other people or relying on yourself. Then choose your technique.

Involving other people

There are four ways (A, B, C, and D) that you can call on other people to help you do what you ought to be doing. Choose one or as many as it takes.

- ✔ **Be accountable:** Tell someone what you're going to do and by when. Accountability is built into many tasks at work, in which you have to report to a boss or a team, but try telling your best friend too. At home, see how you hop to cleaning the garage after you tell your buddy Jerry the garage will be spic and span by Sunday night. Better yet, invite Jerry to stop by around 5 p.m. on Sunday to inspect your handiwork. Fill your office mate in on your plan to finish project XYZ, and by all means, tell your mother about your vow to start saving $200 a month.

- ✔ **Barter:** If you procrastinate because you don't like or know your task very well, simply swap jobs with someone. Maybe you can type like the wind, but don't really get or care how spreadsheet formulas work. Tell your colleague Joyce, the local spreadsheet whiz, that you'll type up a report for her if she'll handle your spreadsheet formulas. It's a win-win!

- ✔ **Collaborate:** Working with someone else can help get the job started and done faster because you now have a shared commitment and two minds or pairs of hands. You may assemble a team to divvy up different parts of a project, or ask a friend to come over for your annual closet cleanout to help you decide what looks good and what can go to charity or the resale shop.

✔ **Delegate:** Why do the task yourself when someone else can? Supervisors should delegate tasks to staff so that employees can grow in their jobs. Parents can teach children household jobs and self-management skills that help them discover the meaning of responsibility and feel like contributing members of the family. (Read "Delegating: The Four Ds" later in this chapter for more.)

Doing it yourself

If you need or prefer to lean on yourself to beat the procrastination trap, there are plenty of solo ways to jump-start your motor. Look for a match with your personality style in the techniques that follow:

✔ **Jump in!:** Have you ever noticed how kids get in the pool? Youngsters generally run to the deep end and just jump in without checking the temperature because there's nothing kids can do to change it and they want to go swimming. The faster you get in, the faster you get used to the water, so just jump.

✔ **Take it step by step:** Of course, under no circumstances will you ever see me jump into the pool. You can find me down at the other end, slowly walking down the steps and taking my time getting used to the water temperature as each part of my body, from my feet to my stomach to my chest, gets wet. Any project can be achieved the same way, one step at a time so take a small step today.

✔ **Choose your starting point:** You don't always have to start at the so-called beginning or proceed in linear order. If you want to start a project on page three, start on page three. If you plan a holiday dinner and you'd rather design the menu before you decide on the guest list, that's fine. Just go back and figure quantities after you know how many you're having.

✔ **Race the clock:** When we were kids, my brother and I used to race to see who could drink their milk the fastest. Chances are you raced the clock in college by pulling an all-nighter to write a paper or study for finals. Deadlines drive achievement, so give yourself one, write down the date and time you want to finish, and race the clock.

✔ **Tie yourself down:** As a last resort, you need to simply tie yourself down. Tell yourself you can't go to the movies, you can't watch TV, you can't even get a cup of coffee until you write that report or paint that room. Pretend there's a real rope holding you there, and you literally can't leave until you do what you have to do. You can even use a tie or scarf to strap yourself to the chair. You may think twice before taking that coffee break.

Interruption busters: Phone calls and visitors

So you finally get going on your project and what happens? Interruptions. Flow's greatest enemy and a pervasive part of modern living, interruptions eat time twice over, both the minutes or hours interruptions take and the time required to regain your focus when they're over. Even if you can stop an interruption in progress, you still need to refocus, so prevent uninvited disturbances before they begin.

- ✔ **Telephone:** The simplest way to stop telephone interruptions is not to pick up the receiver when the phone rings or when you think you'll just clear up a point with a quick call and end up talking for half an hour.

  See Chapter 17 for all the ways to filter and funnel telephone calls. When trying to prevent interruptions, the rule is simple: Don't pick it up.

- ✔ **Visitors:** Visitors may not be as common an interruption as the telephone, but a real live person can be more compelling. You can discover ways to control visitor traffic in the next section.

Strategies for work

Diplomacy is key when carving out quiet time at work. Just remember that at the end of the day, your staff, colleagues, and superiors will respect you more for getting your job done than for being always available.

- ✔ **Screen.** Have an assistant or receptionist greet your visitors and tell the unexpected or noncritical ones that you're in a meeting.

- ✔ **Close.** Sometimes cutting yourself off is hard, but a closed door is a clear signal to all those who pass that you're busy on the other side. For those who still knock, open the door partway only and ask them to come back at a specific time. Don't let the visitor start the conversation.

- ✔ **Stand.** If you don't have a door or closing the door is not appropriate, greet incoming visitors by standing up. Most people won't sit down if you stand.

- ✔ **Walk.** So you're on your feet but your guest is reclining in your favorite chair. Now's the time to suggest that you chat while walking back to your visitor's desk, or say that you have somewhere to go. Then do go, preferably to the restroom, where only the most intrepid will tag along.

- ✔ **Hide.** Who says you have to work where people can find you? Go to a conference room, an empty office, a corporate or offsite library, or your home office for high-intensity times. Only the true bloodhounds will track you down.

✔ **Sign.** Put up a sign on your door or cubicle wall that says, "Do Not Disturb — Important Project." Depending upon your relationship with others in the office, people may respectfully leave you alone or take every opportunity to taunt you.

✔ **Postpone.** For hard cases, schedule an appointment to talk about an issue later, or a lunch to catch up on the social front.

Schedule appointments you'd rather not take before meetings so you have a good excuse to leave. If your time log reveals a particular person who repeatedly interrupts you throughout the day, schedule a daily 15- to 30-minute meeting to answer all the questions at once.

Strategies for home-based businesses

When you work at home, visitor interruptions all too often come from people you love. That doesn't mean you have to let flow go down the drain.

✔ **Business hours.** Inform family members of your work schedule (9 to 5 for most) and ask that they only disturb you for very important matters or emergencies.

✔ **Signs that speak volumes.** Put a sign on the door during important or peak times that says "Quiet, Do Not Disturb." If the sign is printed on colored paper, even children who can't read will know what the words mean. Red, hot pink, neon green — just be sure to share your color code with your cohabitants.

✔ **Outsource meetings.** Hosting a meeting at home can be less than professional and cause you to spend hours cleaning up. Instead, arrange to meet clients or customers at their office. If this isn't possible, rent a conference room or choose a mutually convenient coffeehouse.

✔ **No-pet policy.** Much as you may love them, corral pets away from your office so barking dogs or mewing cats don't interrupt your concentration or telephone calls.

✔ **Nobody's home.** Don't answer the door during working hours unless you're waiting for a special delivery. Use a peephole if you need to know.

Strategies for home

Just because you're home doesn't mean you're available. Remember the value of your time when visitors knock, and don't spend your time on just anyone.

✔ **Who's there?** Peer out your peephole to check the identity of unexpected visitors, and don't answer to those you don't know.

✔ **Not interested.** Don't waste time talking to salespeople when you have no intention of buying something from them. Once you know what they want, politely say "No" and let them go ring someone else's door or phone.

✔ **Stay focused.** If you're doing something that can't be interrupted, such as baking a cake or surfing the Net, just let the doorbell ring. No one has to know you're home unless you're expecting something important. How often does necessary news arrive at your door?

Occupational overload: Just say "No"

Once you beat procrastination and interruptions, you have to get to the meat of the time-management matter: One of the biggest reasons work doesn't get done is that there is simply too much of it. Sometimes the biggest favor you can do for everyone involved is to say "No." Here are four steps that help:

1. **Listen and understand the request.** What's being asked of you and why? You have to really understand the request to say a "No" that will stick.

2. **Say "No."** I know saying "No" is easier said than done, but just start with an *"n"* sound, and then put your mouth in the shape of an *"o"* and say "No, I'm sorry, I can't do it."

3. **Give reasons.** Simply and clearly state the reasons that you can't do the project or go to the meeting or be on the organization's board. "No, I'm sorry, I can't do it because I have three other commitments."

4. **Suggest alternatives.** If you understand the what and why behind the request, suggesting another way or someone else who may be able to do it is easier. "No, I'm sorry. I can't, but Jean knows about that matter and she can help you."

Saying "No" to your boss, of course, is always a bit of a special case. You can suggest someone else to do the project, but if the boss still wants you to do it, then you need to explain the work that you currently have.

"I would need to stop working on Project A to do Project B. Do you want me to do that?" or "I already have Projects A, B, and C to do. What are the priorities?" Your boss may be glad for the assist with prioritizing, and you may be glad to have a workload that allows you to perform at your best.

Delegating: The Four Ds

Of course, there's an alternative to saying "No" that's often the right thing to do: Delegate. Passing a task along to someone else in a more appropriate position to do it can maximize the value of everybody's time. Whether an expert who knows something you don't, somebody under you whose time costs less, or a colleague with time to spare when you're in a crunch, delegating to the right person can be more efficient all around than taking on every task that crosses your path. To delegate is not to dump — delegating is to assign a task in a clear, productive way. To do so, follow the four Ds of Delegation as follows:

- ✔ **Decide what to delegate and to whom**: The right time to pass a job along is when you face any of the following types of tasks: routine, technical, short, those you don't have time for, and those that train others.

  An expert can often do specialized jobs better, from writing a computer routine to serving dinner for 50. Experts may cost more, but if they can do it faster and better than you can, you may save money and time at the bottom line. Calculate what your time is worth and compare it to the cost of hiring out.

  The person with the most expertise is not the best delegate if that person's schedule is overloaded, or if your job requires time more than special skills. At work, consider a colleague or staff person who's not busy right now and/or stands to benefit from learning the job. At home, you may be accustomed to handing tasks off to the oldest child, but a younger sibling may have more free time and be ready to take on more.

  Hesitant to delegate? Have an imaginary chat with your CFO. Would he or she consider you a failure for spending your valuable time on a task that someone else could handle at a lower cost to the company? Quite the opposite. Think about your family. Will you fail them by not spending all your evenings and weekends working on the charity auction or blood drive when you could have shared some of those responsibilities with others? Au contraire, Pierre!

- ✔ **Direct what, not how:** Tell the delegate what you want done — the end objective of the job. But unless you're teaching a brand-new skill, don't dictate how to do the job itself. People learn more and are better motivated when they can figure things out for themselves. Communication is very important when you're delegating, so go to a quiet place such as a meeting room or your office with the door closed so the delegate can listen intently to explanations and ask questions afterward. Get feedback to confirm that your goal is clear.

  You know the saying: Give someone a fish, and you've fed them a meal; teach someone to fish, and you've fed them for life. Empower others and free up your time for more important things by making a small time investment in training.

- ✔ **Define authority:** Tell your delegate exactly how much authority you're granting. Is there a dollar limit on the project? A decision point at which you must be consulted? Defining authority helps the delegate do the best job within the bounds you consider appropriate.

✔ **Deadlines:** I discussed how deadlines help get work completed. Now turn the tables. Let the delegates tell you when they can a) give you a progress report and b) deliver a final product. If you have a deadline on your end, make sure their due date is earlier in case they need extra time or you need to correct something.

It's How You Do It: Strategic Tasking

Say you put procrastination behind you. Eliminated interruptions. Used delegation and the word *no* to trim your task list to a manageable load. It's time to get down to work, so what's the best way? Strategic tasking is the art and science of matching the type of job to your manner of approach.

Single tasking

To single-task is to truly work on one thing at a time. When you want to focus and concentrate on something big, hard, or new, single tasking is the mode to use. See the section on Peak and Pace in Chapter 18 for more about the best times to single-task.

Group tasking

Grouping many tasks that are small and/or routine according to the principle of *like* can allow you to expedite routine work most efficiently. I'll dare to repeat from the section on routines in the previous chapter that the more you repeat an activity, the easier and faster it gets. Want to prove it to yourself? Try writing your name five times with your left hand (or right hand if you're left-handed). Did you do it? Wasn't the fifth time much easier than the first?

Group tasking gets things done faster through the power of repetition. Here are the jobs to group together to make the most of your time: paying bills, opening incoming mail, reading incoming e-mail, tackling correspondence, writing thank-you notes, updating data entry and your contact entry files (name, address, phone), and running errands.

Multitasking: Personal calls and waiting

Then there are the moments in which you can and should be doing more than one thing at once. I'd like to chime in that I sincerely believe that you can only do one thing at a time *well,* but how well do you need to wait in line?

Multitasking has become a way of modern life because people have more to do, including low-grade but necessary jobs that don't deserve full attention. Here's where to double up.

Personal calls plus

Given that no one can seem to spend a nanosecond off the phone anymore, why not take advantage of wireless technology to do two things at once? Enjoy guilt-free social calls by tucking a cordless phone under your chin or donning a headset and completing routine tasks such as cooking a meal, cleaning, straightening up, doing your nails, or watering the plants. This dual task paradigm does not extend to more demanding activities such as interfacing with your children or walking on the treadmill. Nobody needs to hear you panting or playing a game while they're spending their precious time trying to talk to you. And don't double up on business calls. It's a quick way to lose respect and miss important information.

Waiting and in transit

At appointments, in line at the post office, at a lunch engagement, in the subway station — you probably spend hours waiting every month of your life. Get that time back by tasking while you wait.

- ✔ **Read.** Don't go anywhere you'll need to wait without a part of your To Read File or your current book in hand. Not only is this a productive and/or pleasant way to pass the time, but you may find that reading in different environs sparks new ideas. Take a plastic file folder with just as much reading as you think you may have time for.

- ✔ **Write.** Quick notes such as thank yous, birthday, or catch-up cards are a great way to tick items off your list while you wait. Keep a few assorted note cards in a plastic folder and take the folder along for the extra time you find at the doctor's office or before a workshop.

- ✔ **E-mail.** If you have a laptop or handheld computer, reading and responding to e-mail is a good waiting game, because you can usually find an easy stopping point.

- ✔ **Plan.** There's nothing like waiting to help you remember all the things you need to do so take this time to work on your Master or To Do List (see Chapter 18).

Any time you leave the office or home, ask yourself what you can do on the way. Could you drop off the dry cleaning on the way to work, pick up some office supplies en route to a meeting, take advantage of an out-of-the-way appointment to get to your favorite antique store?

Pro Communications

All the time management in the world won't help you get things done if you can't communicate effectively. Whether getting the message across is your job — you could be in sales, a teacher, or a mom — or you work on a committee or team, get or receive assignments, assist someone, administer a program, or are simply trying to get along with your roommates, mastering the art of interpersonal contacts will save you time and make your day much nicer.

Electronic communications have become so elaborate that I devote an entire chapter to using everything from phones and faxes to the Internet. Flip to Chapter 17 for the basics on choosing and using your communications tools.

The phone: Incoming calls and messages

Read Chapter 17 and set yourself up with all the phone lines and features you need. Now how do you use the darn thing? Probably your most powerful productivity tool and your greatest time waster, the telephone can be viewed as a wild animal that you need to tame.

The first question to ask yourself about incoming calls is, "Am I taking them?" A quick reminder from the previous section on interruptions: You don't have to answer the phone just because it rings. Voice mail, caller ID, answering machines, and assistants are all available to put you in control of your incoming calls — which, from a time-management perspective, is the only place to be.

The busiest days for incoming telephone calls are Mondays. If you can screen calls, Monday is definitely the day to do it.

For people in sales, public relations, consulting, and speaking, voice-mail screening may not be a viable option. Prospective clients shopping for services or media people looking for a news lead may choose whomever they reach first on the phone, so you could miss the boat by calling back.

When you talk to new callers, be sure to get their direct-dial number so you can save going through a switchboard or assistant if you ever have to call them back.

The outgoing message on your voice-mail or answering machine is your calling card to everyone who calls you. Make a good impression and elicit important information from your callers with a *power message*. What's a power message? One you script, rehearse, and deliver with enthusiasm. Type up all the messages you use and keep the sheet in your Phone/Voice-mail File. Pull the file out anytime you need to record a new message, and you can have a power greeting in place in seconds.

At the office

Whether you work for a corporation or own your own business, your message should identify both you and your company. This helps callers ascertain whether they've reached the right party and if it's a wrong number, your message is free advertising. Some further power messaging principles for the office:

1. Create three standard messages and type them on your reference sheet:

   - **Standard daily message.** Don't mention a specific day here. Saying that this is Tuesday works great for Tuesday but if you forget to change your message on Wednesday, you look like a loser. Furthermore, who needs the extra work of a daily message swap? Mention days only when you'll be out of town so that callers don't keep trying to reach you when you're not available.

   - **Out of town message.** This is a time for a little white lie: Tell callers you'll be back in the office a day after your actual return. This gives you the time you need to catch up on work, mail, and calls without the world beating down your door.

   - **Vacation message.** Ditto the preceding.

2. If you have an assistant or someone else who can handle calls on your behalf, mention that person's name and extension in your message so your caller has an option for immediate attention.

3. Conclude by specifically inviting the caller to talk: "Please leave your message after the tone and speak slowly." How much time have you wasted playing and replaying incomprehensible messages from people who talk too fast?

4. If it fits yours and your company's style, finish with a friendly tag line to leave your callers with a smile. Mine is "Get organized to enjoy life" — the heart and main mission of my business.

At home

Less is more for home messages. Why tell someone who you are who doesn't already know? And you certainly don't want to alert thieves when you're out of town. "Hi, we're not available right now" does the job. Finish by prompting the caller to speak (slowly) and a cheerful tag if you like.

Playing and taking messages

It absolutely amazes me how many people play their messages back and then save them. Talk about double work. The *save* button should be called *spend* instead, which is what it does with your time. Play the message once, write it down, and then erase it. If you miss a name or number, repeat the message right then and there.

Note the magic words *write it down* in the preceding paragraph. Writing is of course critical if you take messages for others, but even if you listen to a personal answering machine at home and you live alone, you need to write down every message you receive in order to green-light your day.

All messages you need to act upon can go on your Master List as soon as you get them. Skip straight to your To Do List if you plan to act today.

Handling outgoing calls effectively

Before you pick up the phone, stop and ask: Is there a better way? If you only need to disseminate information rather than discuss it, a fax or an e-mail may be faster. Human beings are chatty by nature. If discussion is required simply to set up a meeting time or find out a fact or two, delegate the call to an assistant, if you can. For those calls you do need to make, don't just grab the receiver at random. Have a calling plan.

Use the program and speed-dial features on all your phones, cellular and regular. That's fingertip management of your phone calls! You can also use the dial function on computer contact-management programs connected to your phone, then have that person's record open and ready to receive your notes.

Choosing your time

Prime time for outgoing calls is 9 to 11 in the morning and 2 to 4 in the afternoon. This allows for the average arrival, departure, and lunch hours for most work places, though some stores and doctor's offices don't open until after 10 a.m. and many consumer-oriented businesses are open into the evening.

Calling outside of prime time can be a great strategy if you are a) hoping to reach voice mail instead of the person, or b) trying to reach somebody who's been waylaying you with an assistant. Many executives answer their own phones before or after hours when their assistants aren't in. (Of course if they've read this book, they'll plan their time better. If you were high on their priority list they would have already called you back, and if not they shouldn't be talking to you anyway.)

Note the time zone you call and adjust accordingly. Most phone books have a time zone map in the front, as do many organizers. Remember to take daylight saving time into account in the summer if you call states such as Arizona or Indiana, which don't switch.

Take advantage of off-peak phone rates and time zone differences by making long-distance calls east early in the morning and west in the evening.

Try setting a certain time each day to pick up your messages and return calls. You may want to have one peak and one off-peak time, depending upon whether calls are important or routine.

Organizing and prioritizing your calls

Consider what calls are the most important today and mark their priority order on your To Do List, accounting for any time zone differences. Gather all of the relevant material you need for all your calls, which usually includes your datebook/organizer, any relevant papers, and perhaps your To Discuss List (see Chapter 16). If you have several issues to cover, start with the most important items on the list so that if the other person is suddenly called away, your top priorities have been taken care of.

Balancing incoming and outgoing calls: Stopping phone tag

Just as you plan your time for incoming and outgoing calls, so may the people you try to reach (especially if you give all your associates copies of this book as gifts). If those schedules don't mesh, you could be caught in an endless game of telephone tag. The way to avoid this is to leave messages that say more than "You're it."

Before placing a call, plan the message you want to leave if you get voice mail or an assistant. State what information you have to relay or the question you need to ask, and give a good time to call you back, preferably during a time you expect to be taking calls. If a return e-mail, fax, or call to your assistant would be sufficient, say so.

Appointments and meetings

It seems that nothing can get done without a meeting. Yet, meetings can also be big time wasters. When you plan or decide whether to attend a meeting, use the Five Ws plus How as your guide.

Considering why and who

Why even have a meeting? To decide which meetings you should attend, ask yourself what benefits each one offers you. If you can't come up with a compelling list, drop the meeting from your schedule if you can (discuss this with your boss first if necessary). For recurrent meetings, consider whether you really need to go to every one, or whether there's some way the meetings could be improved.

Good reasons to have a meeting are: to plan or execute a team project, fill everyone in on the status of a project and get feedback, brainstorm ideas, create cohesion, build relationships, or inspire. If your purpose is strictly to disseminate information in one direction, consider a written report instead.

Who needs to attend? The general rule is that the more people in a meeting, the longer the meeting takes and the more resources it diverts from other priorities, so consider your participant list carefully. Many meetings can also benefit from bringing in outsiders. You may want to hire a speaker or trainer in a given area, or engage a consultant for special expertise or a broader perspective. Write down your list of meeting participants and use the list to track who will be there as people respond, and to follow up with those you haven't heard from. When you're invited to a meeting, you may want to check who will be there before deciding whether to attend.

Deciding what and when

What do you need to discuss? Every meeting should have an agenda. Typing up and sending out the agenda in advance can make your meeting run more smoothly, as participants will be better prepared to discuss topics and can ask to add items you may not be aware of.

When should you meet? The three time factors to consider for your meeting are time of day, day of the week, and for recurrent meetings, frequency. Monday morning is a good time to discuss what everyone is doing for the week. Friday afternoon can serve for a wrap-up. A midweek meeting works well for troubleshooting. Evening meetings may get the best attendance on Tuesday, Wednesday, and Thursday, while Sunday night is a good pick for a family meeting. You want to schedule appointments and meetings for your off-peak time. Don't worry about performing; the stimulus of the situation can get you going, and your peak time will remain free for projects requiring concentration.

If you are in charge of the meeting, especially a staff meeting, you may want to survey the participants to find out how many of your staff are morning versus afternoon people, and then set the time to coincide with the majority's off-peak period.

Set an ending time for your meeting and stick to it. Ending the meeting on time not only encourages efficient use of time and a brisk approach to your agenda, but a punctual stopping point shows your consideration toward attendees. Being able to plan the rest of the day is important for people, whether getting to another appointment, completing a project, or getting home in time to spend some time with the kids before tucking them into bed.

Knowing where and how

Where to meet? Is this a small meeting at the table in your office, or do you need a conference room? Maybe going offsite would be better to keep everyone from being distracted or to spark new ideas. Restaurant meetings are great for relationship-building but not so good for actually getting things done. In general, breakfast and lunch meetings are more business-oriented and brief, while dinner may be mostly or purely social and can stretch on for hours, which, depending upon your goal, may or may not be good.

How to meet? The purpose of your meeting will determine the setup of the event — a small table for a brainstorming session, a semicircle of chairs or U-shaped table arrangement for a seminar, separate tables or classroom style for a workshop, an auditorium with media capabilities for a big presentation. If you have a speaker or someone is presenting, be sure to arrange all the technical requirements in advance. These days, many people carry presentations on their laptop computers. Can you all gather around and see, or do you need a special projector? Are there handouts to be reproduced? Should there be water, flowers, company logos or banners, promotional items to take away? If you plan meetings often, create a form covering all these details.

Meetings take up everybody's valuable time, so make sure there are no interruptions unless there's a certifiable emergency. Have the phones covered and ask people to turn off their cell phones and beepers. Close the door and tell visitors you're busy. Remember that the number of people in the room multiplies every minute wasted.

Never go to a meeting without something to take notes with, your planner, and your business cards. See Chapter 21 for more about handling offsite appointments and meetings. Finally, the main point of a meeting is oral communication, so brush up those skills on both the talking and listening side: talk slowly, listen carefully, and take notes — no matter what, give handouts, and talk back.

Finally, if your meeting occurs regularly, consider how frequent it really needs to be. Could you push your weekly meeting to biweekly and still stay on top of the game? If a monthly meeting always seems to run too long and has an overloaded agenda, maybe you need to get together more often.

Reading and writing: Written communication

Have you noticed how much more the computer has encouraged reading and writing? If you're not as skilled in written communications as you'd like to be, you may wish to get up to speed by reading a writing guidebook. In the meantime, here are a few tips from a time-management perspective.

Writing: Draft and revision

Write drafts. Your composition teacher wasn't kidding when he said that writing improves with rewriting, and this is true for everything from a report to a letter, for amateurs and pros alike. Do you know how many drafts of these chapters I've gone through? And you may still think there's room to improve. Though it may sound paradoxical, writing a few drafts of a document can actually save time, and here's the trick: Write the first one fast. How good the draft is doesn't matter, because you're going to come back and revise. Your first draft can even be bad. You'll be amazed how your writing speed picks up when you take a redraft approach and how much better the final product is.

Whenever possible, let a draft sit overnight so you can revise it with a fresh eye. Much longer, though, and you can forget what you meant to say to begin with.

Reading: How to skim

News flash: Just because someone wrote a word doesn't mean that you have to read it. No, I'm not suggesting that you put this book down and walk away. What I mean is that some words mean more than others. Skip the small words like *and* and *the* and cut to the chase of those longer nouns and verbs that give a sentence meaning. If you look at a lengthy article or report, it often helps to skim first, reading the headline, all the subheads, and possibly the first line or two of each paragraph to see if you really want to read the whole thing. An outline, abstract, or table of contents can also tell you where a document is going. Check before plunging in to determine the value of the content and prepare your mind for what's to come.

When reading a reference book in sections like this one, remember that you don't have to read it straight through. Use the table of contents to find the parts you want. In fact, if you look at the front of this book you see that the nice ...*For Dummies* people have provided an ultradetailed table of contents for your speed-reading pleasure. Thank you! The same goes for the newspaper. You're under no obligation to read anything but the columns and articles of interest to you. Use the headlines as your clue.

When you read for content — to find out about something or absorb technical information — keep a clear ruler and a red pen on hand to underline important passages. Then go back to review the underlined parts and use a highlighter to pick out key points only.

When you highlight points as you read, you're likely to go overboard. Have you ever finished a chapter and found most of it was yellow? Underlining first helps you focus on the truly important stuff the second time around.

See Chapter 16 on information flow for how to create a To Read File in the Take Action File system.

Socializing

Humans are social creatures. In fact, for many people one of the big rewards of getting organized is having more time to hang out, and making connections can be as important to your career as it is to your mental health. But accidental socializing or going overboard can eat up your time, perhaps taking up hours you'd really rather spend with someone else. I suggest conscious socializing as a strategy for making the most of your interpersonal time.

Put a coffee warmer on your desk so you don't have to get up for a hot cup every time your coffee cools.

✔ **Schedule regular breaks,** especially a lunch break, to reenergize yourself. You'll work more efficiently as a result, and knowing when your breaks are supposed to be prevents you from using them to procrastinate.

✔ **Keep all the tools you need right at your fingertips** to prevent trips that may entail running into people. See Chapter 15 on setting up your desk for more.

Look at the road ahead — a long expanse of green lights, all perfectly timed. Enjoy the flow and go!

Chapter 20

Maximizing Your Personal Time

*P*rogress is a funny thing. With every new invention for doing things faster and better, people just accumulate more obligations and commitments rather than additional free time. You have to keep up to speed on the speediest way to do things just to stay in place. If you actually want to have more time to enjoy your life, you need to be crafty indeed. This is a shortcut chapter jam-packed with ideas for making the most of the time of your life.

Some time-savers are timeless. Others are new, enabled by technology or a more evolved brain. In the following text you'll find a combination of classic and current ideas to make you better at everything from money to love. Organization is more fun than you may think!

If You're Overwhelmed, Read This First

Many people have a hard time getting organized because carving out the five minutes here, the hour there, or a weekend afternoon needed to start the systems presented in this book can be tough. The quick and easy tips in this chapter can help you create those windows of time by expediting tasks more efficiently. Line up a few together, and you have an hour to start your filing system.

The other advantage of these practical, everyday tips is that each one represents a small step that can take you closer to your goal of getting organized, while improving your quality of life as you go. If you're overwhelmed, spend a month, which is about the amount of time required to train your mind, putting these principles into action, and then you'll be ready to tackle the rest of the book.

Getting Out of the House

For most of us, mornings aren't peak time for clear thinking, so simply getting out of the house can be one of the day's most daunting jobs. You can take the rigor out of rise and shine by planning your morning just like a project. With a morning plan, everything can go smoothly when you need to coast along the most, enabling you to glide out the door and meet the challenges of your day. Table 20-1 can help.

Table 20-1	Your Morning Timetable
Activity	*Time*
Be at your destination:	_____
Subtract: Travel time	- _____
Leave your house at:	_____
Subtract: Time to dress, eat, childcare, pet care, read paper	- _____
Wake up at:	_____
Subtract: Hours of sleep needed	- _____
Go to bed at:	_____

Work walking out the door backward, and you end up with a plan for not just getting out of bed, but for getting into bed the night before. One smooth sweep from today to tomorrow ensures you stay caught up on your sleep.

 Is that late night talk show or novel you can't put down coming between you and your beauty rest? Tape the show and watch the tape while cooking dinner the next day. Find a different time slot for your reading that presents less temptation. Staying up too late tonight mortgages the quality of tomorrow.

With your morning plan in hand, do some preassembly to get you out and about without even needing to engage your brain. The night before, get ready for the next day by doing the following:

✔ Put everything you need by the door you exit from in the morning — briefcase (including reading material, files, and organizer), laptop, keys, purse/wallet, audiotapes, umbrella, and so on. (See Chapter 4 for more on the flight deck approach.)

✔ Plan your clothes the night ahead. (Organizing your closet according to the principles in Chapter 6 can help.) Check the forecast on the late night news or the World Wide Web. If you live in a volatile climate such as my hometown of Chicago, you may want to have two outfits in mind and tune in to the early morning weather report. Know the report time of your favorite radio station so you don't miss the weather while you're in the shower.

✔ Keep a clock in the bathroom and set it five minutes fast.

✔ Organize your toiletries, makeup, and hair accessories according to the principles of P-L-A-C-E (see Chapter 7).

✔ Make a morning routine that you follow in the same order every day. For instance:

  1. Walk the dog

  2. Exercise

  3. Shower (and shave)

  4. Dress

  5. Makeup

  6. Hair

  7. Eat breakfast/read paper

  8. Pack lunches

  9. Outta here!

Ladies, if you'd like to keep lipstick off your clothes and your hair in place, don pullover tops before you apply makeup and style your hair. Button-down blouses, sweaters, and jackets can go on after your grooming routine is complete to prevent showers of powder and stray hairs from landing on your clothes.

✔ Buy a coffeemaker with an automatic timer to make the coffee every morning before you even reach the kitchen. Some even have a self-timed grinder so your beans are ultra-fresh.

✔ Take the train or bus instead of driving to save gas and use the extra time to read the paper, review reports, catch up on e-mail on a laptop, or write thank-you notes.

Shopping and Errands

Even those who are born to shop can use a few ways to get the job done faster. From buying a fabulous new outfit to running routine errands, you can benefit by consolidating your destinations into one fell swoop instead of darting hither and yon. Setting up shopping and errand routines can save time and regularize your schedule. And with home delivery and the Internet, you don't even have to leave the house to accomplish many acquiring missions. Here are some tips to get your shopping done while the clock is ticking:

- ✔ Run all your errands at once to save time and gas. Block the time out in your calendar and go.

- ✔ Run errands on the way to somewhere else. If the dry cleaner is on the way to work, drop your clothes off in the morning and pick them up on the way home. Think like a map.

- ✔ Shop the supermarket only once a week, on the same day. This will help you get your act together as laid out in Chapter 5. Need fresh fish? Decide whether a specialty store or the grocery store offers the best time/money tradeoff. Run out of milk? Hit the convenience store *once* — then adjust your quantity in the future.

Saving your time: Personal services

Why run an errand or do the weekly drudgery when people can come to your house and do chores for you? You're busy with work and/or family, right? In the age of personal services, you can spend less of your life on the little details. Here are some ideas:

- ✔ Order groceries by phone or online and have them delivered.

- ✔ When you're really in a rush to get dinner on the table, hit these stops in the supermarket: the take-out counter, the deli/prepared foods counter, the bakery, the salad bar, the produce section for prewashed salad in a bag, and the refrigerator section for fresh pastas and sauces.

Remember that you always pay extra for convenience — so the more prepared the foods you buy, the higher the price generally is. If you're on a strict budget, study up on the bulk shopping, cooking, and storage techniques discussed in Chapter 5 to cut your food bills significantly.

- ✔ Have prescriptions delivered to your home, ordering by phone to your local pharmacy, by mail, or through one of the many Web sites.

- ✔ Find a hair stylist, makeup artist, or barber who makes house calls.

- ✔ Hire a maid service.

- ✔ Have dry cleaning delivered.

- ✔ Canvass the neighbors for a teenager who can cut your lawn or remove your snow.

- ✔ Get a babysitter so you can go out.

✔ Have music lessons in your home.

✔ Set up an account with your printing/copying center and express delivery service so orders can be picked up and delivered.

✔ Order meals out, whether from a take-out place, a specific restaurant, or a restaurant delivery service.

✔ Bring technology home: Have a computer techie or trainer come to you.

Cybershopping and services

The Internet has seriously revolutionized running errands. Why schlep around in the car when you can shop online for anything from cars to clothes to computer parts and your friendly postal carrier or delivery service can bring the goods to you?

However, some transactions are better suited to cybersolutions than others. Consider two potential virtual shopping trips:

✔ **Scenario one:** You get on the Web, use a price-checking service to find just the toy your nephew has requested for his birthday at the best price in the nation, buy it, and ship it cross-country with a few quick clicks. You then devote the time saved to writing him a nice long letter.

✔ **Scenario two:** You spend an hour flipping through the pages of a national clothing store site searching for a shirt you saw in the window of your local branch. You finally find it, take a guess on the size, and fill out all the forms to buy it, only to have the shirt not fit when the package arrives.

Which of these situations represents the most efficient use of the Internet?

The Internet can make quick work of many errands and save time and money — *if* the right variables are in place. The first scenario is such a case, while in the second, you would have been better off going to the store where you saw the shirt.

Cybershopping makes the most sense when

✔ Your connection speed and navigating skills enable you to complete your transaction faster than you would in person or by phone. This means you don't waste time flipping pages or filling in forms that could be saved by seeing something live or dealing with a real person. For example:

  • **Go virtual** to purchase a particular CD. Just type the name into the vendor's search engine and buy.

  • **Consider traditional** if you live next to a well-stocked CD store with good prices or aren't quite sure what you want.

✔ You can use the Internet to gather information and compare prices. For instance

- **Go virtual** for electronics, computer hardware and software, toys, books and music, and office supplies.

- **Consider traditional** when shopping for something such as unique home-decorating items that can be viewed more quickly and easily and contextualized in a display.

✔ Chances of needing to return it are slim. Such as

- **Go virtual** to buy electronic postage stamps.

- **Consider traditional** to shop for clothes.

✔ You're shipping your purchase somewhere else and can save a trip to the post office too.

✔ You're housebound or live in the country.

Cleaning and Chores

Like many people, you're grateful for vacuum cleaners and all but still waiting for the technological revolution to make keeping the house clean easier. Hello, inventors! Meanwhile, here are old-fashioned ways to get household work done fast.

Hiring help or delegating

One way to get the job done is to let someone else do it. From hiring out to tapping family members or cohabitants for help, you can turn to other people to ease your burden of chores. Here are some specifics:

✔ **Hire household help.** This time-honored tradition makes even more sense in the age of families with two working parents. Whether you hire out on a regular (weekly or monthly) or special-occasion basis (parties and holidays), consider professional help for everything from cleaning to catering, babysitting, elder care, gardening, pool maintenance, and snow removal. You can even hire someone who comes to your house every week and cooks a week's worth of meals, leaving everything packaged and labeled with reheating instructions.

To determine whether hiring out is cost-effective, determine the time you would take (not the professional) to accomplish the job, multiply that number by what your time is worth per hour, and divide the result roughly in half to account for taxes. If the amount is more than the cost of hiring, you're actually paying less by outsourcing — *if* you spend the time saved doing something productive. But then again, sometimes that's not the point.

✔ **Share with a partner.** The days of strict gender lines for household jobs are long gone. Sit down with your mate and work out who's willing to do what, by dividing up tasks and sticking to them or establishing a chore rotation. A kitchen-friendly man may discover that his wife would rather take out the garbage and mow the lawn than cook — so swap already.

✔ **Share with the kids.** Chores are good for kids! Have a family meeting and schedule jobs appropriate to the age level of each child laundry, meal setup, dishes, cooking, garbage patrol, and errands. You may rotate chores, or even have a weekly lottery to add a little excitement factor. Young ones can start by discovering how to pick up toys and crafts, make their bed, and choose their clothing at night as their first time-management assignments.

What you can do in the house

When the job of household cleaning falls to you, find the time by setting up routines and planning ahead. Some suggestions include

✔ Plan the same day each week to clean the house. Depending upon traffic, you can step up to twice a week for a light once-over on the bathrooms.

Okay, if you absolutely must, you can scrub the sinks and sweep the kitchen floor every day.

✔ Set aside time *before* holidays to polish the silver and clean the china cabinets, dishes, and crystal glasses you'll need (see Chapter 8). Nobody needs this stress in full holiday swing.

✔ Separate laundry into two different washdays — one for clothes, one for towels and linens — to lighten the load on each day. Use the same days each week.

✔ Stash a few extra garbage bags at the bottom of your wastebaskets so when you throw away the current one, a new bag is ready and waiting.

Save money by using plastic grocery bags to line small bathroom wastebaskets.

✔ Choose at least one day a year to purge your household files if file purging isn't an ongoing process.

What you can do outside the house

Outside appearances (and functions) do count, so organize your regular outdoor tasks with these tips.

- ✔ Clean the garage floor a couple of times a year. You may like going there much more.

- ✔ Keep the cars in shape by posting repair, tune-up, and tire-rotation schedules on the garage wall. Have a basic maintenance check done before each major trip to head off highway disasters. Wash, wax, even repaint your baby as often as it takes to stay in love. Maintaining the automobile you have is much cheaper than buying a new car.

- ✔ Take the snowblower and lawn mower in for tune-ups before their seasons start. Add these items to your car maintenance schedule so you don't forget.

- ✔ Have blacktop driveways resealed once a year.

Handling and Moving Your Money

Moving money around is easier than ever before. Make sure this works for, not against, you. With a few management techniques you can make the most of your dough. See Chapter 17 for more on bringing balance to your finances. In the meantime, you can be prepared and organized to handle everyday challenges as well as emergencies. Lose the late fees, say goodbye to high interest rates, and have cash on hand where and when you need it with some simple money moves.

Preparing for emergencies

At some point we all need emergency cash, whether the car broke down or whatever. To avoid making hasty phone calls to family and friends at questionable pay phones during personal disasters, it pays to be prepared. Some tips to make troubles easier:

- ✔ Keep a spare $20 bill hidden in your wallet for emergencies only. Replace the bill the next day if you spend it.

- ✔ Carry a spare check in your wallet in case you unexpectedly run out. Keep your check register on hand so you can record checks as you write them.

- ✔ If you can resist the temptation, carry a credit card for big emergencies only.

Being a smart debit-card user

Debit cards are fast; they're the new way to *write a check*. But unlike charge cards, when you reach your limit, you're broke! Yeah, those debit cards are great, but only if you're organized enough to track your balances.

If you don't have your checkbook along to record debit transactions on the spot, be sure to take the receipt and enter the reduction right away when you get home or place it in your To Enter Take Action File to process when you pay bills.

Pay for things with a charge or debit card to prevent having to get and carry cash. A debit card is a better bet than credit if you get tempted not to pay off your charge card balances at the end of the month.

Getting the most from your credit cards

Credit cards can be great to have when making big purchases such as a refrigerator or washer and dryer. However, unless you plan on paying off the balance every month or you're older and have good, established credit that enables you to get the cards with low interest rates, you can be in for an interest-rate roller coaster.

Get a charge card that gives back — cash, airline miles, or points toward something you can use. Pay if off every month so your givebacks aren't negated by interest charges, or worse yet, late fees.

Do your best not to carry credit card debt; it's too expensive. Cancel your extra charge cards to reduce temptation and pay as much as you possibly can each month to keep interest costs down.

Managing your monthly bills

Paying your bills is a monthly ritual that you won't ever be able to escape. That being the case, you may as well make payments as easy and painless as possible. Set up a schedule and a budget. Every month, pay the bills, balance the checkbook, and get your finances in order. Just get comfy and do it. To get you started:

- ✔ Make a monthly budget, including an allocation for savings.

- ✔ Pay all bills at one session, preferably once a week. Don't wait until they are due; just mail them now. The amount isn't going to get any smaller — and if you're late, you could be slapped with an additional fee.

✔ If you don't make a regular salary, cross-check your paychecks with your record of hours worked or invoices.

✔ Keep separate checking accounts for business and personal funds.

Dealing with the big picture

Every once in awhile, shifting your focus from the everyday to the faraway and out of the way pays off. Being proactive can save you money and hassle. On a periodic basis, make an effort to do the following:

✔ Check your credit rating and Social Security status. Correct any errors; they could have major implications for your financial health.

✔ Refinance your mortgage when interest rates are down. Pay extra whenever you can to save interest costs — but not if you're carrying higher-rate consumer debt. Always pay the highest rate balances first.

✔ If you have considerable credit card debt, consider refinancing. Rather than paying the high interest rate of a credit card debt, find a bank that will give you a loan at a low interest rate and pay off the credit card with the loan, saving the difference between the two rates.

✔ Find out about investing for college savings and/or retirement plans as well as ways to reduce your tax bill. For many people, investments in an IRA earn 30 percent off the top simply by not being taxed. *Personal Finance For Dummies* (IDG Books Worldwide, Inc.) can smarten you up fast.

Using electronic financial services

Going to the bank, writing checks, and licking stamps all take up your time. Why not move your money with bytes instead? These financial services can save you time and money. Imagine being able to cut down on your monthly bill-paying paperwork! Consider the following:

✔ Pay while you play (or work) by using automatic debits to your bank account to pay utility, credit card, and loan bills. Keep a running list of debits and days of the month they're made to enter into your checkbook at bill-paying time.

Some Web-based services receive all your bills on your behalf, send you an e-mail as they come in, and then take care of paying them as soon as you e-mail back the go-ahead. You keep control but have no checks to sign or stamps to affix.

✔ Hit pay dirt with direct deposit from your employer. Sign up to have your paycheck electronically deposited into your account and you can spare yourself payday lines at the bank and often waive monthly service charges too.

✔ Bank by wire, using the phone or the Internet to view balances, transfer money between accounts, and explore your bank's financial resources. When you're wired, you can wave goodbye to bankers' hours.

Making Time for Your Family

Ah, the ties that bind . . . Who doesn't want higher-quality, less-stressful family time? A few good habits can help unite your household and create more quality time together, as well as ease the logistics of managing and caring for a group. Give these ideas a try to sweeten up your home life.

Savoring together time

With family members coming, going, and lining up for the bathroom, some houses feel more like Grand Central Station than a home. The solution is to schedule routine tasks and fun family time so everyone knows what to expect. These togetherness tactics can help.

✔ Make a schedule for the morning to plan bathroom time and breakfast to get everyone out the door.

✔ Eat dinner together with no television and discuss everyone's day. A shared meal is both emotionally important and an efficient time for communication, so make eating dinner together a priority and schedule it in.

✔ Have a family meeting once a week to set up chores or schedules and provide an open forum for everyone to talk about whatever's on their mind. Sunday night is often free of other commitments.

✔ Have a family day once a month with a fun group activity — a picnic, sports event, amusement park, museum, bowling, skating, miniature golf, and so on.

✔ Establish a family reading time, a no-TV night, or a game night.

✔ Stick little notes in school kids' lunch or school bags every so often with "I love you" or "Have a great day." Keep your college students' mailboxes full. Write a letter to each child upon high school and/or college graduation about growing up and the future.

✔ Make time for relatives. They're more precious than you may realize in the course of busy days. Visit grandparents, drop a card to cousins. They share your gene pool and your past — but can share your present only if you let them.

Finding support systems: Kid care

Kids are bundles of energy, fountains of joy — and in need of constant care. Prevent parental burnout with ways to keep children happy and well cared for while you get some well-deserved grown-up time.

✔ Carpool! There's always another child going where yours is . . . and another parent who can drive next time.

✔ Join a playgroup to meet other parents and share ideas and support while the kids amuse themselves.

✔ Drop a child at a park district program, preschool, or library program for an hour or two so you can have some free time or run errands.

✔ Shop at stores with play areas to keep little ones occupied while you browse.

✔ Find a gym with child care. No more excuses.

✔ Trade babysitting hours with another parent.

✔ Ask grandparents to take the kids overnight so you can have a night alone with your partner. (If you're lucky, maybe they'll even invite them for a week so you can have a romantic vacation!)

✔ Send all the kids to summer camp or relatives and tackle a big project you couldn't otherwise get done.

Elderly or dependent care

Whether you're a primary caregiver, offering major custodial care around the clock, just helping out with errands, or simply lending a hand or preparing for emergencies, keeping affairs organized can ease caregiving. The following can help you help others:

✔ Make a file for each relative for whom you have responsibility, including a copy of the will and files for bank, insurance, charge card, bill, and investment information. Include brokers, bank locations, safe deposit boxes, and so on.

✔ Add your name to the bank accounts, safe deposit box, checks, and charge cards of the person you are caring for so that you can handle financial affairs if necessary.

✔ Keep a full set of residence keys, including outside doors to apartment buildings and storage sheds. Know at least one neighbor who you can call in an emergency and give that person a house key.

✔ Go along on doctor's appointments and track treatment and care. Make sure the doctors have met you and have your phone number in their file.

✔ Establish a day of the week for grocery shopping. See the section in this chapter for more on expediting errands and shopping.

✔ Get a charge card for phone orders, such as having pharmacy or groceries delivered.

✔ If you pay the bills, have them mailed directly to you.

✔ Sign up for automatic withdrawals and deposits at the bank.

✔ If your loved one doesn't drive, get a state picture ID good for everything from airplane travel to writing checks at the grocery store.

✔ If appropriate, consider a facility where other people, bus services, and activities can improve your loved one's quality of life and take a burden off you.

Managing Your Health

It seems everybody is managing their own medical care these days, and the job can get overwhelming. Protect the precious asset of your health with a few proactive habits. Here are some to get you started:

✔ Keep a list of all your doctors in your date book, including name, phone number, and type of practitioner. Add all medicines you regularly take, including grams and what they're for. Throw in your insurance policy number and the number to call to authorize procedures and admissions. This is a quick reference for you — and for someone else in case of an emergency.

✔ Make annual doctor appointments just before your birthday or at the same time each year. This includes general practitioner, dentist, optometrist, gynecologist, and possibly the dermatologist for a mole check.

✔ Schedule school physicals in July so that you're not caught in the August appointment rush and to be sure your child is covered for the full year for any sports.

✔ Keep all open insurance claims in a dedicated file so you know to follow up and can pull papers quickly.

✔ Create a medical history for each family member by keeping a running list of major injuries or illnesses such as chicken pox, broken bones, surgeries, and so forth. Pitch the rest of the documentation; no doctor needs to know that you took penicillin for strep throat in 1983.

✔ If you take more than two pills on a daily basis, including supplements and vitamins, get a weekly pillbox. Fill each compartment on Saturday so you can cruise through the week without thinking. Call the pharmacy for a refill when the last week's worth is sorted. Use the drive-up windows at some pharmacies for quick service or have medicines delivered.

✔ Take vitamins and medications at the same time each day. Write it in your planner if you're trying to get in the habit of something new.

✔ Consumers are flooded with health information every day, so hold on only to things that are helpful today. Yes to a diet you're currently on, no to one that didn't work. Toss documentation on any illness or disease you don't have. The information will be outdated if you should ever need it.

Scheduling Physical Fitness

I know there are people who love to exercise. I sure wish I were one of them. Because I'm not, I refer to the compelling reasons to keep a move on: to be more productive, enjoy better health, live longer, and think clearer. There's no point in investing in an IRA if you're not investing in your muscles and bones to last long enough to reap the benefits. Furthermore, an hour at the gym tonight could improve your performance in tomorrow's important presentation and even bolster your resistance to next week's virus. It's never too late to start on fitness and enjoy daily and long-term rewards. There's just no way out — and this is where a well-organized approach to fitness comes into play.

✔ Join a health club or class. Watching and working out with others can help keep you going.

✔ Find a workout buddy to walk, jog, swim, or play tennis with, or make a standing date to meet at the gym.

✔ Do you love watching basketball, baseball, or hockey? Get off the bench and play.

✔ Bike to work to take care of your commute and your workout at the same time. A set of panniers over your rear wheel can hold your briefcase and laptop.

✔ Work out over your lunch hour. There's no need to worry about getting child care or cutting into your evening, and you'll return to work reenergized and sharp.

✔ Mix up your exercise from one session to the next — running, yoga, weights, swimming, kickboxing, biking, hip hop dance — for cross-training and to keep from getting bored.

✔ Studies have found that any bouts of physical activity at any time of day all contribute to your fitness level — so take the stairs, park farther away, take a quick walk, wash your own windows. Every little bit counts!

Entertainment and Recreation

Yes, it's true: You can even have fun more efficiently, and do you know what that means? More fun! Scheduling recreation into your life is as important as anything else. Pleasure is good for your health, strengthens bonds with family and friends, and can even up your productivity.

At least once a month (and more if you can manage), block off some time in your calendar to do something you love. Whether going to the movies or climbing mountains, singing karaoke or going to hear a concert featuring your favorite singer, do whatever floats your boat with no ulterior motive but feeling good.

In our hyperachieving society, it can be surprisingly easy to forget about fun or get stuck in an entertainment rut, so I recommend making and keeping a list in two categories: a) things that you know give you pleasure, and b) new things you want to try. Schedule at least one of each into each month. Here are some ideas to get you started:

- Make a lunch date with a nonwork friend. Invite a small group to gather for dinner at a restaurant. Stage a dinner party with your dream menu, but don't do all the cooking yourself — assign each guest a dish and send the recipe with the invite.

- Take up a musical instrument. Sign up for lessons or join a group.

- Join a club or take a class to share your existing or potential passion — bowling, golf, bridge, painting, writing, reading, collecting coins, computer gaming, and so forth.

- Indulge your inner child with a visit to a water park, the zoo, a mini golf course, or entertainment parks. Ride the roller coaster — or not.

- Go to museums or art institutes. They're much more fun than you may remember. Traveling art exhibits are turning out to be the place to see and be seen, while science museums have become highly entertaining, interactive playgrounds. Okay, so you may discover something too.

- Go roller blading, ice-skating, horseback riding, sledding, or skiing on snow or water.

- Get into the swing of things and go dancing. Salsa, swing, country line, techno rave — it burns calories and boosts mood!

- Use your favorite form of entertainment as a reward for a goal achieved (see Chapter 18 on setting and achieving goals).

Finding a Special Someone

Being organized leaves more time for love . . . and being in love makes the rewards of being organized all the sweeter. Don't neglect this important part of life.

Finding love

Love is a goal like any other, and you don't want to leave it to pure chance any more than you may expect to find a needle in a haystack or a paper in a pile on your desk. Here are some organized approaches to the amorous task:

✔ Join a singles club or an organization of people with similar interests. Whether you go to a dance, a gourmet dinner, or a group hike, getting out and chatting is half the battle.

✔ Hit the Internet. Personal ads have gone high-tech and gained legitimacy with all the Web-based ways to post everything from what sort of person you're looking for to your tastes in music and food to a photo or video clip — and then you can search it all by keywords. Chat rooms and news groups are another place to hook up with like-minded people. If you don't like singles bars, skip the rooms and groups aimed at singles and find one allied with one of your interests or hobbies instead.

You know even less about people you meet on the Web than those you encounter in singles bars, so be cautious. Schedule initial meetings for public places and don't give out your address or phone number until you know a person well.

✔ If your work is currently the love of your life, go to a networking group for your field. *Networking* has many meanings.

✔ Tell your friends and family that you'd like to date. The old-fashioned matchmaker is still alive and well.

Making time for love

You need a To Do List to expedite your projects, your tasks, and your love life. If love always comes last in your busy life, perhaps you schedule everything but the very thing you live for. Make prioritizing your paramour easy by writing up a Love List of all the special things, big and small, that you can do to make the most of your time together. Keep your list on hand for easy reference both for spontaneous moments and for when you're sitting down to plan your week or month. Make time for love, and all the time of your life will be nicer.

✔ Schedule a date night, even — especially! — if you're married or have been together so long that your idea of a night out is in with the VCR. Follow all the proper steps: Call your partner on the phone and ask him or her out. Make a reservation for dinner. Plan a movie. Get dressed up.

✔ Send flowers. This works for both sexes.

✔ Send a card — cute, funny, flowery, an inspirational poem — for no reason at all.

✔ Tuck a love note in your partner's purse or briefcase, or mail the note to their place of work.

✔ Have a scavenger hunt to find a rose or a poem.

✔ Make a book of gift certificates for items from a hug to a hand-delivered massage to a romantic getaway weekend. Give it for Valentine's Day or the anniversary of the day you met.

✔ Put on some sultry music and have a romantic dinner by candlelight at home.

✔ Go out dancing, whatever style you like.

✔ Rent a romantic video and cozy up on the couch or carpet with a bottle of wine.

✔ Rent a rowboat or canoe and spend a lazy afternoon afloat.

✔ Go on a picnic and lie around in the grass looking at the sky.

✔ Trade off fantasy nights — yours one time, your partner's the next.

✔ Share a candlelit bubble bath.

✔ Put a red light bulb in the lamp and Johnny Mathis on the stereo.

✔ Circle the full moon on your calendar and take advantage of the evening to sneak away and sit in a convertible or on a blanket on the grass. Stare at the stars, bask in the moonbeams, and talk all night!

Chapter 21

Going Mobile: Trips Near and Far

These days, high-performance living is all about being mobile and taking your whole life with you when you go. Everybody seems to be in the business of accumulating miles, whether commuting, carting kids, taking business trips, seeing the world, or simply rushing from one engagement to the next.

Staying organized while you move and interfacing the systems you use on the road with those at the office and home can make all your mobile operations more efficient. You'll get out the door stress-free, grease the wheels of your trip, and come back home with a smile on your lips.

The Power Briefcase and Purse

Organized people are always prepared but they're not packhorses. The first move in your mobile lifestyle should be assessing what you need to take along for the ride, and then assembling the power briefcase, purse, or chic over-the-shoulder bag that puts everything at your fingertips without slowing you down.

Your carry-along bag and its contents can keep you comfortable and productive everywhere you go if you take an organized approach to putting your tote together. Do you really need your full cosmetic kit if all you ever touch up is your lipstick? Could you do more efficient work on your commute if you had a small ruler and red pen for underlining within easy reach? Why carry separate laptop and briefcases when you can get a model that combines both functions? Tap the power of packing right for each day.

Feeling things first: The wallet

By definition, your wallet generally holds your most valuable assets. You want to be able to quickly spot what's there and what's not. Start your quest for a smart wallet by choosing a model that keeps your assets organized and in view. Of the dozens of shapes and sizes available, four basic features comprise a wallet that works:

- ✔ A section for unfolded currency
- ✔ Slots for charge cards (about eight)
- ✔ An ID/driver's license window holder
- ✔ A closed (zipper or snap) change pocket

Guys, skip the money clip. Every time you need to put cash on the table it takes two steps to pull off the money clip and unfold the money, and likewise in the other direction. A wallet, on the other hand, is like a minifiling cabinet where you can easily slip the twenty behind the ten and find it when you need it in one quick move, which can be critical when you're trying to smoothly pick up the tab.

Next, take a hard look at your cards. You may have 20, even 30 cards that do everything from proving who you are to earning you a discount on a restaurant meal or frequent-flyer miles on your trip to New York. Do you really need to carry every one with you every day?

Most people can get through the average day with about eight cards in their wallets:

- ✔ Driver's license
- ✔ ATM card
- ✔ Charge card
- ✔ Grocery check cashing/discount card
- ✔ Medical insurance card
- ✔ Prescription card
- ✔ Discount club store card (Sam's Club, Costco, and so on)
- ✔ Library card (You do have one, don't you? It gives you instant access to all those books and magazines that you don't need to store on your own shelves!)

Some cards come in miniature form to add to your keychain, leaving your wallet space free. This can be convenient, depending on the size of your keychain, but if you have to open your wallet to complete the transaction anyway, do you really want to reach for your keys too?

The rest of your cards can stay at home — backup charge cards, restaurant discount cards, membership cards, and so forth. You can keep airline cards in a cardholder tucked into your carry-on luggage, in case you have to swap flights (keep a list of numbers in a file for making reservations). If your health club membership card is in your gym bag, you'll always have it when you need it. And do you really regularly shop more than one supermarket? Keep just your primary supplier's card in your wallet.

You can use a major credit card at any gas station or department store — so cut up those single-vendor cards! They just take up space and complicate your finances.

If you're a professional, you probably want to carry one other all-important card you always want: your business card. You never know who you'll meet, so whenever you hit the street, make sure you have about 20 business cards on hand. Have cards will travel!

Use a separate holder to carry your business cards so you can whip your cards out quickly and leave your wallet unstuffed and safely put away.

Packing less than the kitchen sink: The purse

Women love their purses — and why not? A fashion accessory that can hold everything you think you may need (whether you really need it or not), a purse is like a best pal. Women's purses are also notorious for packing away far more stuff than any person needs in a day. If yours has become a piece of luggage, the time has come to pare down to the basics. I suggest you carry only the following:

  ✔ Wallet

  ✔ Checkbook (two if you have a separate business account)

  ✔ Datebook/organizer

  ✔ Keys

  ✔ Glasses (sunglasses if you're not operating out of your car)

  ✔ *Only* the cosmetics you regularly touch up with during the day

- Comb and mirror
- Nail file, if you use one
- 3-x-5-inch notepad, for your Master List and/or notes
- Two pens: One blue or black (for normal use) and one red (for high-priority entries in your calendar and underlining as you read)
- Six-inch ruler for underlining as you read
- Business cards

Choosing the right purse is the next step to polishing up your mobile look. A round purse wastes space, just as anything else round does (think about all those stolen corners). When selecting a purse, start with a rectangle, and then look for

- **The right size** to hold just what you need and no more. Murphy's Law states that you'll fill any available space, so resist temptation by keeping your purse on the small side. The weight of a small purse will be easier on your back and you'll find things faster too.

- **A reader's pocket** if you like to carry a book to read. This outside pocket, which is wide enough to hold a paperback, allows you to grab your book without digging through other things.

- **A front zipper pocket,** that extends about halfway up the purse, to hold pens, a ruler, and business cards. Again, the pocket gives you quick access without having to open the main compartment.

- **A zipper or locking flap closure** at the top to keep thieves' hands out of your purse and valuable items in.

Though separate compartments inside a purse may *seem* organized, what happens if you look for something in the wrong compartment? You have to start all over again by looking in another one. I prefer a single section so you can see everything at once.

Taking care of business: The briefcase

Business of any sort calls for a briefcase, which is sized and shaped to hold and protect papers and files. Basically an abbreviated suitcase, your briefcase should get you through all the day's business with efficiency and ease.

Finding the briefcase that best suits your needs is half the battle. Basic designs include hard suitcases, soft bags, and double-duty computer cases. To choose your briefcase, consider the weight and nature of what you carry (read on for a checklist). Leather briefcases look better than vinyl, but they also weigh more, especially if you're looking at a combination laptop case/briefcase. Here are some considerations in the briefcase debate:

✔ **Hard case:** A hard exterior does a good job of protecting its contents from bumps and bends, and also provides a writing surface while you ride the train or perch in a chair at a tableless meeting. Most hard briefcases don't come with any place for pens or pencils, so a small holder helps to keep them all together.

Need an immediate fix to keep your pens and pencils from floating all over your briefcase? Try a cardboard pen or pencil box or a resealable plastic bag.

✔ **Soft case:** Usually equipped with sections and pockets to hold pens, pencils, files, and a pad of paper, soft cases have some organizational advantages. They're generally lighter in weight, and many also come with a strap for wearing over your shoulder. Soft spots of the soft case: a more casual look (which may be just fine, depending on your profession), no handy writing surface, and the things inside can get banged and bent — especially if you overstuff the bag, which those soft walls can tempt you to do.

✔ **Computer case/briefcase:** If you use a laptop outside of the office, you can benefit from combining your computer case and briefcase, which gives you just one thing to carry and one item to track during busy, high-mileage days. Here are features to seek:

• **Padded laptop section** with room for the power cord and cable lock.

• **Briefcase section** that holds file folders and writing pads and provides pockets for pens, pencils, and business cards.

• **Pockets for disks and/or CDs.**

• **Slot for a CD drive** if you need to exchange it with your floppy drive.

• **Strong zipper closure** that can be locked if necessary.

Some briefcases are specially designed for public-transport commuters, with external straps to hold a newspaper and an umbrella. After all, you always need the news, and you never know when the weather is going to turn to rain.

Keep a luggage tag with your business card on your briefcase. If someone else at the office, a meeting, or the airport has one that looks the same, you can easily identify yours without opening it. (Keep a business card inside your briefcase too, in case the luggage tag falls off.)

A power briefcase is targeted to the task at hand, so it shouldn't be stuffed full of shoes or cosmetics or files from yesterday's projects. Essentials to pack in your briefcase include

- Datebook/organizer
- Business cards
- Two pens: One blue or black (for normal use), one red (for high-priority entries in your calendar and underlining as you read)
- Six-inch ruler for (underlining as you read)
- Highlighter
- 8½-x-11-inch writing pad
- A few spare file folders
- Current project files
- Customer/client files
- Reference files
- To Read File
- Company or product literature

Optional add-ins include

- Small stapler
- Staple remover
- Paper clips
- Scissors
- Sticky note flags
- Rubber bands (to hold anything but paper)

You can buy plastic file folders to keep in your briefcase permanently for select papers from your To Read, To Discuss, To Do, and To Write Files. Alternatively, you can use a large plastic expandable wallet with separate sections to keep these papers organized.

Taking Control of Your Commute

Many of us need to get from here to there and back again every day of the working week. Commuting, whether literally or virtually, is a contemporary reality. It can contribute to or sap your productivity, depending on your approach.

Commuting options

Your best commuting choice involves a weighted equation of variables, from availability of your own wheels to proximity to public transportation routes, traffic conditions, workplace needs, and personal style. To sort them out, use the following list to consider your priorities. Is it time for a change?

- ✔ **Public transportation** (train, subway, bus): You don't have to be an environmentalist to know that taking the bus, subway, or train wherever you want to go saves gas over driving. You can be a realist and realize it saves you money too. You also gain time, as you switch your attention from the life-or-death task of driving to reading the morning newspaper or a book, working on your laptop, or catching up on the day's project or client files.

- ✔ **Car:** If you drive, check different routes and do a time/benefit analysis based on actual traffic flow at the time you need to go. The most direct route may also be the busiest and take the longest. Expressways may move faster because they have no stoplights, but not if they're clogged with other cars with the same idea.

  Technology developers are starting to sell devices to help drivers plot the best routes based on time and traffic conditions. Stay tuned, and drive carefully.

- ✔ **Carpool/vanpool:** You can combine the best of public transport with private destinations by joining a carpool or vanpool. In addition to saving gas, you can relax when you don't have to drive and use the time to socialize or discuss business.

  If you carpool or vanpool with business associates, beware of turning every morning commute into a morning meeting. You don't want to be mentally drained before you even see your desk.

- ✔ **Bike:** If you possess cycle-savvy, biking to work can give you the best of many worlds, as you double up your commute with a workout and morning wakeup. Bicycles can carry bags behind the seat or mounted on a rack over the rear tire, baskets in the front or back, and even hold water bottles on the frame. Look for the accessories you need to turn your bike into an eco-friendly commuting machine.

Just don't go: Telecommuting

If you work at home, travel time is about 30 seconds — so do you even need to go to the office? Telecommuting presents some tangible benefits: no interruptions, no set schedule, no travel, and you get to wear what you want. The challenges include keeping on top of your time, working effectively with your team or clients, and perhaps convincing your boss.

Variables to factor into your telecommuting decision include

- **Commute time:** Can you save a lot of time by not commuting to work? If so, consider staying home.

- **Office appointments and meetings**: Do you need to be at the office to see clients or attend meetings? Running back and forth may be more hassle than staying based at the office.

- **Delegating that needs to be done face-to-face:** If you oversee projects or frequently delegate tasks to staff, you may find face-to-face contact is more effective than telecommuting.

- **Technical and technological resources**: Do you need equipment, people, or books available at the office and not accessible from home? Can you borrow the books or equipment or talk to the people by phone or e-mail?

- **Subtle interpersonal factors:** Will physical distance keep you out of mind at promotion time? Are you comfortable and productive working alone? Does your boss actually believe you work as hard as you do?

I suggest two popular ways to strike a telecommuting compromise:

- Schedule all your office obligations for one day a week and work the remaining four from home.

- Choose one day each week to stay home and dedicate to your high-focus projects, and then head for the office the other four.

Working and Playing from the Car

Whether or not you use the car for your daily commute, the horseless carriage may take you shopping and on errands, to meetings and appointments, to movies and meals out. Hanging out with friends, heading for the beach or gym, and driving children to and from school or activities all involve getting in the car. In fact, your car may seem like a second home or office, which means you need systems to make the space work in your favor without storing a warehouse's worth of stuff in your vehicle.

Functional necessities: Car checklist

Your car may take you far from the comforts of home, so you want it to be well stocked. A few supplies will make your car trips smoother, safer, and more productive. Make sure to put these supplies neatly in their places, however, rather than strewing them over passenger seats or piling them on the floor.

Glove compartment

The glove compartment is a great built-in way to contain basic car supplies. Bear in mind that you don't want to try to open your glove compartment and sort through things while you drive, so if you know that you'll want a cassette or your change purse on the road, pull it out before you start. Some things you may want to store in your glove compartment for easy access include

- ✔ Manuals for car, sound system, and electronics
- ✔ Tool for unlocking tires
- ✔ Two-sided change purse for meters and tolls (quarters on one side, dimes and nickels on the other, about $3 total)
- ✔ Small travel package of tissues
- ✔ Pocket flashlight
- ✔ Auto mileage book (for business write-offs)
- ✔ Receipt envelope (for business expense reports)
- ✔ Cassettes or CDs (optional)
- ✔ Scissors (optional; great for trimming stray threads)

Driver's seat area

Some items you want right at your fingertips while you drive, such as sunglasses, a pad to jot down quick ideas, some change, and perhaps your mileage log. Some cars come with a divided section between the two front seats to hold such items. If this organizer is optional when purchasing a new car, I recommend you get it to keep things neat and minimize driving distractions. Keeping the following items in your driver's seat area can make your ride nicer.

- ✔ Sunglasses
- ✔ Garbage can or bag
- ✔ Water bottle (in hot weather)
- ✔ 3-x-5-inch notebook or small padfolio (optional)
- ✔ Pen/pencil (optional)
- ✔ Small tape recorder (optional)
- ✔ Cardboard sun visor (optional)

Who knows what aspect of driving sparks ideas, but have you ever noticed how many genius thoughts come to mind on the road? Don't lose them! Keep a small pad of paper or minitape recorder on hand to record your brainstorms while you wait for the light to change. A hard-backed pad, sometimes called a "padfolio," is easier to write on than a soft notebook.

Nothing messes up a car more than trash, so be sure to have a place in which to stash yours. Auto supply stores stock different types of trash cans to sit on the floor, some with built-in cup holders.

Because I don't have a front seat storage section in my car, I use a small trash can on the floor instead. There, you'll find my sunglasses, tissues, scissors, pen and pencil, pocket flashlight, and auto mileage book all nicely contained and easy to access.

Most people don't wear sunglasses in the house, so where do you suppose you usually reach for them? That's right, in the car. So why not just keep them there so you don't have to search the house every time you leave? You can stop by your vehicle to grab them if you're hitting the street directly or if someone is picking you up. Or just keep a spare pair in the hall table drawer.

Trunk

The trunk is the place for anything big or bulky, as well as the easiest-access spot in the car. Why wrench your back reaching for or wrestling with something on a seat or the car floor if you can put it in the trunk instead? On the other hand, the trunk should not become a permanent storage site simply because it's out of sight.

A collapsible crate is a great addition to your car trunk, whether you're an apartment-dweller toting things upstairs or just generally have a lot to carry from the car. The crate may fold up small, but it makes a big difference. An alternative to the collapsible crate is a collapsible shopping cart or just a big canvas bag with handles into which you can throw all the bags from your errands and carry them with one hand.

Round out your trunk take-alongs with emergency equipment: flares, a blanket, tennis shoes, energy bars, water, some spare cash, and, in winter, tire chains, snow scrapers, sand and/or salt, and a shovel, and you're good to go.

Electronics

Cars are increasingly electronic machines, both in terms of basic functions and a growing array of gadgets you can get to turn your auto into a home office, rolling entertainment center, or smart vehicle with extra safety and navigational capabilities. The overriding concern with any electronics in your car, whether a cell phone, CB radio, or video, is that they not distract from driving. Some gadgets that may make working or playing from the car better include

- A port to connect a handheld computer with a cell phone.
- Wireless connections to the Internet.

- ✔ A dashboard CD/CD-ROM player, digital address book, and voice-activated phone system.

- ✔ Wireless concierge systems that do everything from looking up directions to making dinner reservations to locating and unlocking your car.

- ✔ A night vision system that sees farther ahead than your headlights.

- ✔ A system that notifies local authorities when your air bags are deployed.

- ✔ Rear-seat entertainment systems for videos and games.

Extra goodies can turn your automobile into a magnet for car thieves. Purchase an antitheft device, whether a car alarm, a tracking device, or both, to prevent thieves from going mobile with your property.

And don't forget the old-fashioned cell phone and even older-fashioned CB radio for calling for help when you're stuck, lost, or wondering about road conditions.

Do use a cell phone to make driving safer by carrying it for emergency calls when you need help on the road. *Don't* diminish the safety of your driving by talking on the phone while behind the wheel, which experts estimate to be more dangerous than driving drunk. If you must make a call, pull over.

Appointment accessories and protocol

If you work out of your car, doing sales, making calls, or attending meetings, you can turn your wheels into a rolling office with a few tricks and tools.

Equipment: Taking info with you

A number of manufacturers make special organizers just for people who work from the car. From a simple file wallet that you can easily carry around, to a plastic box for hanging files that you can leave in the trunk, to various other formats and features, there are many ways to keep files, literature, and everything you need to be effective organized neatly in the car.

You may want to buy a minidesk that includes a table for writing or working on a laptop and even has a built-in section for hanging files, as Figure 21-1 shows. A small tape recorder is great for taking notes as you drive away from a meeting. You may wish to explore some of the electronics discussed in the previous section for help storing addresses, getting directions, hooking up to the Internet, and so forth while you're in the car.

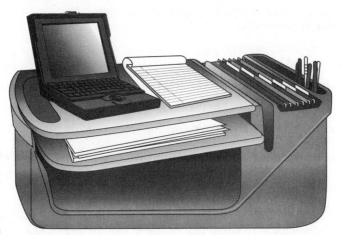

Figure 21-1:
An organizer
for working
from the car.

Scheduling appointments: Making use of distance and time

When you're on the road, each appointment has higher stakes due to the time you've invested getting there, so make sure your drive time pays off. If you're in sales, for example, and you spend a lot of time on the road, your productivity depends on making calls to clients efficiently. Here are some tips to speed you on your way:

- **Try to make all your appointments in the same geographical area —** one suburb today and another tomorrow. Be flexible enough to allow for last-minute changes.

- **Confirm appointments the day before.** You don't want to drive an hour only to find out the person forgot to write the meeting down and isn't available.

- **Determine if you want a morning, afternoon, or mealtime appointment** before you call to arrange it. You may choose a lunchtime slot for a social, get-to-know-you appointment. If you plan to make a formal presentation, a morning meeting may be better than the afternoon, when the contact has more on his or her mind.

- **Plan your appointment.** Decide what topics you want to cover and what materials you need to have with you. Schedule follow-ups after the appointment, and be sure to document what happened in a contact-management program or file immediately after leaving.

Trips for Business or Pleasure

Making tracks out of town can be very fun and productive after you're under way, but getting going can bring even a seasoned traveler down. Whether your trip is an overnight jaunt or a monthlong vacation, equip yourself by getting organized out of the gate.

Every trip needs a plan, and you can make yours fast with our old friends the Five Ws plus How. Each time you prepare to set out, sit down with a piece of paper and jot down the answers to these questions.

- ✔ *Why* go? Is your trip for business? For fun, adventure, hedonistic pleasure, a romantic getaway, to see the world? To visit family or friends? For research? Answering this question will help you sort out your travel plan priorities.

- ✔ *What* type of trip is it? A conference, trade show, meeting, vacation? Analyzing what you'll be doing can help answer some of the other questions, especially what to pack.

- ✔ *Where* to go? Do you want to travel to your client's headquarters, or have them meet you at your manufacturing plant? Is visiting Grandma at her house always best, or might she love to meet you at the beach? Should the attractions be tailored to adults, children, or both? Do you want to stay at a hotel or someone's house?

- ✔ *When* should you go? A convention comes with a set date, but do you want some extra time before or after to visit the city? For a vacation, consider what's the best or most economical season for your destination, when getting away from work is easiest, and whether you need to consult school break schedules for kids.

- ✔ *Who's* going? Are you traveling alone or with a business associate? Will your partner or children come along? This can affect how you choose to travel and where you want to stay.

- ✔ *How* to get there? Planes can save time, driving can save money, and the train or bus is a cost-effective way to let someone else handle the driving while you relax. A quick analysis of your transportation options can help you make the most of any trip, and Table 21-1 provides a view of the variables.

Table 21-1	Transportation Options	
Ride (Train or Bus)	*Drive*	*Fly*
Eco-friendly	Not fuel-efficient if you're alone	Fuel-efficient for long trips and/or large groups

(continued)

Table 21-1 (continued)

Ride (Train or Bus)	Drive	Fly
Most cost-effective for a single rider	Most cost-effective for a group; often more time-effective than bus or train	Most time-effective for long trips; getting to and from airport may make it a draw for short ones
Time for relaxing, sleeping, thinking, working	Time for listening to music or spoken audio, thinking, or chatting with passengers; can't sleep, read, or work	Time for relaxing, sleeping, thinking, working
No traffic on the train; someone else worries about the traffic on the bus	Traffic!	Traffic on the way to and from the airport
Not mobile when you get to your destination	Mobile when you get to your destination	Easy to rent a car or grab a taxi or limo

Power packing

Having the right things with you when you travel can make the difference between comfort and misery, making a great impression and a poor one, getting a good night's sleep or staying wide-eyed all night, sorry that you left your jammies and toothbrush at home. When you get organized, packing the right stuff is painless, and the pleasure of having everything on hand and in its place will pay off throughout your trip.

Dealing with luggage

Most luggage today is made with wheels, which is definitely what you want for easy handling and taking a load off your back. The drawback? All those darn rollaways look alike! Distinguish your luggage by tying a brightly colored ribbon or piece of cloth around a handle or pasting on a sticker in a prominent place. The second step to tracking your luggage is to put a tag on the outside and a business card inside, so you can check to make sure you have the right one. The piece can be returned to you if it gets picked up by someone else, lost, or delayed in flight.

If your luggage was lost, what would you go nuts without? That's what you should carry on. A change of underwear, medicine, cosmetics, a shaving kit, and something to sleep in may make your carry-on list. A travel alarm clock and small flashlight can also be helpful. You never know when the power may go out, and if you have an important meeting, a plane to catch, or a wedding to attend the next day, time is of the essence.

Many hotels provide basics such as toothbrushes, shaving cream, hair dryers, and irons. Call ahead before you count on extra amenities.

Packing list

I recommend a 1-2-3 packing process to save space and time and maximize your traveling appearance and attitude: (1) Choose two or three colors of clothes to mix and match for the entire trip. (2) Run through each day of your trip and what outfit you'll be wearing when. (3) Make a list! See the one in this chapter for an example, and customize it for your own wants and needs.

Set up your packing list on the computer, in a word-processing table or spreadsheet. Print the list any time you're heading out; write in specific items after each category; check things off as you pack; and you can hit the road without reinventing the wheel!

Clothes

___Underwear

___Socks

___Nylons/tights

___Sleepwear/loungewear

___Robe

___Tops

___Shorts

___Pants/jeans

___Sweatshirt

___Skirts

___Dresses

___Suits

___Sport coat/pants

___Dressy outfits

___Sweaters

___Shoes (dress, gym, daily)

___Boots

___Jackets

___Raincoat

___Workout clothes

Accessories

___Jewelry

___Watches

___Hair ornaments

___Scarves

___Belts

___Ties

___Tie clips

___Purses/totes

Toiletries

___Toothbrush

___Toothpaste

___Comb/brush

___Shampoo/conditioner

___Soap

___Shower cap

___Hair dryer

___Curling iron

___Deodorant

___Makeup

___Nail polish/remover

___Razor

___Shaving cream

___Cologne/aftershave

___Suntan lotion

___Medicine

Other necessities

___Airline tickets

___Passport

___Itinerary

___Hotel/car papers

___Organizer/planner

___Glasses/sunglasses

___Driver's license

___Money/checks

___Traveler's checks

___Charge cards

___Airline cards

___Travel alarm

___Luggage keys

___Umbrella

___Camera/videocamera/film/tape/batteries

___CD or tape player/CDs or tapes/batteries

Office supply and drugstores sell plastic envelopes that are a little bigger than #10 envelopes and are just right for carrying airline tickets, hotel papers, and car-rental papers all in one place. Add the receipts you need to track for expense reports or charge-card reconciliations, and you have one-stop record keeping while on the road.

Trip tips — before and after

Travelers know it's not the trip that's stressful and difficult — it's the day before you leave and the one after you get back. Here's how to put everything in order so the world will keep turning while you're gone and welcome you back upon your return.

The day before: Pull it all together

You know the feeling — you're supposed to leave tomorrow and you couldn't possibly have more loose ends. Use this list to tie them up.

- ✔ Tell clients, customers, and friends/associates you're leaving the day before you really are to give you time to get ready.

- ✔ Pack clothes, accessories, and business materials.

- ✔ Arrange for transport to the airport if needed.

- ✔ Stop mail and newspapers, or arrange for a neighbor to pick them up.

- ✔ Make three copies of your itinerary for you, your assistant/boss, and your spouse or another primary person.

- ✔ Change your voice mail message (office only).

- ✔ Give instructions to an assistant, family members, or housesitter.

- ✔ Confirm arrangements for plant care, pet care, and snow or lawn care (set up a week in advance).

- ✔ Prepare documents you need, from passports to expense forms.

- ✔ Complete or delegate work.

- ✔ Compile a To Read File for the trip.

- ✔ Assemble files, books, magazines, and tapes.

- ✔ Put together your laptop, power pack, batteries, and lock.

- ✔ Set light timers.

The day after: Buy some recovery time

Home sweet home! Unfortunately, the pressures of returning after time away can sometimes sour your arrival. Here are some hints for a soft landing.

- ✔ Tell everyone that you're returning the day after you really are so you can get back up to speed.
- ✔ Unpack and refile.
- ✔ Pick up animals and plants.
- ✔ Open mail, read e-mail, and review phone messages.
- ✔ Follow up on trip-related business.
- ✔ Complete expense reports.
- ✔ When you're good and ready . . . return phone calls.

Footloose and fancy-free — organized is the way to be when the road calls your name. Add order to your movements, and you can go mobile at the top of your game.

Part VI
The Part of Tens

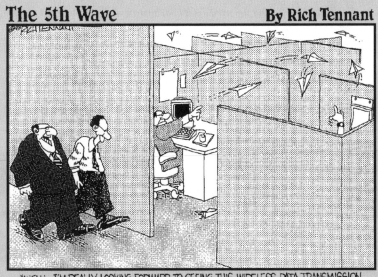

The 5th Wave — By Rich Tennant

"WELLL, I'M REALLY LOOKING FORWARD TO SEEING THIS WIRELESS DATA TRANSMISSION SYSTEM OF YOURS, MUDNICK."

In this part . . .

Organized people love lists, and here are five to make your life easier. Whether you're squeezing more storage out of a small living space, moving without tears or fears, clearing out clutter with a garage sale, picking and caring for a pet, or dealing with what even the best organizational systems can't entirely prevent: emergencies, each of the following chapters provides a ten-point litany of tips for a high-impact organizing issue. These quick references are handy when you're in a hurry and make great reading when you're on hold. Hang ten!

Chapter 22

Storage for Small Spaces: Apartments, Condos, and Compact Houses

• •

In This Chapter

▶ Making the most of vertical space

▶ Hiding or displaying household items in a space-efficient way

▶ Doing double duty with your furniture

• •

*O*kay, so you're space-impaired — that's no excuse for not putting every-thing into its place. Tight perimeters can provide the right motivation for cleaning up your act: More room to breathe. This chapter offers ten tips to help all of you apartment, condo, and small-house dwellers find space in unlikely places and peace in your compact abodes.

Purging Like You Mean Business

Just as one of the best ways to make money is to save instead of spending it, nothing creates space more efficiently than protecting it from the attack of clutter. Review the P-L-A-C-E section for each room in your home as described in Chapters 4 through 13 and purge like crazy. Ask the five W-A-S-T-E questions (outlined in Chapter 3) of every item that crosses your threshold. If you grew up in a big house, now's the time to resize your mind and trim your posses-sions to fit your current space.

Stacking and Tiering

Think vertical. Most people naturally perceive on a horizontal plane, but that could represent half or less of your available space. Stacking up cans of tuna fish and tomato soup in the pantry is the way to start. Then get advanced with the stacking and tiering systems described in Chapter 5 and Chapter 6.

Stackable trays and racks offer shelves to stack items so that you can pull things from lower ones without having to unpile everything on top. (See Figure 5-3.) Stacking solutions are great in kitchen and bathroom cupboards, which often have feet or even yards of unused vertical space. Tiered layers or steps raise each row higher than the one in front of it so you can see everything (the same way it's supposed to work with seating at the movie theater). Tiering works well for canned goods and spices in the kitchen, as you can see in Figure 5-5. The same principle applies to tiered hangers for skirts, shirts, or pants in the clothes closet. (See Figure 6-3 for an example of tiered shirts.)

Shelving It

Another way to think vertical is by adding shelves on walls and in cabinets and closets. From the front hall and bedroom closets to under-sink cabinets and empty walls waiting to hold books, entertainment media, or collections, every additional shelf is that many more square feet of space. Use wooden shelves instead of coated wire racks to aid balance for small items. Even short shelves can help expand floor space, as shown by the shoe shelving in Figure 6-5.

If you're not particularly handy but have a wall to spare, purchase a freestanding shelving unit. It's self-installing.

Tucking Under: Space Beneath the Bed

Make space while you sleep. There are a number of containers, cardboard and plastic, designed for storing things under the bed. This is the place for off-season clothes and other infrequently accessed storage items. Want even more under-bed space? Use risers to lift the bed higher, as pictured in Figure 6-6.

Using Countertops Constructively

Space-impaired people are the only ones to whom I grant the right to leave things out on the counter. If you have more appliances than cupboard space in the kitchen, put them on counters according to the rule of access. In a drawer-deprived bathroom, you could arrange cosmetics on the countertop, or create even more space and prevent a cluttered look by using freestanding pullout drawers instead. See Figure 7-1 for an example of countertop drawers.

Containing with Cabinets

One simple solution can do a lot of containing: cabinets. With the space-expanding properties of shelves and the aesthetic advantages of closed doors, cabinets can spruce up and expand the space of any apartment or condo. Install one above your desk for all your office supplies. Add a free-standing unit to the living room to hide your CDs and videos.

Decorative screens can hide all sorts of things and separate a room into different functions.

Hanging with Hooks

Thinking vertical again, you really can't have too many hooks. Install them in your closets to hold purses, hats, recycled plastic grocery bags. Put a big one on a patio or balcony wall to hang a bicycle. Hooks on the back of the bathroom door can keep robes, clothes, or towels off the floor, while small hooks screwed into the bottom of a cupboard shelf can suspend cups and mugs above your stacks of plates and bowls.

Behind Closed Doors

Speaking of the backs of doors, there are a number of coated wire racks designed to hang on the back of doors and double up their function as storage space. This might be a shoe storage system inside your bedroom closet door, additional food storage space on the back of pantry doors, or a holder for sponges or a trash bag hanging from your under-sink cabinet door in the kitchen.

Carting and Rolling

Every apartment resident should know the art of carting — containing things in a mobile unit that rolls with the punches. Try a microwave cart in the kitchen, a filing cart in the office, or a set of rolling drawers in the bathroom.

Double-Duty Furniture

Who can afford single-use furniture when space is at a premium? Look for drawers, doors, and shelves in every piece you buy so it has a second use as storage. Your night table might have a drawer for reading material and a cabinet beneath where you can stock sweaters. An efficient end table includes enclosed shelves to hold photo albums, CDs, or your current craft project. Sourcing a computer workstation? Seek one that can hold the fax machine and files along with the basic equipment.

Chapter 23

Ten Moves to Make Your Move Hassle-Free

- -

In This Chapter

▶ Fighting moving panic with a plan

▶ Asking the movers the right questions

▶ Tossing out that zebra-patterned humidor

▶ Eating your edibles in advance

▶ Getting your new home ready

- -

Perhaps the ultimate organizational challenge, moving has a way of making you wish you'd organized a long time ago. Not to worry. There's no time like the present. I'm moving across the country while I write this, so these tips are guaranteed hot and fresh.

Making a Plan

The minute you know when and where you're going to move, make a plan per the detailed instructions in Chapter 18. Remember to work the plan backward from your target (move) date. If you do everything according to the chapter, you'll end up with all the checklists and dates you need.

Choosing a Mover

Nobody moves alone, so decide who will be on your team well in advance. The decision of whether to lean on friends or go pro probably depends upon how far you're going and whether you're moving items from a small apartment or a huge house. You also want to consider whether you have a lot of heavy furniture to move, the number of stairs on either end, and your friends' muscle power.

If you're going to hire out, call several movers and ask about

- **Pricing:** Does the quote cover packing costs, mileage, and time? Are there additional costs for special items such as pianos?
- **Insurance coverage:** Is insurance automatically included, and is it enough?
- **Packing charge:** Does it cover the whole place or just the fragile or large items?
- **Transport time:** If you're moving out of town, how many days will it take the truck to arrive?
- **Holding charge:** If you'll arrive after the movers, what is the charge to hold your shipment before unloading?

Closing the Old Place

Call all utilities — electric, gas, telephone, water, sewer, and garbage — and stop service the day *after* you plan to leave. Also stop other services, such as newspaper delivery, lawn or snow care, bottled water delivery, and so on, with adequate notice.

Fill out the postal service form to have your mail forwarded and send change of address notes to all people, business and personal, who you want to have your new address. Check with the telephone company about relaying a message with your new number.

Begin using up food in the refrigerator and pantry at least two months in advance. Cut back to the bare minimum when grocery shopping and plan your meals around food on hand. Don't plan on packing any perishables, and limit other food items as much as possible.

Getting Insurance

Call ahead for insurance quotes for all the coverage you'll need at your new place — cars, medical, home or renters', liability. Have a current appraisal of jewelry, art, and other valuables before moving.

Planning Ahead for Travel

Arrange any necessary travel a long time before your move so a plan is made and that task is out of the way. If you're driving, renew your auto club membership for roadside assistance and maps to your destination. Have the cars checked for tires, tune-ups, oil changes, and any other maintenance services.

Covering Your Financial Assets

Leave bank accounts open until the last check clears the account. Don't cancel ATM cards until the account closes, so you have access to your money. Close out your safe deposit box and transfer it to a new bank. Close all charge cards at local stores. Send address changes to all investment accounts. If you'll be on the road for awhile, purchase traveler's checks and take a charge or debit card so you don't have to travel with too much cash.

Collecting Personal Records

Collect school transcripts; medical, dental, and vision records (including X rays) as well as legal documents such as trusts and wills before you leave town.

Purging Before You Pack

As soon as you make the move decision, start seriously asking the five W-A-S-T-E questions (explained in Chapter 3) of all your possessions and tossing or donating what you don't need. Here's your golden opportunity to donate that albatross of a gift whose giver has since moved on. There's no point in taking the time and money to pack and move clutter. Remember that you may have different wants and needs in your new place. If you're moving to a warmer climate you can toss most of your winter clothes and consider whether you want some new light-colored furniture. If you're moving from a house to a condo, all that lawn and snow equipment can go.

Packing What You Need

Start packing at least a month ahead of your move. If the house is large, or you have quite a bit to pack and only weekends to do it, start two to three months in advance. You'll need boxes before you can pack item one, so put that on the schedule first. If you're moving locally, boxes that have been used before are fine, and you can start scouring local stores for extras. However, you should ship only in new boxes, which you can buy at truck rental places or shipping stores. Hit the office supply store for file boxes. Be sure they're sturdy, and don't buy them so big that you won't be able to lift them after you pack them.

Special wardrobe boxes with a bar across the top are great for packing clothes. Professional movers can supply wardrobe boxes as part of your price estimate, or you may find it cheaper to purchase your own.

Pack like items together by the room they'll go in. Don't mix things up just because they might fit better in another box. *Exception:* Go ahead and use your towels and linens for packing material to cushion fragile items. You'll save space and weight.

Use a permanent marker and in bold letters on at least two sides and the top of the box write the room and the box's main contents. Mark any boxes that are fragile with a fragile sticker. If you don't have any, run some off on your computer, preferably in *bold red ink*. Number all the boxes, and then make a separate list by number of what's where. If you need something, locating it will be much faster if you refer to your numbered list and find the corresponding box rather than reading all the box names.

Preparing the New Place

Make arrangements to clean up the new place, replace carpeting, paint walls, and complete any other work you want done before move day. If your future home is in another city, is there someone who can let service people in and out? Call the telephone company and arrange for a new number(s). If it's a new home, the phone company can install the jacks before you get there so you're wired upon arrival. Call the electric, gas, water, sewer, and garbage company and arrange to start utilities the day before you get there. You can also have rental furniture delivered before your arrival if there's someone available to open the door. New home sweet home!

Chapter 24

Ten Tips for Great Garage Sales

*T*here's nothing like a garage sale to turn clutter into cash flow. The trick is to *give* garage sales — not go to them yourself. Whether you're selling from the garage of your house or out on the front lawn of your apartment complex, here are ten ways to make your garage sales great.

Scheduling Your Sale

May and June start the garage sale season in winter climates, with sale activity generally peaking in August and early September all across the country as everyone cleans up for the new school year. Join the club and plan to have yours at peak time, when people are out and about hitting the garage sale circuit.

Advertising

If you're selling a large number of items or something valuable, consider placing an ad in the local newspaper to bring in eager buyers. There's usually a two-week deadline for ad placement, so plan accordingly. If you don't want to pay for an ad, just be sure to post signs on major cross streets and all the way to the site of your sale.

You can buy preprinted signs that say "Garage Sale" or use posterboard to make your own. Bright colors and decorative borders help draw attention, but don't overcrowd your message. Make the words short and sweet and print with a large permanent marker with letters big enough to easily read while driving by. Note special features, such as toys or a complete bedroom set for sale, to add extra advertising appeal.

Being Neighborly

Teaming up with neighbors can add impact to your garage sale because you can advertise on signs and in ads "three homes . . ." or "the block of . . ." and put out plenty of stuff to entice passers-by to stop. The group approach can also make a garage sale easier and more fun. Sellers can rely on each other to run the show while one shuttles a child to soccer practice or takes a break. If you don't know your neighbors, here's a great way to get acquainted. Some developments make a group garage sale an annual event the same weekend each year.

Bagging and Boxing

Start collecting brown and plastic grocery bags as soon as you decide to have a sale so that your best customers have a way to carry their loot away. Also assemble as many boxes as you can to use for display. Pile one full of stuffed animals, or stand an open box on its side to act like a bookcase. Arrange the books with the spines out. As boxes are emptied, give them to buyers to carry their purchases.

Collecting and Marking

A week in advance, collect everything you plan to sell in one room so you can see what you have and start pricing. Group like items together — clothes in one place, toys in another, jewelry in a third — and get going on deciding how much you want to sell them for. Put a low price tag on that old moosehead that's been collecting dust in the attic in the hope that it will move.

Give yourself at least two days to price and mark everything. Start with a sheet of paper and a general price list: T-shirts $2, pants $3, games $4. Once you have your list, mark each item with colored stickers. You can use different colors for different dollar amounts, or code them to family members or neighbors if you plan to divide up the proceeds by sales of individual items.

Setting Up

Borrow tables from neighbors — long tables, card tables, anything you can tote — the day before. Set up the tables in the garage the night before so you're ready first thing the next morning. Pull things out into the driveway the day of the sale so people can see you're having one, but if there's a chance of rain, stick to just a few big items so you can get them under cover quickly if you need to. Display smaller items on tables, which are the right height for easy viewing and browsing. Arrange big things in two parallel rows so people can walk between — perhaps lining both sides of the driveway.

Changing Money

Go to the bank the day before the sale and buy a roll each of quarters, dimes, and nickels, and at least 20 $1 bills. Find a covered box to use for cash; one with dividers or sections is best for keeping different denominations sorted out. Write down your initial change amount on a slip of paper and store it in the box, so you can subtract it from the total to figure your profit at the end of the day. As soon the box hits $50, start taking additional cash into the house.

To track revenues for different sellers, use colored price stickers for each seller and write each person's name on a separate piece of paper. As you sell things, pull the sticker off the item and paste it directly on that person's list. Tally up the totals at the end of the day.

Selling Toys

If your house is in toy overload, target your sale to children and sell only toys. Let the kids use the money made to buy something new. It's amazing how they'll suddenly agree to part with old and outgrown things with a promise like that on the horizon. Ka-ching!

Involving the Kids

If you have a family, your garage sale should be a family affair, both in principle and to keep you sane. Have the kids handle the money if they're old enough; it's a great mini-lesson in math and commerce. Younger children can have a small lemonade stand. At a quarter a glass, the math is easy and mistakes don't matter much.

Making Items Sell

If your garage sale is two days long, mark things down the second day by putting up a sign: "25% Off!" At noon, change the sign to "50% Off!" or "Best Offer!" You're in the business of selling here.

When the garage sale is over, do *not* put leftovers back into the house. Leave it all in the garage (or in boxes in a storage unit if you're in an apartment), and then call Goodwill, Salvation Army, or some other charity to come and pick it up. Take the tax deduction and enjoy all the extra space.

Chapter 25

Ten Pointers about Pets

*H*aving a pet is like being a parent. House pets aren't wild animals, so forget the romantic idea that they'll take care of themselves. Whether you're deciding to get a pet or trying to improve your relationship with the woolly one in your house, these pet-parenting tips can help.

Time

Pets take time, so take a good look at your schedule and the timetables of other household members before you take the plunge. If you have children, realize that even if the dog *belongs* to young Katie, much of the burden of care will probably fall on your shoulders.

Don't just go to the pet store and buy whatever is cutest. The primary criterion for adding a pet to your family (even if the family is just you) should be whether you have the quality time available that the pet needs to flourish. Read up on the needs and habits of different animals to find one that fits your schedule. How long can your pet be left alone and how much time does it demand while you're home? Dogs need several walks per day and loads of affection, while cats can occasionally take care of themselves for a few days in a row (though they may be mad when you get back). Fish need daily feeding and occasional cleaning but little else. Iguanas, guinea pigs — all have different wants and needs, but all appreciate predictable daily routines and interaction with their owners. Some pets' needs can seem subtle. You might think a bird doesn't need much attention, but Skippy, our family canary, stopped singing when we kids got busy and spent less time at home.

Nothing is more tragic than when people get a pet only to later discover they don't have enough time to make it happy. Make a realistic assessment of the time your pet requires on a daily, weekly, and monthly basis; who in the household can devote the time to the pet's needs; and whether you can continue this level of care well into the future. Once you find the pet that fits your schedule, write daily times for cleaning, care, and play into your calendar. If you made the right choice, your pet time will be time well spent.

Space

Match the size of your indoor and outdoor space to the size of the animal and how much it moves around. A small apartment is ill-suited for a big, rowdy dog that needs room to run and romp, but fine for hamsters that hang out in their cage. Of course, hamsters have a tendency to have babies, so account for reproduction. Plan for projected growth too. That little 6-inch iguana can grow to several feet, going through a few different cages and taking up more space in the process.

You also want to organize your space to give your pet a good home that works with your household setup. Do you want the pet in the living room, family room, or bedroom; outside; or everywhere? Where's the best spot for a dog basket, kitty litter box, birdcage, or fish aquarium? Can you build a backyard fence to give a dog free-range play? Where can you leave out food and water dishes that is convenient for people and pets alike?

Cost

So far, we're not required to send pets to college, but they can still rack up a long list of expenses. First there's the initial purchase cost, which can be steep if you prefer purebred dogs, free if your neighbor's cat just had kittens or you get your pet from a shelter, and somewhere in between at the pet store. Next consider cage and equipment, supplies, food, care while you're out of town, and veterinarian costs from initial shots to ongoing care. Don't skimp on supplies necessary to keep the animal healthy and clean, like a good filter system for fish.

Plan a pet budget to prevent financial surprises. Start with initial costs: buying the pet, equipping its home, and basic supplies. Calculate the cost of food on a weekly basis. Add in veterinarian care and medications — regular checkups, procedures such as shots and de-clawing, and a contingency for illness and injuries. If you travel and expect to board the pet often, figure those costs too. Add these allocations to your overall household budget, cutting back in other areas if you need to. Finally, track your pet bills and compare them to your initial budget, making adjustments as necessary. For more on budgeting, see Chapter 17.

Family Harmony

If you have a family, a pet is a new member, so don't take on the added responsibility without group approval. To assess young children's interest in animals, watch them at the homes of people with pets or at the park. Do they approach and pet the dog or want to hold the hamster? Does your family want a friendly animal that wanders the house like a cat or dog; a bird, that may have the run of the house but isn't particularly cuddly; or a creature that stays in a cage? You may all go to the pet store together to view the possibilities, but do your research first. Few families leave a pet store empty-handed, so be prepared with your parameters before you go.

Records

Make a pet file to keep all health records, including shots, and a history of illnesses and injuries. Establish a schedule for checkups and immunizations, perhaps when you're making appointments for yourself. If you bought the pet from a breeder, keep a record of its bloodlines and family history in case of illness and for any future breeding. Research your pet's habits and life cycle, from eating and sleeping to when it grows a fur coat for winter, goes into heat, and has a growth spurt or slowdown. Organize this information into one hanging file per pet, subdivided into separate folders for medical records, breed information, and habits. Keep your pet records with your personal files as described in Chapter 16.

Training

Decide on house rules for the pet, and begin training immediately (puppy kindergarten is a great start) so there are no mixed messages. You can't let a puppy jump on the couch for the first week and then change your mind. Be sure all family members are communicating the same rules, and consider obedience school for a little help from the pros.

One day at a time is a good way to tackle pet training. Whether you're taking a class or going it alone, schedule some time each day to train your new pet. Write it into your calendar, keep the commitment, and enjoy the payoff of a happy pet relationship.

Pet Supplies

Treat pet toys like kids' toys: Contain! An open basket works well, so kids and pets can find what they want and you can move it around as needed. Create a pet center to keep all supplies on a shelf in the kitchen, laundry room, or basement. Keep leashes by the door for easy access when it's time to walk the dog.

Grooming and Cleaning

Most pets get plenty dirty, so create a regular cleanup schedule. A longhaired dog may need to be brushed every day, while once a week is enough for a short-haired pooch. How often does the box or tank or cage need to be cleaned? Pick regular days and/or times for pet chores and write them down in your calendar until these tasks become habit.

Feeding Time

Buy a closed plastic container for storing pet food to keep Sylvester's chow from smelling and protect it from insects, and then decide where to feed your pet and keep the food close by. The kitchen is often convenient, as you can rustle up a meal for Fido while you prepare your own. If you have young children, be sure to keep food and water out of the way of their play. Some animals regulate their own food, so you can just leave meals out and let pets nibble at will. Others subscribe to the see-food-and-eat-food diet, wolfing down anything they can get their teeth into, in which case you need to control the supply so pets don't become overweight, which is no healthier for animals than it is for people. Many pets need water all day long, so keep that bowl full with fresh water. Make feeding and replacing water a routine at the same time each day, perhaps before or after your own meal.

Travel

If you want to take a trip with a pet, check out the variables first. Take a cruise around town before trying a major car trip. Make plane travel arrangements well in advance and find out what kind of cage you need. Pets can't travel in plane cargo holds in cold weather, so take the season into account. Some pets can't travel in planes at all because of the air pressure, as my daughter discovered when she wanted to bring her pet turtles home from college for the summer.

If you're traveling without your animal companion, leave plenty of time to set upboarding or pet-sitting, or you may find yourself with a needy animal on your hands the morning of your departure.

Chapter 26

911! Emergency Strategies

In This Chapter

▶ Stopping emergencies before they start

▶ Stepping up to the plate with supplies and knowledge

▶ Strategies for medical, fire, snow, and car emergencies

▶ Empowering yourself against power outages

*N*obody likes emergencies, but those who are unprepared like them the least. You never think it could happen to you, but it does and they do. I've driven through certifiable blizzards to give organizing workshops and powered through more power failures and floods than I can count. Elizabeth, the coauthor of this book, survived the Northridge, California, earthquake and lived to complain about it. Emergency preparedness is as important to your peace of mind as it is to your basic health and safety, so here are ten ways to be prepared.

Money

Money can't buy love or happiness but it can solve a host of problems if you find yourself in urgent circumstances. Always, always carry a spare twenty-dollar bill in a separate compartment in your wallet for the unexpected moments you need cash, from being stranded on the freeway to dashing out of a house on fire. If you spend it, replace it that day. My father taught me this trick the day I started driving, and it can bail you out of countless jams.

Keep a charge card, even if you prefer not to, so you can always order what you need over the phone and have it delivered. Whether you're sick in bed and need a prescription or you're suddenly attending to an emergency and can't get out to the grocery store, you need an electronic money supply.

Hate credit? Get a debit card instead. It works the same way, but instantly pays the balance from your bank account.

Medical

Make a list of phone numbers of the closest emergency room covered by your insurance, the pharmacy, and the poison center in your area. Post it in a prominent spot. If you have children, give them a copy when they become teenagers and be sure they know where to find the one in the house.

Put together two first aid kits, one for the house and one for the car. See Chapter 7 for basic necessities. Add a first aid book for quick reference so you don't have to think hard under pressure. Try *First Aid & Safety For Dummies* by Inlander and Norwood (IDG Books Worldwide, Inc.)

Communication

Carry a calling card, a few quarters, or a cell phone everywhere you go, even if you're hiking in the mountains, working out at the gym, or driving your usual commute. The phone is your lifeline. Stay connected!

Car

You're as likely to be in your car as anywhere when emergencies strike, so be sure your basic needs are covered by keeping a warm blanket, bottled water, packaged snacks, a flashlight, and a pair of comfortable shoes in the trunk at all times. That new pair of formal dress shoes may dazzle on the dance floor but "dapper" doesn't cut it if you find yourself fixing a flat in a rainstorm.

No amount of car preparedness can help if you can't get into the car, so prevent lockouts with one or two tactics. Hit the hardware or auto supply store for a small, magnetized box that holds an extra car and/or house key and sits just inside the front or rear bumper of your car. Another option is to carry a spare car key, separate from your key ring, in your wallet or purse. Now you're covered when the front or trunk door slams shut with your key ring inside.

Use preventive maintenance to keep your car in good running order and head off freeway meltdowns. Check the tires regularly, making sure they're in good shape and filled with air. Rotate them for even wear, and always carry a spare. Even if you don't know how to change it, someone else will. Ditto for jumper cables.

Keep your insurance card and registration in the glove compartment, along with a pad and pen for noting all details in case of an accident. A disposable camera can document the scene after an accident and facilitate your insurance claim. Add a coin purse with at least $3 in change, which will cover everything from tolls and meters to emergency pay-phone calls.

Fire

Flames can burst forth anytime, anywhere, so install smoke detectors on every floor of your home and keep the batteries fresh. Have at least one fire extinguisher on hand, including in the kitchen where most fires start. You also want a box of baking soda there, for a less-mess quench to smaller kitchen fires.

If you should find yourself in a fire, the basic lifesaving procedure is to *stop, drop,* and *roll.* Stay under the smoke. If you have kids, teach them the steps and make it a game.

Keep a fireproof box in the house for valuables such as jewelry or legal documents while not in the safe deposit box at a bank. Have a pet? Alert firefighters by putting a special sticker in your window.

Children's Safety

As early as possible, teach your children that strangers may be dangerous, but police and firefighters are their friends. As soon as they're using the phone, teach them to call 911 in an emergency and clearly state the problem. Try a practice session with a toy phone. Children should also know their home phone number in case they get lost or have an emergency.

When ordering a new phone number, ask for a pattern, such as 962-1616, to make it easier for kids to memorize.

Create a babysitter's information sheet including your cell phone or pager number, all the emergency numbers, including poison control, and the name, number, and address of a helpful adult neighbor. Leave a house key with a neighbor and tell your kids who to get it from if they should ever be locked out.

Power Failures

Keep a flashlight in every bedroom, the kitchen, and the basement, stoked with working batteries, where you can easily find them in pitch darkness if the lights should suddenly go out. Have a supply of extra batteries and replace them annually. Also keep candles and matches on every floor, but don't light them if you suspect a gas leak (as after an earthquake).

Keep firewood on hand if you have a working fireplace. Get a Sterno camp stove and keep a cache of canned and packaged foods that can be eaten with little or no cooking.

Snow Emergencies

Every winter, stock your trunk with a snowbrush, shovel, and rock salt, as well as tire chains for heavy snowfall areas. At home, clean and prepare the snowblower before the season begins and empty it of gas when it ends. Have a snow shovel in case the snowblower breaks down.

Valuables

Keep originals of important legal documents in a safe deposit box at the bank. This includes birth and marriage certificates, passports, divorce agreements, real estate closing papers, wills, trusts, stock certificates, CD notes, car titles, etc. Keep copies at home for quick reference. This is also the place to store computer backups and valuable jewelry.

Get birth certificates as soon after kids are born as you can manage. Renew your passport; it's easier than starting all over again.

Insurance

Take out replacement, not regular, insurance on your household possessions. A replacement policy pays for lost items at today's prices, not the original purchase price, which can make a world of difference if you get wiped out by disaster.

Have your valuables appraised so you have ready proof if you need to make an insurance claim. These include jewelry, crystal, good silver, and artwork. Add equipment and appliances such as computers, VCRs, cameras, and so forth to the list and keep it in your safe deposit box.

Index

• Z •

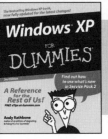

SPORTS, FITNESS, PARENTING, RELIGION & SPIRITUALITY

0-7645-5146-9

0-7645-5418-2

Also available:
- Adoption For Dummies
  0-7645-5488-3
- Basketball For Dummies
  0-7645-5248-1
- The Bible For Dummies
  0-7645-5296-1
- Buddhism For Dummies
  0-7645-5359-3
- Catholicism For Dummies
  0-7645-5391-7
- Hockey For Dummies
  0-7645-5228-7

- Judaism For Dummies
  0-7645-5299-6
- Martial Arts For Dummies
  0-7645-5358-5
- Pilates For Dummies
  0-7645-5397-6
- Religion For Dummies
  0-7645-5264-3
- Teaching Kids to Read For Dummies
  0-7645-4043-2
- Weight Training For Dummies
  0-7645-5168-X
- Yoga For Dummies
  0-7645-5117-5

TRAVEL

0-7645-5438-7

0-7645-5453-0

Also available:
- Alaska For Dummies
  0-7645-1761-9
- Arizona For Dummies
  0-7645-6938-4
- Cancún and the Yucatán For Dummies
  0-7645-2437-2
- Cruise Vacations For Dummies
  0-7645-6941-4
- Europe For Dummies
  0-7645-5456-5
- Ireland For Dummies
  0-7645-5455-7

- Las Vegas For Dummies
  0-7645-5448-4
- London For Dummies
  0-7645-4277-X
- New York City For Dummies
  0-7645-6945-7
- Paris For Dummies
  0-7645-5494-8
- RV Vacations For Dummies
  0-7645-5443-3
- Walt Disney World & Orlando For Dummies
  0-7645-6943-0

GRAPHICS, DESIGN & WEB DEVELOPMENT

0-7645-4345-8

0-7645-5589-8

Also available:
- Adobe Acrobat 6 PDF For Dummies
  0-7645-3760-1
- Building a Web Site For Dummies
  0-7645-7144-3
- Dreamweaver MX 2004 For Dummies
  0-7645-4342-3
- FrontPage 2003 For Dummies
  0-7645-3882-9
- HTML 4 For Dummies
  0-7645-1995-6
- Illustrator CS For Dummies
  0-7645-4084-X

- Macromedia Flash MX 2004 For Dummies
  0-7645-4358-X
- Photoshop 7 All-in-One Desk Reference For Dummies
  0-7645-1667-1
- Photoshop CS Timesaving Techniques For Dummies
  0-7645-6782-9
- PHP 5 For Dummies
  0-7645-4166-8
- PowerPoint 2003 For Dummies
  0-7645-3908-6
- QuarkXPress 6 For Dummies
  0-7645-2593-X

NETWORKING, SECURITY, PROGRAMMING & DATABASES

0-7645-6852-3

0-7645-5784-X

Also available:
- A+ Certification For Dummies
  0-7645-4187-0
- Access 2003 All-in-One Desk Reference For Dummies
  0-7645-3988-4
- Beginning Programming For Dummies
  0-7645-4997-9
- C For Dummies
  0-7645-7068-4
- Firewalls For Dummies
  0-7645-4048-3
- Home Networking For Dummies
  0-7645-42796

- Network Security For Dummies
  0-7645-1679-5
- Networking For Dummies
  0-7645-1677-9
- TCP/IP For Dummies
  0-7645-1760-0
- VBA For Dummies
  0-7645-3989-2
- Wireless All In-One Desk Reference For Dummies
  0-7645-7496-5
- Wireless Home Networking For Dummies
  0-7645-3910-8